Eleventh Edition

Combat Leader's Field Guide

Revised and updated by
CSM James J. Gallagher
USA (Ret.)

STACKPOLE
BOOKS

First edition, 1956, © Military Service Pub. Co.
Second edition, 1960, © The Stackpole Company
Third edition, 1961, © The Stackpole Company
Fourth edition, 1962, © The Stackpole Company
Fifth edition, 1964, © The Stackpole Company
Sixth edition, 1966, © The Stackpole Company
Seventh edition, 1967, © The Stackpole Company
Eighth edition, 1973, © The Stackpole Company
Ninth edition, 1980, © The Stackpole Company
Tenth edition, 1987, © Stackpole Books
Eleventh edition, 1994, © Stackpole Books

ISBN 0-8117-2425-5

Contents

Preface

This manual is designed to assist leaders or prospective leaders of combat infantry units or other groups that, in an emergency, must fight as infantry. The content is tactical and logistical, administrative matter mostly being omitted. When in the field, especially under stress of combat or simulated combat, the combat leader cannot instantly recall everything he has been taught. Rapid changes in the situation may cause him to assume a position for which he has not yet been trained. He will then appreciate some brief reference material to guide him. He cannot carry a "five-foot shelf" of field manuals, and unlike the staff officer or higher commander, he does not have ready access to organizational files or library. What he needs he must carry in his pocket, condensed yet in a form approximating at-a-glance capability. This field guide has been compiled from current field manuals and field circulars with those requirements in mind.

You will note that much of the reference material is in fact a comprehensive checklist to ensure that you have not overlooked some important consideration of troop leading.

As with the tenth edition, the material in this edition is in two parts, unit combat operations and soldier combat skills. The material in Part I introduces the new army doctrine and focuses on dismounted infantry operations, including battle drills—collective actions rapidly executed without applying a deliberate decision-making process. A small unit's ability to accomplish its mission often depends on soldiers and leaders to execute key actions quickly. In the post–Cold War era, forces will be called upon to deploy almost anywhere in the world on short notice to confront an opponent whose weapons may be as good as our own. This guide includes the considerations applicable to the U.S. Army in its 1993 role of force projection.

Part One
UNIT COMBAT OPERATIONS

1

The Battlefield

The Army is in the process of transition from the doctrine of AirLand Battle to that of a new strategic era. This new doctrine recognizes the end of the Cold War and the change in the nature of the threat. It reflects a shift to stronger joint operations, retains the best of all the doctrine that has gone before, extends AirLand Battle into a wider interservice integration, is more aware of the increasing incidence of combined operations, and recognizes that Army forces operate across the spectrum of war and operations other than war. This doctrine allows for an Army more disposed to force projection than to forward defense.

ARMY DOCTRINE

Fundamental to operating across the full range of possible operations is an understanding of the Army's doctrinal foundations—the principles of war and the tenets of Army operations. Small-unit leaders must understand the concepts and fundamentals of Army doctrine to effectively lead in combat.

Principles of War

The enduring bedrock of Army doctrine, the principles of war have stood the test of time. Only slightly revised since first published in 1921, today's force-projection Army recognizes the following nine principles of war.

Objective

Direct every military operation toward a clearly defined, decisive, and attainable objective. The ultimate military purpose of war is the destruction of the enemy's armed forces and its will to fight. In operations other than war, the ultimate objective might be more difficult to define, but it must be clear from the beginning.

Offensive

Seize, retain, and exploit the initiative. Offensive action is the most effective and decisive way to attain a clearly defined common objective.

Mass

Mass the effects of overwhelming combat power at the decisive place and time. Synchronizing all the elements of combat power where they will have decisive effect on an enemy force in a short period of time is to achieve mass.

Economy of Force

Economy of force is the judicious employment and distribution of forces in order to achieve mass elsewhere. Allocate minimum essential combat power to secondary efforts.

Maneuver

Place the enemy in a position of disadvantage through the flexible application of combat power. Maneuver is the movement of forces in relation to the enemy to secure or retain positional advantage.

Unity of Command

For every objective, seek unity of command and unity of effort. At all levels of war, employment of forces in a manner that masses combat power toward a common objective requires unity of command and unity of effort.

Security
Never permit the enemy to acquire unexpected advantage. Security results from the measures taken by a commander to protect his forces.

Surprise
Strike the enemy at a time or place or in a manner for which it is unprepared. The element of surprise can allow forces to achieve success well out of proportion to the effort expended.

Simplicity
Prepare clear, uncomplicated plans and concise orders to ensure thorough understanding. Other factors being equal, the simplest plan is preferable.

Tenets
Success in battle will depend on the ability to fight in accordance with five basic tenets.

Initiative
Initiative means setting or changing the terms of battle by action. Infantry forces attempt to maintain their freedom of action while limiting the enemy's. This requires an offensive spirit in all operations. Decentralized operations in which small units aggressively fight through enemy resistance with the immediately available resources support the seizure or retention of the initiative. Individuals act independently within the framework of their commander's concept. Leaders and soldiers must understand the intent of commanders two echelons above. Commanders use mission-type orders and clear, concise instructions to ensure that subordinates understand the concept and how they fit within it.

Agility
Infantry forces seize or retain the initiative by acting and/or reacting faster than the enemy. This begins with the commander, who must have the mental agility to rapidly analyze tactical situations, thinking through many possible courses of action and the enemy's likely reaction to them, and determining the most effective and least costly course. SOPs and drills enable the unit to rapidly execute assigned missions without long, detailed orders.

Depth

Depth is the extension of operations in time, space, and resources. A commander seeks to fight the enemy throughout the depth of the enemy's formations by properly positioning his forces or by skillfully maneuvering his unit. This allows the unit to seek out and concentrate against enemy weaknesses. By swiftly concentrating against first one, then another enemy weakness, a skilled commander can begin to seize the initiative on a local level, allowing a higher commander to then exploit the opportunity.

Synchronization

Synchronization is the arrangement of battlefield activities in time, space, and purpose to produce maximum combat power at the decisive point. A commander synchronizes his subordinates' actions on the battlefield by assigning clear missions, making understood the timing required in the operation, and focusing all actions toward achieving overwhelming combat power at a decisive point. Issuing mission orders, identifying the main effort, and assigning each subordinate element clear tasks and purposes are the best means of maintaining synchronization in a fast-paced, fluid environment.

Versatility

Versatility is the ability of tactical units to adapt to different missions and tasks. In a force-projection army, the demands for versatility increase. Forces must be prepared to move rapidly from one region to another, one type of warfare to another, and one form of combat to another.

Combat Power

Army forces seek to apply overwhelming combat power in order to achieve victory at minimal cost. Four primary elements—maneuver, firepower, protection, and leadership—combine to create combat power.

Maneuver

Maneuver is the movement of forces supported by fire to achieve a position of advantage from which to destroy or threaten destruction of the enemy. Maneuver is the primary means of gaining or retaining the initiative. Forces use stealth, camouflage, dispersion, terrain, and fires to support their movement and close with the enemy. Infantry takes advantage of its ability to move across difficult terrain in any weather to surprise the enemy. The indirect approach guides movement planning: avoiding the enemy's strengths, moving through gaps or weaknesses or around its flanks, and striking at critical locations to rapidly destroy the enemy's will and ability to fight.

Firepower
Firepower is the capacity to deliver effective fire on a target. Firepower and maneuver are complementary. It is the effect of fires on the enemy that matters. A few weapons firing accurately from a location that surprises the enemy are more effective than many weapons with a large volume of fire but without the element of surprise. Before attempting to maneuver, infantry units must establish a base of fire. Leaders must understand the capabilities of organic and supporting weapons, how to position and employ them, and the techniques of integrating and controlling fires.

Protection
Protection is the conservation of the fighting potential of the force. It includes all actions that degrade the enemy's ability to maneuver against or place fires on the friendly force. These include security measures; use of limited visibility, cover, and concealment; air defense; camouflage; and dispersion. Protection also includes maintaining the soldiers' health and morale. Maneuver provides protection for the force by preventing the enemy from fixing it and concentrating firepower against it. Firepower, such as suppressive fire during an assault, can also provide protection. Infantry gains protection by avoiding detection during movement and by digging fighting positions when stationary.

Leadership
The combat power generated by infantry forces is dependent on the concepts and plans developed by the commanders and subordinate leaders. Infantry leaders are expected to lead by personal example and to provide purpose, motivation, and direction for their soldiers. Leaders must know their profession, their soldiers, and the tools of war.

Basic Rules of Combat

These rules appeared in Army doctrine for a short time but are no longer included in recent publications. At small-unit level, however, they encompass the essence of the above fundamentals.

Secure
- Use cover and concealment.
- Establish local security and conduct reconnaissance.
- Protect the unit.

Move
- Establish a moving element.
- Get in the best position to shoot.
- Gain and maintain the initiative.
- Move fast, strike hard, and finish rapidly.

Shoot
- Establish a base of fire.
- Maintain mutual support.
- Kill or suppress the enemy.

Communicate
- Keep everybody informed.
- Tell soldiers what is expected.

Sustain
- Keep the fight going.
- Take care of soldiers.

2

Command and Control

LEADERSHIP

Military leadership is a process by which a soldier influences others to accomplish the mission. The commander's leadership and the company's command and control system operate in a dynamic and complex environment that commanders and leaders must understand. Because leadership is essential to the successful use of combat power, leaders must motivate their soldiers and give direction to their efforts.

The traditional principles of leadership are excellent guidelines for developing leaders, subordinates, and units. These principles and the *be, know,* and *do* attributes provide a philosophy of professional leadership that will help you address the challenges every leader faces.

Principles

1. Know yourself and seek self-improvement.
2. Be technically and tactically proficient.
3. Seek responsibility and take responsibility for your actions.
4. Make sound and timely decisions.

5. Set the example.
6. Know your soldiers and look out for their well-being.
7. Keep your soldiers informed.
8. Develop a sense of responsibility in your subordinates.
9. Ensure that the task is understood, supervised, and accomplished.
10. Train your soldiers as a team.
11. Employ your unit in accordance with its capabilities.

Attributes

BE

- Be committed to the professional Army ethic (loyalty to the nation's ideals, loyalty to unit, selfless service, personal responsibility).
- Possess professional character traits (courage, competence, candor, commitment, integrity).

KNOW

- Know the four factors of leadership and how they affect each other (follower, leader, communication, situation).
- Know yourself (character strengths and weaknesses, knowledge, skills).
- Know human nature (human needs and emotions; how people respond to stress; character strengths and weaknesses, knowledge, and skills of your people).
- Know your job (technical and tactical proficiency).
- Know your unit (how to develop necessary individual and team skills, how to develop cohesion, how to develop discipline).

DO

- Provide direction (set goals, solve problems, make decisions, plan).
- Implement (communicate, coordinate, supervise, evaluate).
- Motivate (apply principles of motivation, such as developing morale and esprit in your unit; teach, coach, and counsel).

Infantry Leaders

An infantry leader is closest to the fight and must be a resourceful, tenacious, and decisive warrior as well as a tactician. He must understand and use initiative in accomplishing a mission; he cannot rely on a book to solve tactical problems. He is expected to lead by example, be at the point of decision to maintain control, understand the situation, and issue orders if required. This means that he must know how to quickly analyze a situation and make decisions in light of the commander's intent. He must be prepared to take independent action if necessary. The art of quickly making sound decisions lies in the knowledge of tactics, the estimate process, and small-unit techniques and procedures.

Mission Tactics

Mission tactics is a term used to describe the exercise of command authority by a leader; it puts the relationship of command, control, and communications in proper perspective by placing the emphasis on command. This provides for initiative, the acceptance of risk, and the rapid seizure of opportunities on the battlefield. Mission tactics reinforced by knowledge of the higher commander's intent and focused on a main effort establish the basis for small-unit leadership. Leaders must be provided the maximum freedom to command and have imposed on them only that control necessary to synchronize mission accomplishment. The more complex an operation, the more control needed. The challenge to leaders is to provide the minimal amount of control required and still allow for decentralized decision making.

THE COMMAND AND CONTROL PROCESS

The commander accomplishes a mission through the command and control process. He uses this process to find out what is going on, to decide what action to take, to issue orders, and to supervise execution.

Troop-leading Procedure

The basis of the command and control process is the troop-leading procedure—a series of actions used for planning, coordinating, executing, and supervising tactical operations. Its interrelated components are the commander's estimate of the situation and the METT-T (mission, enemy, terrain and weather, troops and equipment, time available) analysis. (See accompanying chart.)

The troop-leading procedure is a continuous process that begins when a mission is received and ends when the mission is accomplished. The actions are continuous and do not necessarily occur in the order shown in the chart. All actions will be accomplished regardless of the amount of time available. The goal is to provide your subordinates their missions within one-third of the available time so that they have two-thirds of the time for their planning and preparation.

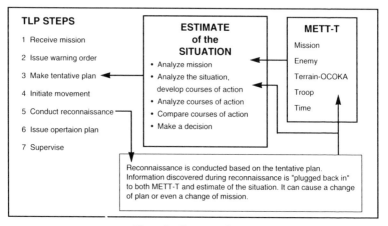

Troop-leading procedures.

Commander's Estimate of the Situation

The commander analyzes relevant information, based on his analysis of METT-T, to develop the most effective solution to a tactical problem. At company level, the commander's estimate of the situation is a rapid mental process that provides a format for the logical analysis of all relevant factors.

The total tactical environment is covered by the METT-T factors, which are analyzed in relationship to each other. These factors must be considered rapidly.

- MISSION—specified tasks; implied tasks; limitations and/or constraints; intent; essential tasks; restated mission.
- ENEMY—type; composition; organization; identification; strengths and weaknesses; morale; capabilities; likely courses of action; intentions.
- TERRAIN—observation; fields of fire; key or decisive terrain; obstacles; cover and concealment; avenues of approach.
- WEATHER—trafficability; visibility; effect on soldiers; effect on equipment; effect on friendly and enemy aircraft.
- TROOPS—number and types of platoons; state of training and discipline; strength (men and materiel); condition of men; morale; past performance; location and disposition of adjacent units; state of maintenance and supply; combat support available; combat service support available; effectiveness of leadership.

- TIME AVAILABLE—planning and preparation; line of departure; movement; start point, critical point, release point; hold or seize key terrain; enemy reaction.

Leaders use the estimate for every tactical decision. The estimate has five steps:

Step 1. Conduct a detailed mission analysis. During the analysis, the commander determines the following:

- Commander's concept and intent (two levels above).
- All tasks his unit must accomplish.
- All limitations on his unit's freedom of action.
- His unit's restated mission statement.

Step 2. Analyze the situation and develop courses of action. During this step, the remaining factors of METT-T are analyzed. The next factor analyzed should be the terrain, not the enemy, for several reasons:

1. Understanding the terrain will provide a better understanding of the enemy's capabilities and limitations. Terrain is considered from both the friendly and enemy viewpoints. Weather factors are considered at the same time.

2. The focus of enemy analysis is to locate the enemy's strengths (to avoid them) and weaknesses (to exploit them). The end result of the enemy analysis should be a detailed statement of the enemy's most probable course of action.

3. The commander's analysis of available troops considers the current status of his men and equipment—including key leaders, morale, weapons, and ammunition—and how adjacent and supporting units may affect the mission.

4. The commander considers the times specified in higher-headquarters orders and any key times resulting from his analysis of the situation.

5. As the commander conducts his analysis, he begins to develop one or more courses of action. Each course of action must be feasible, accomplishing the mission and supporting the commander's concept; reasonable, in that the unit will remain an effective force after completing the mission; and distinguishable, not just a minor variation of another course of action.

Step 3. Analyze the courses of action. This analysis is accomplished by war-gaming these courses of action against the enemy's most probable course of action. Upon completing the war game of each course of action, the leader should have determined its advantages and disadvantages and have identified any critical events that would determine success or failure.

Step 4. Compare the courses of action. The leader now considers the advantages and disadvantages of each course, how the critical events affect each course, and significant factors based on his mission. There are two types of significant factors: mission-specific, which includes casualty evacuation, soldier's load, physical condition of soldiers, effectiveness in accomplishing the mission, and time usage; and more general factors, based on doctrinal guidelines, including security, simplicity, surprise, exploitation of enemy weaknesses, risk, disruption of enemy attack, concentration at the decisive point, use of limited visibility, and employment of key weapons. Although most of these apply in every tactical operation, certain ones will be more important to the mission at hand.

Step 5. Make a decision. The leader selects the course of action he believes has the best chance of accomplishing the mission.

COMBAT ORDERS

Either written or oral, combat orders are used to transmit information and instructions to subordinates. The use of combat orders, expressed in standard formats or containing essential elements, ensures that instructions are conveyed clearly, concisely, and completely. Standing operating procedures (SOP) complement combat orders. Reference to SOP for tasks and situations that occur often expedites issuance of orders.

Warning Orders

Commanders use warning orders to alert subordinate units of an impending mission and to provide initial instructions so that subordinates have a maximum amount of time to prepare. Although not a prescribed format, the warning order contains five essential elements:

- The mission.
- Who is participating in the mission.
- Time of the operation.
- Any special instructions.
- Time and place for issuance of complete order.

Operation Orders

The operation order (OPORD) supplies needed instructions and information to subordinates. It outlines what must be done to accomplish a mission and how the commander intends to fight the battle. It ensures that subordinate platoons and support elements know everything necessary to accomplish the mission. The standard OPORD format is used to organize thoughts in a logical sequence:

Paragraph 1: SITUATION

Subparagraphs:

a. Enemy forces.

b. Friendly forces.

c. Attachments and detachments.

Paragraph 2: MISSION

A clear, concise statement expressed in the *who, what, when, why,* and *where* of the tasks to be accomplished. There are no subparagraphs.

Paragraph 3: EXECUTION

Subparagraphs:

a. Concept of operation. (The commander's visualization of the operation from start to finish. It accurately describes the commander's intent so mission accomplishment is possible in the absence of further instructions.)

(1) Maneuver.

(2) Fires.

b. Missions for assigned and/or attached units are stated in separate subparagraphs, including details of specific missions for each.

c. Coordinating instructions.

Paragraph 4: SERVICE SUPPORT

Contains a statement of CSS instructions and arrangements that support the operation.

Paragraph 5: COMMAND AND SIGNAL

Subparagraphs:

a. Command. (May include CP location, liaison requirements, succession of command.)

b. Signal. (Discusses communication-electronics instructions.)

Fragmentary Orders

The fragmentary order (FRAGO) is issued to make a change in an existing order; therefore, it addresses only those items from the OPORD that

are changed. Although no standard format exists, the essential items normally included are as follows:
- Situation (enemy and friendly).
- Changes to the organization.
- Orders to subordinate units.
- Fire support.
- Coordinating instructions.

OPERATIONS SECURITY

All measures taken to maintain security and achieve tactical surprise constitute operations security (OPSEC). These measures include countersurveillance, physical security, signal security, and information security. OPSEC also involves the elimination or control of tactical indicators that can be exploited by the enemy. To provide the most effective OPSEC, you must see the enemy before it sees you. The following measures can be used to provide OPSEC:
- Use hide and defilade positions habitually.
- Position observation posts to observe enemy avenues of approach.
- Camouflage positions, vehicles, and equipment against both visual and infrared detection. Break up silhouettes, reduce glare, reduce vehicle signatures caused by dust, exhaust smoke, and tracks.
- Reduce infrared and thermal signatures by parking in shadows, turning off engines and heaters, and using terrain masking.
- Maintain noise and light discipline.
- Patrol aggressively to prevent enemy surveillance and to gather information about the enemy.
- Use smoke to screen movement.
- Enforce proper radio operating procedures: authentication, encoding, limiting transmission time, using low power, and tying down antennas.
- Use radio operators trained in antijam, interference, and deception procedures.
- Overwatch friendly barriers and obstacles.
- Maintain contact with adjacent units.

FRATRICIDE

Fratricide is frequently experienced in combat and is defined as fire upon friendly units, personnel, or equipment resulting in suppression, damage, or destruction. Fratricide incidents can be caused by direct or indirect fire and are more common in night attacks. They are due in large measure to a lack of positive target identification.

Many tactical techniques and procedures that have been established over the years for other battlefield purposes also minimize fratricide incidents. These include fire planning and fire control measures, such as sectors of fire, target reference points (TRP) and engagement areas (EA), restrictive fire control measures, priorities of engagement, pyrotechnics and visual markers, checkpoints and trigger points, boundaries, limiting stakes, range cards, and sector sketches. Fratricide incidents can also be reduced by rehearsals, emphasis on target identification, and situational awareness. Individual soldiers and unit leaders must know at all times who is to their flanks, front, and rear and must be kept informed of changes in the tactical situation. Technology, lethality of weapons, and dispersion on the modern battlefield all tend to increase the possibility of friendly-fire-related casualties. Even with the availability of identification devices currently under development, it is still the responsibility of leaders and soldiers to adhere to established control measures combined with situational awareness to ensure that fire is not placed on friendly troops.

CONTINUOUS OPERATIONS

The company must be prepared to fight, fix, fuel, arm, and man vehicles and weapons twenty-four hours a day. Plan to fix, refuel, rearm, and man every time the tactical situation permits.

Sleep plans must be enforced. Use the buddy system so that each man can look after another. Train soldiers to recognize signs of fatigue. Troops, and especially leaders, require rest in order to remain effective. Mental tasks are degraded more by lack of sleep than by physical exertion.

Use of the one-third/two-thirds rule is critical. Warning orders must include order issue and movement times so that sleep and rest schedules can be set. Orders must be given in a deliberate manner and should be simple, specific, and very directive in nature. Subordinates should briefback to ensure the order is understood.

COMMUNICATIONS

Communications are necessary to control subordinate elements, to receive and to disseminate information, and to coordinate combat support and combat service support. The commander is responsible for the discipline of the communications system within his unit and for its operation in the system of the next higher headquarters. Responsibilities for establishment of communications are as follows:

- Senior unit to subordinate unit.
- Supporting unit to supported unit.
- Reinforcing unit to reinforced unit.
- Left to right and rear to front.
- Both units take prompt action when communications cannot be established or when they are disrupted.

Five Basic Means of Communications

The commander has five basic means to communicate:

FM Radio

The company commander operates on the company net and monitors the battalion net; the XO operates on the battalion net and monitors the company net; the first sergeant operates on the battalion admin/log net and monitors the company net; platoon leaders operate on platoon nets and monitor the company net. Use of the radio is avoided until enemy contact is made.

Wire

Wire hot loops are established within and between platoons and the company when the unit is stationary. OPs should be included within a hot loop.

Messenger

To reduce electronic signals, messengers are used whenever possible prior to battle. Normally battalions send messengers to the company, and platoons send messengers to the company commander.

Visual Signals

These normally include hand-and-arm signals, flag signals, pyrotechnics, flashlights, and chemical lights. Visual signals should be planned together with, or as a backup to, voice communications. They are normally used either when other communications are lost or to overcome jamming.

Audible Signals

These are normally used to transmit prearranged messages, to attract attention, and to spread warning alarms. They should be simple to understand, and prearranged meanings should be covered in SOPs.

3

Movement

Infantry's key strength is its ability to cross almost any terrain during all weather conditions. When infantry can move undetected, it gains an advantage over the enemy. Movement fundamentals, formations, and techniques assist the leader in providing security during movement.

FUNDAMENTALS

- Ensure that movement supports a rapid transition to maneuver.
- Conduct reconnaissance of the terrain and the enemy to the extent possible.
- Move on covered and concealed routes and, if the situation permits, during limited visibility.
- Select routes that avoid natural lines of drift, likely ambush sites, and other danger areas.
- Establish security during movement and halts. Avoid moving directly forward from covered positions. All weapons should be prepared to engage targets. Enforce camouflage, noise, and light discipline.
- Designate air guards.
- Make enemy contact with the smallest element possible.

FORMATIONS

Formations describe the relationship of soldiers and elements to each other and are used to provide control, flexibility, and security. There are five basic moving formations: column, line, vee, wedge, and file.

Column

The column formation provides good dispersion laterally and in depth without sacrificing control, and also facilitates maneuver. It allows a limited volume of fire to the front and rear and a large volume to the flanks. Squads can move in either a column wedge or a modified column wedge.

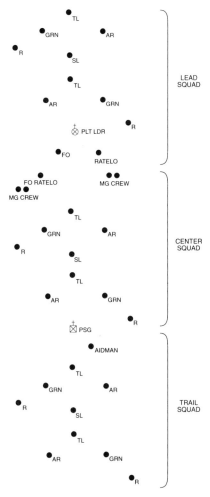

Platoon column.

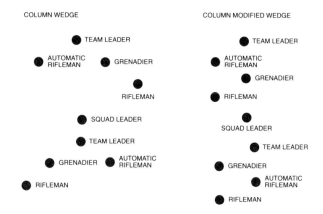

Squad column wedge and modified wedge.

Line

The line formation allows the delivery of maximum fire to the front but little to the flanks.

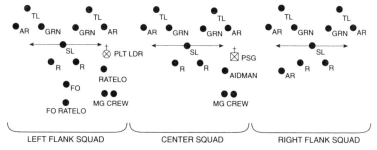

NOTE: Squad Leader (SL) positions himself where he can best control the squad.

Platoon on line, squads on line.

Squad line.

Vee

The vee formation allows a heavy volume of fire on contact, but it moves slowly and is difficult to control.

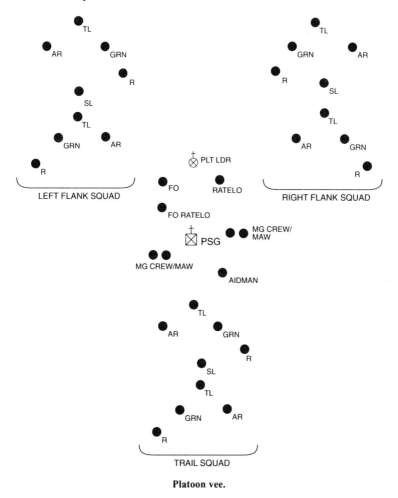

Platoon vee.

Wedge

The wedge formation allows a large volume of fire to the front and flanks. It makes contact with a small element. This formation is able to move faster than the vee but is also hard to control.

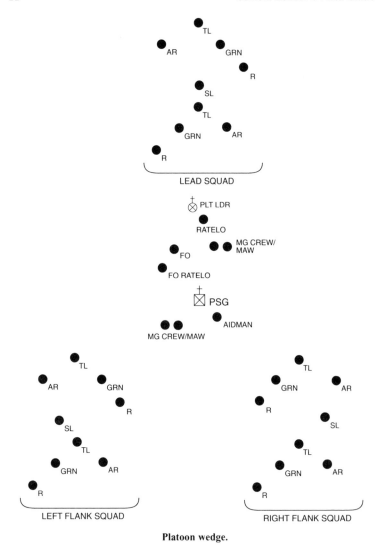

Platoon wedge.

File

The file formation allows a large volume of fire to the flanks but provides the least security. It is used when moving in close terrain or limited visibility.

● TEAM LEADER

○ SQUAD LEADER (OPTIONAL)

● GRENADIER

● AUTOMATIC RIFLEMAN

● RIFLEMAN

● SQUAD LEADER (NORMAL)

● TEAM LEADER

● GRENADIER

● AUTOMATIC RIFLEMAN

○ TEAM LEADER (OPTIONAL)

● RIFLEMAN

Squad file.

MOVEMENT FORMATION	WHEN NORMALLY USED	CHARACTERISTICS			
		CONTROL	FLEXIBILITY	FIRE CAPABILITIES/ RESTRICTIONS	SECURITY
SQUAD COLUMN	SQUAD PRIMARY FORMATION	GOOD	FACILITATES MANEUVER, GOOD DISPERSION LATERALLY AND IN DEPTH	ALLOWS LARGE VOLUME OF FIRE TO THE FLANK— LIMITED VOLUME TO THE FRONT	ALL-ROUND
SQUAD LINE	WHEN MAXIMUM FIRE POWER IS REQUIRED TO THE FRONT	NOT AS GOOD AS SQUAD COLUMN	LIMITED MANEUVER CAPABILITY (BOTH FIRE TEAMS COMMITTED)	ALLOWS MAXIMUM IMMEDIATE FIRE TO THE FRONT	GOOD TO THE FRONT, LITTLE TO THE FLANKS AND REAR
SQUAD FILE	CLOSE TERRAIN VEGETATION, LIMITED VISIBILITY CONDITIONS	EASIEST	MOST DIFFICULT FORMATION FROM WHICH TO MANEUVER	ALLOWS IMMEDIATE FIRE TO THE FLANK, MASKS MOST FIRE TO THE FRONT AND REAR	LEAST

Comparison of squad formations.

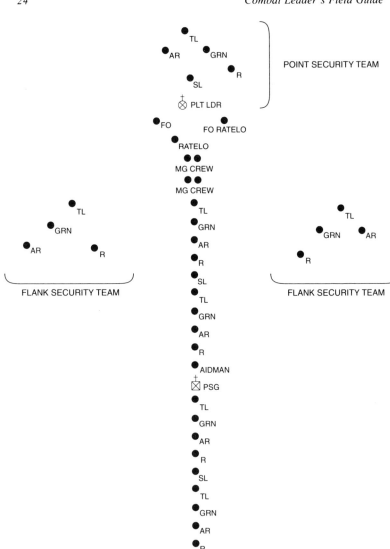

Platoon file.

TECHNIQUES

The three movement techniques are traveling, traveling overwatch, and bounding overwatch. The choice of technique is based on the likelihood of enemy contact and the need for speed. Any of the three techniques can be used with any formation. Soldiers should be able to see their leader and the leader should be able to see at least his lead element.

MOVEMENT TECHNIQUES	WHEN NORMALLY USED	CHARACTERISTICS			
		CONTROL	DISPERSION	SPEED	SECURITY
TRAVELING	CONTACT NOT LIKELY	MORE	LESS	FASTEST	LEAST
TRAVELING OVERWATCH	CONTACT POSSIBLE	LESS	MORE	SLOWER	MORE
BOUNDING OVERWATCH	CONTACT EXPECTED	MOST	MOST	SLOWEST	MOST

Movement techniques.

Traveling

Traveling is used when contact with the enemy is not likely and speed is needed.

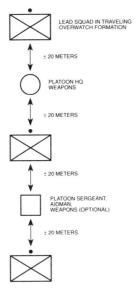

Platoon traveling.

Traveling Overwatch

Traveling overwatch is used when contact is possible. The trailing element may pause briefly to overwatch the lead element.

Bounding Overwatch

Bounding overwatch is used when contact is expected or when a large, open danger area must be crossed. The bounding element moves forward while the trailing element overwatches from a position from which it can support the bounding element by fire. The key is the use of terrain. The overwatch position must dominate the route that the bounding element will take, and the bounding element must stay within the supporting range of the overwatching element.

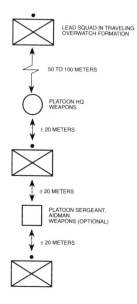

Platoon traveling overwatch.

Elements can bound successively or alternately. Successive bounds are easier to control, while alternate bounds can be faster.

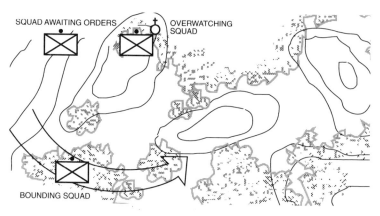

Platoon bounding overwatch.

DANGER AREAS

A danger area is any place on the movement route where the unit might be exposed to enemy observation, fire, or both. Units try to avoid danger areas. If a danger area must be crossed, it should be done with great caution and as quickly as possible.

Do the following before crossing a danger area:
- Designate near- and far-side rally points.
- Secure the near side (both flanks and rear).
- Reconnoiter and secure the far side.

The unit halts when the lead elements signal "danger area." The leader confirms the danger area, then selects and informs subordinate leaders of near- and far-side rally points. Near-side security is posted to overwatch the crossing. The far-side security team crosses the danger area and clears the far side. Once the far side is cleared, the main body moves quickly and quietly across the danger area. A small unit may cross all at once, in pairs, or one soldier at a time. A large unit normally crosses its elements one at a time. As each element crosses, it moves to an overwatch position or to the far-side rally point. The near-side security element then crosses and resumes its place in the formation as the unit continues its mission.

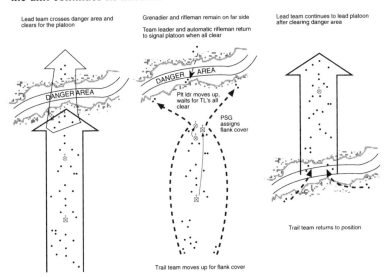

Crossing a danger area.

Crossing Techniques
Open Areas

When crossing an open area, stay concealed and observe carefully from the near side. Post security to give early warning, and send an element across to clear the far side. When cleared, quickly cross the rest of the unit at the shortest exposed distance.

To cross large open areas, a combination of traveling overwatch and bounding overwatch is used. Bounding overwatch is used at any point in the open area where enemy contact may be expected or when the element comes within small-arms range (250 meters) of the far side.

Small open areas may be bypassed, by either using the detour bypass method or contouring around the open area. In the detour bypass method, the force moves around the open area using 90-degree turns to the right or left until the far side is reached. To contour around the open area, the unit uses the wood line and vegetation for cover and concealment as it moves around the open area until reaching the far-side rally point.

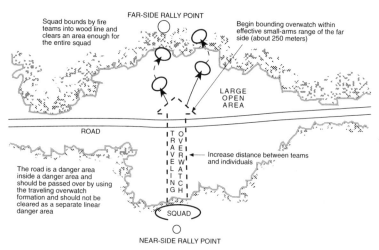

Crossing a large open area.

Roads and Trails

Cross a road or trail at or near a bend, a narrow spot, or on low ground to reduce enemy observation and minimize the unit's exposure.

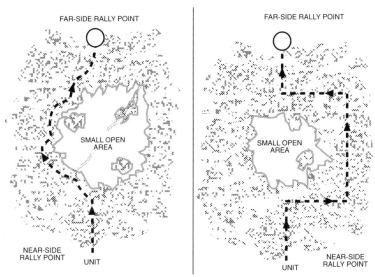

Crossing a small open area.

Villages

Pass on the downwind side and well away from a village. Avoid animals, especially dogs, which might reveal your presence.

Enemy Positions

Pass enemy positions on the downwind side (the enemy might have scout dogs). Be alert for trip wires or other warning devices.

Minefields

Bypass a minefield even if it means changing your route by a great distance. If you *must* pass through a minefield, the lead elements clear a lane for the rest of the unit. Soldiers use their hands to detect trip wires and use sharpened sticks to probe for mines.

Streams

When crossing a stream, select a narrow spot that offers concealment on both banks. Observe the far side carefully, and place security out for early warning. Clear the far side, then cross quickly but quietly.

Wire Obstacles

Avoid crossing wire obstacles if possible; they are normally under observation. If wire must be breached during daytime, use the method that exposes the unit for the shortest amount of time. Check the wire for mines, booby traps, and warning devices. To breach wire at night, either cross over or go under the wire using the following procedures:

To cross over the wire, grasp the first stand lightly, and cautiously lift one leg over. Lower your foot slowly to the ground, feeling carefully for sure footing, then lift the other foot over the wire. Quietly release this wire and feel for the next strand. Cross it in the same way.

To go under the wire, move headfirst. Lie on your back and slide under the bottom strands, pushing forward with the heels. Carry your weapon lengthwise on the body, steadying it with either hand. To prevent the wire from catching on clothing or equipment, let it slide along the weapon. Inch along, holding the wire up with one hand. Do not jerk or pull on the wire. Feel ahead with your free hand for low strands or trip wires.

If the wire must be cut, cut only the lower strands to minimize discovery of the gap. Soldiers should work in a team if possible. Wire should be wrapped with a cloth near a picket, cut partway through, and then bent back and forth until it breaks. The loose end is carefully rolled back to clear the lane. Concertina is hard to control after cutting and can snap back. If concertina must be cut, stake down two loops far enough apart so that a soldier can crawl between them. Then cut partway through and break as previously described.

Enemy Contact at Danger Areas ·

If the unit makes contact in or around a danger area, the leader determines whether to assault the enemy or break contact, depending on the situation and mission. If the unit becomes disorganized, the near-side and far-side rally points are used to link up and reorganize. Ideally, using movement fundamentals, the unit will see the enemy first, remain undetected, and ambush it.

ASSEMBLY AREA PROCEDURES

An assembly area is a location where the unit prepares for future operations. Here the unit receives and issues orders and supplies, services and repairs vehicles and equipment, and feeds and rests soldiers. When an assembly area is used to prepare for an attack, it is usually well forward.

Before occupying an assembly area, the leader designates a quartering party, which reconnoiters the assembly area to ensure no enemy are

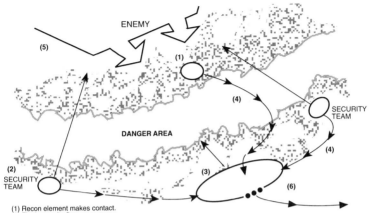

ENEMY

(5)

(1)

(4)

SECURITY
TEAM

DANGER AREA

(4)

(2)
SECURITY
TEAM

(3)

(6)

(1) Recon element makes contact.
(2) Flank security fires on enemy.
(3) Main body takes overwatch position and fires on enemy.
(4) Security and recon return to main body.
(5) Smoke and indirect fire used to break contact.
(6) The platoon moves to different place to cross danger area.

Enemy contact on far side.

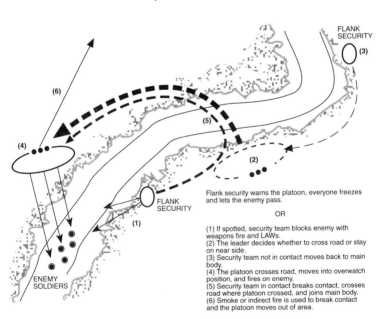

FLANK
SECURITY

(3)

(6)

(5)

(4)

(2)

FLANK
SECURITY

(1)

ENEMY
SOLDIERS

Flank security warns the platoon, everyone freezes
and lets the enemy pass.

OR

(1) If spotted, security team blocks enemy with
weapons fire and LAWs.
(2) The leader decides whether to cross road or stay
on near side.
(3) Security team not in contact moves back to main
body.
(4) The platoon crosses road, moves into overwatch
position, and fires on enemy.
(5) Security team in contact breaks contact, crosses
road where platoon crossed, and joins main body.
(6) Smoke or indirect fire is used to break contact
and the platoon moves out of area.

Enemy contact on road or trail.

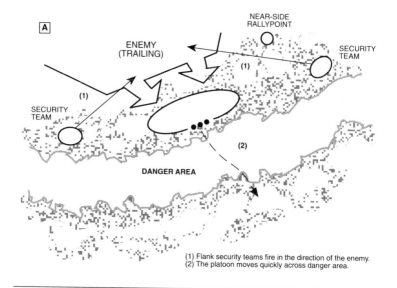

A

NEAR-SIDE RALLYPOINT

ENEMY (TRAILING)

SECURITY TEAM

(1)

SECURITY TEAM

(1)

(2)

DANGER AREA

(1) Flank security teams fire in the direction of the enemy.
(2) The platoon moves quickly across danger area.

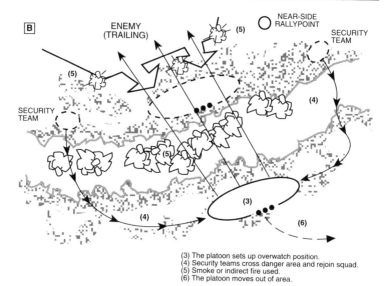

B

NEAR-SIDE RALLYPOINT

ENEMY (TRAILING)

(5)

SECURITY TEAM

(5)

(4)

SECURITY TEAM

(5)

(3)

(4)

(6)

(3) The platoon sets up overwatch position.
(4) Security teams cross danger area and rejoin squad.
(5) Smoke or indirect fire used.
(6) The platoon moves out of area.

Enemy contact on near side.

present and to establish initial security. The quartering party determines initial positions for all elements, continues to secure the area, occupies covered and concealed positions, and as the main body approaches, moves out and guides elements from the release point to their initial positions. The unit occupies its positions in the assembly area and maintains local security. All elements are assigned a sector of the perimeter to ensure mutual support and to cover all gaps by observation and fire. Observation posts are designated and manned.

A priority of work is established to complete the assembly area:

- Positioning crew-served weapons and chemical-agent alarms, and designating principal directions of fire (PDF), final protective line (FPL), and final protective fires (FPF).
- Constructing individual and crew-served fighting positions.
- Setting up wire communications between the elements. (Radio silence is observed.)
- Preparing range cards.
- Camouflaging positions.
- Clearing fields of fire.
- Distributing ammunition, rations, water, supplies, and special equipment.
- Conducting preventive maintenance checks and services on weapons and equipment.
- Preparing night sights.
- Test-firing small-arms weapons (if the tactical situation permits).
- Conducting personal hygiene and field sanitation.
- Instituting a rest plan.

Leaders conduct adjacent-unit coordination and assign security patrols, if necessary.

SOLDIER'S LOAD

The soldier's load is of crucial concern to leaders. Research has shown that a soldier can carry up to 30 percent of his body weight and still retain a high percentage of his agility, stamina, alertness, and mobility. For the average soldier, weighing 160 pounds, that would be a 48-pound load. The soldier loses a proportional amount of his functional ability for each pound over 30 percent.

Use the following techniques for load management:

- Distribute loads evenly over body and load-bearing equipment (LBE).

- Don't carry anything on the front of the LBE that would prevent the soldier from taking well-aimed shots.
- Distribute loads throughout the unit. If it is necessary to man-pack bulk ammunition, water, rations, or demolitions, divide them into small loads.
- Rotate heavy loads (radios, MGs, mortars, and AT weapons) among several soldiers.
- Always consider transportation assets to carry loads.
- Upon enemy contact, drop rucksacks or leave them in an ORP, an assault position, or the assembly area.
- Share or consolidate items. Carry only enough sleeping bags for those who will sleep at the same time. In the same manner, two or three soldiers can share a rucksack and take turns carrying it.
- Consider carrying fewer rations for short operations.
- While carrying rucksacks, use water and rations carried in it first. Then rucksacks can be dropped and soldiers will still have a full supply on their LBE.

Combat Load

The combat load consists of the mission-essential equipment required for soldiers to fight and survive immediate combat operations, plus items needed based on METT-T. When possible, this load should not exceed 60 pounds. There are two components: fighting load and approach march load.

Fighting Load

The fighting load includes only what is needed to fight and survive imme-diate combat operations.

Load	Weight (pounds)
Helmet, ballistic	3.4
Pistol belt, suspenders, and first-aid pouch	1.6
Canteen, 1-quart, and cover with water (2 each)	5.6
Case, small arms (2 each)	1.8
Bayonet with scabbard	1.3
Protective mask with decontamination kit	3.0
Rifle, M16A2 with 30 rounds 5.56 Ball	8.8
Magazines (6) with 180 rounds 5.56 Ball	5.4
Grenade, fragmentation (4)	4.0
Total	34.9

Approach March Load

The approach march load contains the items needed for extended combat operations. On long operations, soldiers must carry enough equipment and munitions to fight and exist until a planned resupply can take place. They are dropped at an assault position, an objective rally point (ORP), or other point before or upon enemy contact.

Load	Weight (pounds)
ALICE, medium with frame	6.3
Rations, MRE (2 each)	2.6
Canteen, 2-quart, and cover with water	4.8
Toilet articles	2.0
Towel	0.2
Bag, waterproof	0.8
E-tool with carrier	2.5
Poncho, nylon	1.3
Liner, poncho	1.6
Total	22.1

Sustainment Load

The sustainment load consists of the remaining equipment and material needed for sustained combat operations. This must be carried by company and battalion assets.

FOOT MARCH

Foot marches are the movement of troops and equipment mainly by foot, with limited support by vehicles. They are characterized by combat readiness, ease of control, adaptability to terrain, slow rate of movement, and increased personnel fatigue. Foot marches do not depend on the existence of roads.

A dismounted company moves in a column of twos, a file on each side of the road. *Distances:* day, 2 to 5 meters between men, 50 meters between platoons; night, 1 to 3 meters between men, 25 meters between platoons. *Rates:* day, 4 kmph; night, 3.2 kmph. (Cross country: day, 2.4 kmph; night, 1.6 kmph.) *Halts:* 15 minutes after the first 45 minutes, 10 minutes out of every hour thereafter.

Road Space (RS), Foot Column

The road space of a company foot column, used in determining time length of the column, consists of two parts: the space occupied by the men alone (including the distance between them), and the sum of distances between elements of the foot column. (Total RS=RS men + RS platoon distances.)

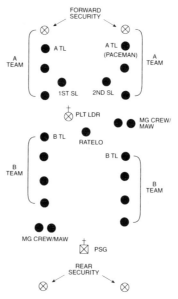

NOTE: 3rd Sqd can be on either side of the road.

Road march formation.

The road space of the men alone is determined by multiplying the number of men by the appropriate factor selected from the table below:

Formation	2 meters per man	5 meters per man
Single file	2.4	5.4
Column of twos	1.2	2.7

The total road space between platoons is obtained by multiplying the number of platoons (minus one) by the platoon distances.

Time Length, Foot Column

Rate	Formula
4.0 kmph	TL (min.) = RS (meters) x .0150
3.2 kmph	TL = RS x .0187
2.4 kmph	TL = RS x .0250
1.6 kmph	TL = RS x .0375

Completion Time

The completion time of a foot march is determined by using this formula: Completion time = SP (start point) time + TL (time length) + scheduled halts.

4

Offense

Offensive operations are undertaken to destroy the enemy and its will to fight; to learn enemy strength and disposition; or to deceive, divert, or fix the enemy. Offense is the decisive form of war.

CHARACTERISTICS

All successful offensive operations use the elements of surprise, concentration, speed, flexibility, and audacity.

Surprise

Units surprise the enemy by striking at a time or place or in a manner for which it is unprepared. Surprise delays enemy reaction, overloads and confuses its command and control, reduces the effectiveness of its weapons, and induces psychological shock in its soldiers and leaders. To achieve surprise, keep your locations, movements, and plan of attack hidden; take advantage of close terrain and/or limited visibility; use camouflage; and move silently.

Concentration

Because tactical offensive operations often expose the attacking force, the attackers need local superiority of combat power, or concentration.

This does not necessarily mean a numerical advantage. If the attacker has used surprise and is attacking at an enemy point of weakness, it may achieve overwhelming combat power with a relatively small force.

Speed
Speed promotes surprise, keeps the enemy off balance, contributes to the security of the attacking force, and prevents the enemy from taking effective countermeasures. Speed in the attack is increased through simple plans, decentralized control, mission orders, thorough reconnaissance, selecting good routes, proper formations and movement techniques, and keeping soldiers' loads to a minimum.

Flexibility
At some point in most attacks, the original plan must be adjusted to meet the changing situation. The attacker must expect uncertainties and be ready to exploit opportunities. Thorough war-gaming, use of the reserve, and mission orders enhance flexibility.

Audacity
Audacity means bold, aggressive actions in dangerous situations. Leaders must calculate risk, act boldly on the calculations, and surprise the enemy. Audacious leaders throughout history have used the indirect approach, maneuvering to maintain a position of advantage over the enemy, seeking to attack the enemy on its flank or rear, and exploiting success at once.

FORMS OF TACTICAL OFFENSE
The four general forms of tactical offense are movement to contact, attack, exploitation, and pursuit.

Movement to Contact
A movement to contact is conducted to develop the situation and to establish or regain contact. Search and attack, approach march, and reconnaissance in force are typical of this form of offense.

Attack
An attack usually follows a movement to contact and is intended to defeat, destroy, or neutralize the enemy. Attack options include hasty

attack, deliberate attack, spoiling attack, counterattack, raid, feint, demonstration, or any combination thereof.

Exploitation

An exploitation extends the destruction of the enemy by maintaining offensive pressure. Opportunities for local exploitation may occur even while the attack continues elsewhere in the same area.

Pursuit

The object of pursuit is the annihilation of the enemy. The difference between pursuit and exploitation is the coherence of the enemy force. When enemy resistance has broken down and the enemy is fleeing the battlefield, any type of offensive operation may give way to pursuit.

OFFENSIVE FRAMEWORK

All tactical offensive operations have a framework of reconnaissance and security operations, main attack plus supporting attacks, and sometimes reserve operations.

Reconnaissance and Security

Before an attack can begin, the enemy flanks, gaps, and weaknesses in its position or formations must be found. At the same time, friendly forces must be protected from surprise. Reconnaissance is performed to obtain information about the enemy or terrain and is focused on information critical to the attack. Security is often maintained through the use of maneuver, observation posts (OPs), and fires to provide early warning or to protect another element from enemy observation or direct fires.

Attacks

Closing with the enemy by maneuver to destroy or capture its troops is the primary task of infantry in warfare. The main attack accomplishes the mission. A platoon is the main attack force for the company if the platoon's attack accomplishes the company mission. Supporting attacks help to ensure the success of the main attack. Supporting attacks are used to fix or suppress the enemy, to seize key terrain, to breach obstacles to support the main attack's maneuver, to protect the main attack from counterattacks, or to deceive the enemy.

Reserve Operations

Reserves exploit success, reinforce or maintain momentum, repel enemy counterattacks, provide security, or complete the destruction of the enemy. The reserve is committed at the decisive point in the battle to ensure success of the mission or to capitalize on opportunities generated by a successful attack.

FORMS OF MANEUVER

The forms of maneuver are envelopment, turning movement, infiltration, penetration, and frontal attack.

Envelopment

In the envelopment maneuver, the attacker avoids the enemy's front and uses supporting attacks to fix the defender's attention forward, while maneuvering its main effort to strike at the enemy's flanks or rear.

Turning Movement

The turning movement uses maneuver to avoid the defense entirely, by moving through terrain not occupied by the enemy or under enemy observation, and to strike deep in the enemy rear.

Infiltration

Infiltration uses covert movement of forces through enemy lines to a favorable attack position in the rear.

Penetration

Penetration is used when the enemy's flanks are not assailable or when time does not permit some other form of maneuver. Its purpose is to rupture enemy defenses on a narrow front to create a breach, hold open the shoulders, and allow access to the enemy's rear.

Frontal Attack

The frontal attack is the least desirable form of maneuver. It is also the simplest form of maneuver, however, and is useful for overwhelming weak defenses, security outposts, or disorganized enemy forces.

BATTLE DRILLS

Infantry battle drills describe how platoons and squads apply fire and maneuver to commonly encountered situations. The battle drill is not intended to replace the estimate of the situation but to reduce the estimate of the situation and the decision-making process to the essential elements. (Experience at the Army's combat training centers revealed a deficiency in the action and reaction of small units.) The emphasis on drills is intended to instill an immediate, aggressive response.

Platoon or Squad Attack Drill

The platoon or squad attack drill is a comprehensive exercise that includes actions from planning the action to reorganizing after defeating the enemy. Within the drill, the platoon members may have to execute other drills—for example, the react to enemy contact or break contact drills. These drills can occur in several situations. The discussion given below for those specific drills also applies to the platoon attack drill, if appropriate situations develop.

Step 1. Prepare for combat. In the assembly area, leaders do the following:

1. Receive the order, issue the warning orders to start preparation, and complete the order or fragmentary order.
2. Check that troops have the right equipment, in sufficient quantities, and that the equipment is serviceable.
3. Check for resupply of ammunition, food, water, and medical supplies in prescribed quantities.
4. Make-sure communications equipment is operable and in prescribed quantities.
5. Make sure that soldiers and equipment are camouflaged.
6. Conduct rehearsals and inspections.

Step 2. React to enemy contact. (The platoon is moving as part of a larger unit in a movement to contact or a hasty or deliberate attack.)

1. Seek cover and concealment. Soldiers being fired on take up the closest positions that afford protection from enemy fire (cover) and observation (concealment).
2. Return fire. Automatic riflemen and machine gunners immediately return a heavy volume of suppressive fire on the enemy position. Using all weapons, the lead squad initially places heavy suppressive fires in the direction of the enemy.
3. Position and control soldiers to provide observation, cover and concealment, and fields of fire. Leaders control distribution of fires to place maximum effective, sustained fire on the enemy.

COMBAT DRILL STEPS

1. Prepare for combat
2. React to enemy contact
3. Locate the enemy
4. Gain fire superiority
5. Attack (knock out bunker, clear trench line)
6. Consolidate and reorganize

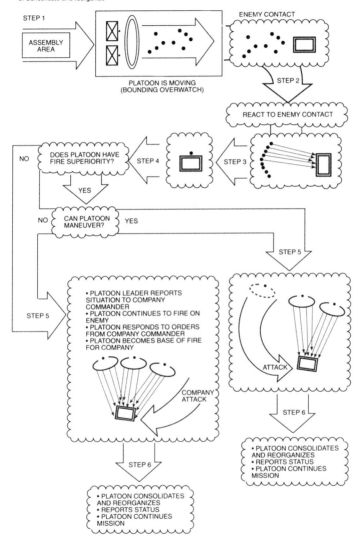

Platoon attack drill.

Step 3. Locate the enemy.

1. Observe. Squad members use sight and hearing to find known or suspected targets.
2. Reconnoiter by fire. The squad places well-aimed, sustained fire on suspected enemy positions.
3. Employ fire and movement. Squad members move in fire teams, buddy teams, or singly by rushing or crawling. A support element covers the moving element, and the assault element seeks covered firing positions.

Step 4. Gain fire superiority. The platoon leader determines if the lead squad can gain fire superiority over the enemy based on the volume and accuracy of the enemy's return fire.

- If *yes,* he continues to suppress enemy weapons returning the most effective fire, normally crew-served weapons. He uses smoke to conceal the maneuver element's movement from the enemy and prepares to attack.
- If *no,* he deploys another squad and all machine guns to suppress the enemy position and calls for indirect fire.
- If still *no,* he deploys the last squad to provide flank and rear security and to guide the rest of the company forward as necessary. He reports the situation to his commander, continues to place suppressive fire on the enemy, and prepares to become the base-of-fire element for the company's maneuver element.

Step 5. Attack. If the squad in contact and the machine guns can suppress the enemy, the platoon leader determines whether the remaining squad(s) not in contact can maneuver.

- If *yes,* the platoon leader maneuvers the other squad(s) into the assault. He determines the enemy weakness based on vulnerable flanks, distance to the enemy, location of enemy positions, and covered and concealed flanking route to the enemy position. Indirect fires and fire from the base-of-fire element are shifted to the opposite side of the enemy position. The assaulting squad(s) fight through the enemy position using fire and maneuver. They try to conduct a flank attack, knocking out bunkers and clearing trench lines.
- If *no,* the platoon leader reports the situation to the company commander. The platoon continues to fire on the enemy and react to orders from the company commander. The platoon may become the support element for the company's assault.

Step 6. Consolidate and reorganize.

1. During consolidation, the platoon leader establishes local security, places OPs, positions key weapons, occupies hasty defensive positions, and prepares for counterattack.
2. During reorganization, the platoon reestablishes the chain of command; redistributes ammunition, weapons, and communications equipment; treats casualties; and evacuates the wounded, search, silence, safeguard, and speed EPWs to collection points.
3. The platoon leader reports his status and continues the mission.

React to Contact Drill

The react to contact drill takes place when a squad or a platoon is receiving fire from enemy riflemen or an automatic weapon.

Step 1. Soldiers take cover and return fire.

Step 2. Leaders locate known or suspected enemy positions and engage with well-aimed fire. Leaders control fire using the following standard fire commands: alert, direction, description of target, range, method of fire, and command to commence firing.

Step 3. Soldiers maintain contact to left and right, as well as with leaders, and report enemy locations.

Step 4. Leaders check status of their men.

Step 5. Platoon leader moves to squad in contact. He brings with him his ratelo, FO, the squad leader of the nearest squad, and a machine gun team. The platoon sergeant moves forward with the second machine gun team and links up with the platoon leader, ready to assume control of the base-of-fire element.

Step 6. The platoon leader determines whether he must move out of an enemy engagement area. If he is not in an engagement area, he determines whether he can gain and maintain suppressive fire with his element in contact, based on the volume and accuracy of the enemy fire.

Step 7. The platoon leader makes an assessment of the situation, identifying the following:

1. The location of the enemy position and obstacles.
2. The size of the enemy force. (The number of automatic weapons, the presence of vehicles, and the employment of indirect fires are indicators of enemy strength.)
3. Vulnerable flanks.

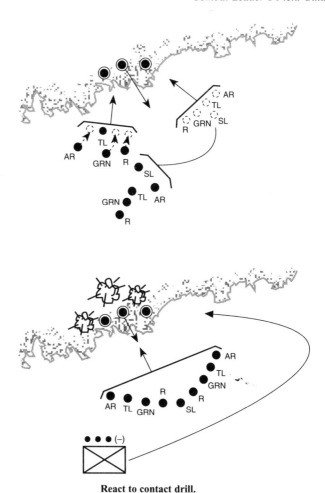

React to contact drill.

4. Covered and concealed flanking routes to the enemy position.

Step 8. The platoon leader then determines his next course of action, such as fire and movement, assault, breach, knock out bunker, or enter and clear a building or trench.

Step 9. The platoon leader reports the situation to the company commander and begins to maneuver, calling for and adjusting artillery or mortar fire.

Break Contact Drill

The break contact drill takes place when the squad or platoon is under enemy fire and must break contact.

Step 1. The platoon leader directs one squad in contact to support the disengagement of the remainder of the platoon.

Step 2. The platoon leader orders the first squad to move a certain distance and direction, or to a terrain feature or the last objective rally point. Meanwhile, the base of fire (supporting) squad continues to suppress the enemy.

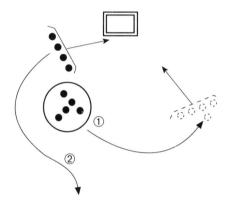

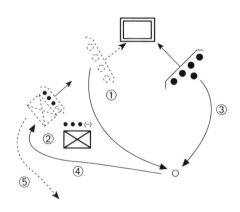

Break contact drill.

Step 3. The moving element uses smoke grenades to mask its movement until it takes up its designated position and engages the enemy position.

Step 4. The platoon leader then directs the base of fire squad to move to its next location.

Step 5. While continuing to suppress the enemy, the platoon bounds away from the enemy until it either breaks contact or passes through a high-level support-by-fire position.

Step 6. Once contact is broken, the platoon should change direction, if possible, to avoid indirect enemy fire.

Step 7. Leaders account for soldiers, report, reorganize as necessary, and continue the mission.

React to Ambush Drill

In a near ambush (within hand grenade range), use the following procedures:

Step 1. Immediately return fire.

Step 2. Take up covered positions.

Step 3. Throw fragmentation, concussion, and smoke grenades.

Step 4. Immediately after the grenades detonate, the soldiers in the kill zone assault through the ambush using fire and movement, while soldiers not in the kill zone identify enemy positions, initiate suppressive fire, take up covered positions, and shift fires as soldiers in the kill zone assault through the ambush.

In a far ambush (beyond hand grenade range), use the following procedures:

Step 1. Soldiers receiving fire immediately return fire, take up covered positions, and suppress the enemy by destroying or suppressing enemy crew-served weapons first, obscuring the enemy position with smoke, and sustaining suppressive fires.

Step 2. Soldiers not receiving fires move by a covered and concealed route to a vulnerable flank of the enemy position and assault using fire and movement.

Step 3. Soldiers in the kill zone continue suppressive fires and shift fires as the assaulting element fights through the enemy position.

In both near and far ambushes, the platoon leader then calls for mortar or artillery fire to isolate the enemy or to attack them as they retreat. Leaders account for soldiers, report, reorganize as necessary, and continue the mission.

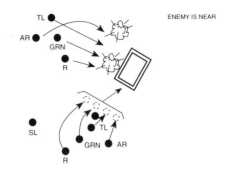

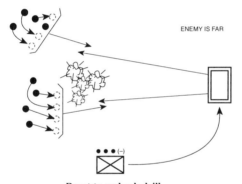

React to ambush drill.

Knock-out Bunker Drill

The knock-out bunker drill is used when the platoon identifies enemy in bunkers.

Step 1. The platoon initiates contact.

1. The squad in contact establishes a base of fire.
2. The platoon leader, ratelo, FO, and one machine gun team move to the squad in contact.
3. The platoon sergeant moves the second machine gun team forward and takes charge of the base of fire.

Step 2. The base of fire element destroys or suppresses enemy crew-served weapons first and uses smoke to obscure the enemy position. The FO calls for and adjusts indirect fire.

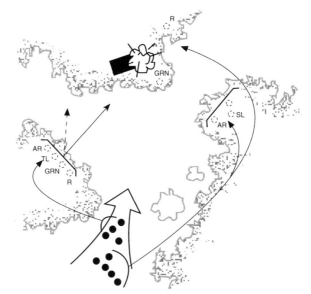

Knock out a bunker—squad.

Step 3. The platoon leader determines whether he can maneuver by identifying the following:

1. The enemy bunkers, other supporting positions, and any obstacles.
2. The size of the enemy force engaging the platoon.
3. A vulnerable flank of at least one bunker.
4. A covered and concealed flanking route to the bunker.

Step 4. The platoon leader determines which bunker to knock out and directs a squad not in contact to assault it.

Step 5. If necessary, the platoon sergeant repositions elements of the base of fire to isolate the enemy bunker.

Step 6. The assault squad, along with the platoon leader and FO, moves along the covered and concealed route.

1. The squad leader moves with the assaulting fire team.
2. The assaulting fire team approaches the bunker from its blind side.
3. Soldiers constantly watch for other bunkers or enemy positions in support of the known bunker.
4. Upon reaching the last covered and concealed position, the fire

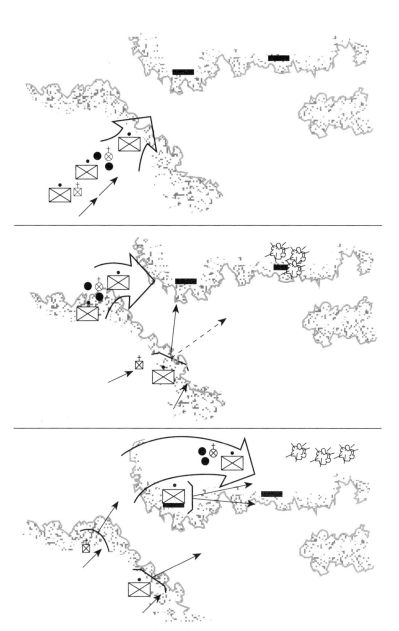

Knock out a bunker—platoon.

team leader and automatic rifleman remain in place and add their fires to suppressing the bunker, while the squad leader positions himself where he can best control his teams.

5. On the squad leader's signal, the base of fire element lifts or shifts fires to the opposite side of the bunker from the assaulting team's approach.

6. A rifleman and grenadier continue forward to the blind side of the bunker. One soldier takes up a covered position near the exit, while the other cooks off (two seconds maximum) a grenade, shouts "Frag out!" and throws it through an aperture.

7. After the grenade detonates, the soldier covering the exit enters the bunker, firing short bursts to destroy the enemy.

8. The squad leader inspects the bunker to ensure that it has been destroyed.

9. The squad leader then reports, reorganizes as needed, and continues the mission.

Step 7. The platoon leader repositions the base-of-fire element as necessary to continue to isolate and suppress the remaining bunkers as squads are maneuvered to knock them out.

Enter and Clear a Trench Drill

The enter and clear a trench drill is used when the platoon is moving and identifies enemy in a trench line, and the platoon leader determines that he can maneuver and assault the trench line.

Step 1. The platoon leader directs one squad to enter the trench and secure a foothold.

Step 2. The platoon leader designates the entry point of the trench line and the direction of movement once the platoon begins clearing.

Step 3. The platoon sergeant positions soldiers and machine guns to suppress the trench and isolate the entry point.

Step 4. The squad leader of the assaulting squad designates one fire team to assault and another fire team to initially support by fire, then follow and support the assaulting team.

1. The squad leader and the assault team move to the last covered and concealed position short of the entry point.

2. The squad leader marks the entry point.

3. The base of fire element shifts fires away from the entry point and continues to suppress adjacent enemy positions or isolate the trench as required.

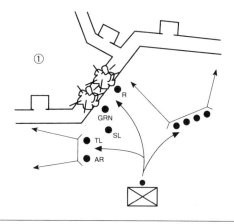

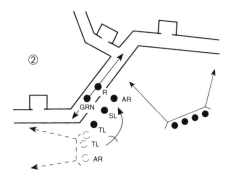

Entering a trench—squad.

4. The fire team leader and an automatic rifleman remain in a position short of the entry point to add suppressive fire for the initial entry, while the remaining soldiers move by crawling or in rushes to the entry point.

5. The first two soldiers of the assaulting fire team move to the edge of the trench, parallel to the trench and on their backs, cook off grenades, shout "Frag out!" and throw grenades into the trench.

6. After ensuring that both grenades detonate, the soldiers roll into the trench, landing on their feet and back to back. They fire their weapons down the trench in opposite directions, then immedi-

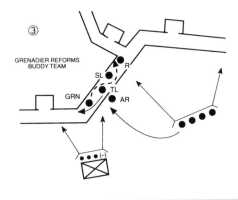

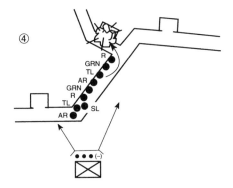

Clearing a trench—squad.

ately move in opposite directions down the trench, firing three-
round bursts. Each soldier continues until he reaches the first
corner or intersection. Then both soldiers halt and take up positions
to block any enemy movement toward the entry point.

7. After detonation of the grenades, the assault fire team leader
   and the automatic rifleman enter the trench and relieve the rifleman at one of the secured corners or intersections.
8. The squad leader reports to the platoon leader that he has
   secured a foothold.

Step 5. The platoon leader now directs one of the base-of-fire
squads to move into the trench and begin clearing it.

1. The squad in the trench separates into a lead team and a trail team.
2. The squad leader moves with the lead team to the secure corner or intersection.
3. The lead soldier of the fire team moves abreast of the soldier securing the corner and announces, "Taking the lead." The soldier securing the corner or intersection acknowledges and is bypassed.
4. The lead fire team starts clearing.

Step 6. Using the buddy system, the second soldier cooks off a grenade, yells "Frag out!" and throws a grenade around the corner.

1. Upon detonation of the grenade, the lead soldier moves around the corner firing three-round bursts and advancing as he fires.
2. The entire fire team follows him to the next corner or intersection.

Step 7. At each corner or intersection, the lead fire team performs the same actions described above. The squad leader ensures that the trail team moves and is prepared to take the lead when rotated.

Step 8. The squad leader calls for indirect fire if necessary and reports his progress to the platoon leader.

Step 9. The platoon leader rotates squads to keep soldiers fresh and to maintain the momentum of the assault. He reports to the company commander that the trench line is secure or that he is no longer able to continue clearing.

Enter Building and Clear Room Drill

This drill is used in urban combat.

Step 1. The fire team initiating contact establishes a base of fire and suppresses the enemy in and around the building.

Step 2. The squad leader determines whether he can maneuver by identifying the building and any obstacles, the size of the enemy force engaging the squad, an entry point, and a covered and concealed route to the entry point.

Step 3. The squad leader directs the fire team in contact to support the entry of the other fire team. He designates the entry point. The platoon and squad shift direct fires and continue to suppress the enemy in adjacent positions and to isolate the building. Indirect fires are lifted or shifted, as necessary.

Entering a room.

Step 4. The squad leader and assaulting fire team approach the building and position themselves at either side of the entry point. (Doors and windows should be avoided because they will normally be covered by enemy soldiers inside the building.)

Step 5. The lead soldier of the assaulting fire team cooks off a grenade, shouts "Frag out!" and throws a grenade into the building. (If the building has thin walls and floors, soldiers must take protective measures from grenade fragments.)

Step 6. After the grenade detonates, the next soldier enters the building and positions himself to the left or right of the entrance, up against the wall, engages all identified or likely enemy positions with rapid, short bursts of automatic fire, and scans the room. The soldier may have to move to the left or right because of the size or shape of the room.

1. The first soldier decides where the next man should position himself and gives the command "Next man in!" (left or right).
2. Once in position, the second soldier shouts "Next man in!" (left or right).
3. Depending on the enemy situation and the size of the room, two soldiers may be able to enter the room simultaneously after the grenade detonates. If so, the soldier on the right side enters, fires from left to right, and moves to the right with his back to

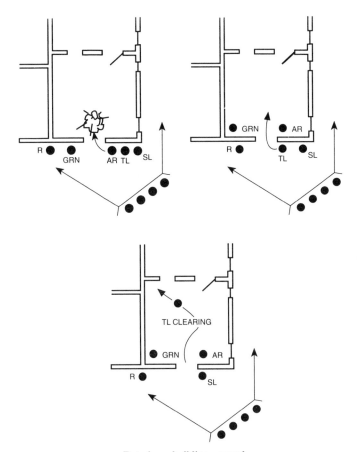

Entering a building—squad.

the wall, while the soldier on the left enters from the left, fires from right to left, and moves to the left with his back to the wall. When both soldiers are in position, the senior soldier shouts "Next man in!" (left or right).

Step 7. The assaulting fire team leader now shouts "Coming in!" (right or left), enters the building, and positions himself against the wall and where he can control the actions of his fire team. He makes a quick assessment of the room's size and shape and begins to clear the room.

Step 8. Once the room is cleared, the squad leader enters the building and marks the entry point according to the SOP.

Step 9. The squad leader and assault fire team move to the entrance of the next room to be cleared and position themselves on either side. This room and all subsequent rooms are cleared by repeating the procedures described above.

Step 10. The squad consolidates its position in the building and then reorganizes as necessary.

Breach an Obstacle Drill

The breach an obstacle drill is used when the lead squad identifies a wire obstacle, reinforced with mines, that cannot be bypassed, and there are enemy positions on the far side of the obstacle.

Step 1. The platoon leader moves forward with his FO and one machine gun team.

Step 2. The platoon leader determines whether he can maneuver.

Step 3. The platoon leader directs one squad to be the base-of-fire element, another to be the breach squad, and a third to be the assault squad once the breach has been made.

Step 4. The base-of-fire squad is joined by the platoon sergeant and the second machine gun team, and together they begin to suppress the enemy and obscure the enemy positions with smoke.

Step 5. The platoon leader leads the breach and assault squads to the breach point.

1. The breach squad leader designates a breach fire team and a support fire team.
2. The breaching fire team moves to the breach point using the covered and concealed route. The squad and fire team leader obscure the breach point, using smoke grenades.
3. The breaching fire team leader and an automatic rifleman are positioned on one flank of the breach point to provide security.
4. The grenadier and rifleman of the breaching fire team probe for and mark mines and cut the wire obstacle, marking their path as they proceed. (If available, bangalore torpedoes are preferred for clearing a lane through a minefield.)

Step 6. Once the obstacle has been breached, the fire team leader and the automatic rifleman move to the far side of the obstacle and take up covered and concealed positions with the rifleman and the grenadier.

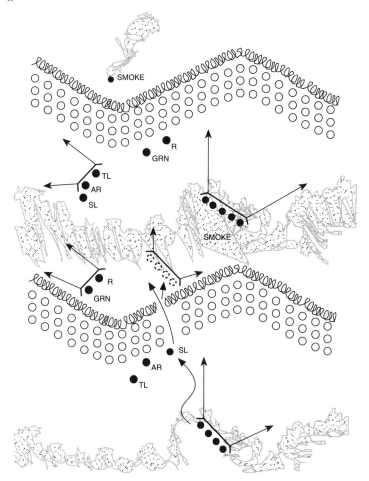

Initial breach of a mined wire obstacle—platoon.

Step 7. The squad leader signals the supporting fire team to move up and through the breach to the far side, where it takes up covered and concealed positions. The squad leader then moves through the breach and joins the breaching fire team.

Step 8. The squad leader reports to the platoon leader and consolidates as needed.

Step 9. The platoon leader leads the assault squad through the breach and positions it to support the movement of the remainder of the platoon or assaults the enemy position covering the obstacle.

Step 10. The platoon leader reports to the company commander.

TECHNIQUES AND PROCEDURES FOR OFFENSIVE MISSIONS

Movement to Contact

There are two techniques for conducting a movement to contact: search and attack or approach march. Search and attack is used when the enemy is dispersed, when the enemy is expected to avoid contact or quickly disengage and withdraw, or to deny the enemy movement in an area. The approach march is used when the enemy is expected to deploy using relatively fixed offensive or defensive formations.

Search and Attack

Search and attack involves the use of multiple squads and fire teams coordinating their actions to make contact with the enemy. Platoons attempt to find and then fix and finish the enemy. They combine patrolling techniques with the requirement to conduct hasty or deliberate attacks once the enemy is found.

Find the Enemy. The initial focus of every search and attack is to find the enemy, its caches, and its support bases. Normally, the platoon is assigned an area of operation (AO) and focuses attention within this AO on specific locations such as key terrain, roads or trails, waterways, villages, or other places where the enemy or its supplies may be found.

Fix the Enemy. If the enemy is found, as part of fixing the enemy, a platoon may be tasked to follow the enemy. If the enemy is not moving, the platoon establishes surveillance to observe and report enemy activities. If the enemy is moving, the platoon tracks it and reports its activities; this may lead to the location of a larger force.

When the purpose is to fix the enemy, the platoon uses direct and indirect fires, maneuvers, and hasty attacks to deny the enemy the ability to maneuver. The squad in contact with the enemy fixes it with all available fires. Ideally, every squad and platoon has the freedom of action to destroy the enemy using ambushes, raids, indirect fires, and hasty attacks. Their leaders must ensure, however, that their plan allows

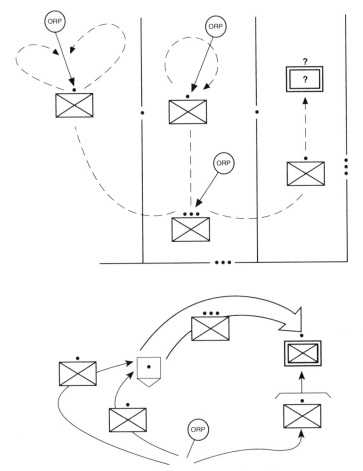

Finish the enemy—concentrate and attack.

for a rapid linkup of reinforcing elements. If the squad fails to destroy or capture the enemy, the platoon leader concentrates forces to attack and destroy the enemy.

Finish the Enemy. An attack to finish the enemy is most successful when the squad or platoon is able to make contact without being detected. This allows for a more complete reconnaissance and coordination of the attack. The unit may be able to finish the enemy without assaulting. By blocking likely escape routes and then calling for indirect fires, the unit may be able to destroy the enemy without exposing itself to enemy fires. If the unit making contact with the enemy is detected or if the initial hasty attack is unsuccessful, the squad in contact becomes a supporting element for the platoon. The platoon leader must personally see the situation, ensure the rapid linkup of his squads, and apply over-whelming combat power against an enemy weak point.

Approach March

The concept behind the approach march is to make contact with the smallest element, allowing the flexibility of maneuvering or bypass-ing the enemy force. During an approach march, platoons may act as the advance guard, flank, or rear guard or may move with the main body.

The *advance guard* locates the enemy and finds gaps, flanks, and weaknesses in its defense. The advance guard attempts to make contact on ground of its own choosing, to gain the advantage of surprise and to develop the situation (to either fight through or support the assault). The advance guard operates within the range of the main body's indirect fire support weapons.

The *flank or rear guard* maintains the same momentum as the main body. This security task requires the platoon to provide early warning, destroy enemy reconnaissance elements, and prevent direct fires or observation of the main body.

When operating with the *main body,* platoons may be tasked to assault, bypass, or fix an enemy force, or seize, secure, or clear an assigned area. The platoon may also provide stay-behind ambushes.

Deliberate Attacks

Deliberate attacks are conducted by platoons as part of a larger force. The platoon can be a base-of-fire element or an assault element. In the movement to the objective, appropriate formations and movement tech-niques are used to avoid contact and achieve surprise.

Line of Departure

The platoon moves from the assembly area to the line of departure (LD) under company control. Machine guns and antiarmor weapons may pre-cede the platoon to overwatch positions near the LD. The LD must be crossed at the right time and place. An attack position may be designated for last-minute coordination and deployment into initial attack formations. If an attack position is not used, the platoon must deploy into the attack formation and fix bayonets before crossing the LD.

Assault or Support Position

The assault or support element moves from the LD using covered and concealed routes to the assault or support position. The support element occupies the support position, locates the enemy positions, is assigned sectors of fire, establishes necessary fire control measures, and maintains communications with the assault element. Direct and indirect fires are placed on the objective. If the attack is not detected, the support element may hold fires until the assault element approaches the assault position. The assault position is normally the last covered and concealed position before reaching the objective.

Assaulting the Objective

As the assault element passes through the assault position, the squads and fire teams deploy to place the bulk of their firepower to the front as they assault the objective. Soldiers use individual movement techniques, and fire teams retain a shallow wedge formation. They increase the volume and accuracy of their fires as they move onto the objective. The assault element assaults the objective from a flank, gap, or known weakness. Fire teams are assigned specific targets or objectives. As the assault elements get closer to the enemy, there is more emphasis on suppression and less on maneuver. Ultimately, to allow one fire team to break into the enemy position, all the other fire teams may be suppressing. As the platoon moves to the objective, supporting fires are lifted and shifted to suppress areas adjacent to the objective, to destroy retreating enemy, or to prevent enemy reinforcement of the objective. On order, the support element moves onto the objective and assists in clearing the objective of any remaining enemy.

Consolidation and Reorganization

Once enemy resistance has ceased, the platoon quickly takes steps to consolidate and prepare to defend against a counterattack. Either the clock technique or the terrain technique is used in consolidating on the objective. In both techniques, key weapons are positioned along the most likely avenue of approach, and squad sectors of fire overlap each other and provide mutual support.

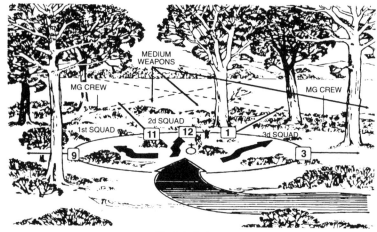

MEDIUM
WEAPONS

MG CREW

MG CREW

2d SQUAD

1st SQUAD

11   12   1

3d SQUAD

9   3

Clock technique.

In the *clock technique,* the platoon leader designates either a compass direction or the direction of attack as twelve o'clock. He then uses clock positions to identify left and right boundaries for squads.

In the *terrain technique,* obvious terrain features are identified as left and right boundaries for squads.

After platoons have consolidated, they begin reorganization activities.

Hasty Attack

In the hasty attack, when a platoon makes unexpected contact with the enemy, the platoon executes the react to contact drill (see page 45).

Raids and Ambushes

Raids and ambushes are special-purpose attacks that may be either hasty or deliberate.

A *raid* is a swift, violent attack to destroy or capture enemy personnel or equipment, to rescue friendly personnel, to gain intelligence, or to gain the initiative. It is a limited-objective attack for a specific purpose other than gaining or holding ground.

An *ambush* is a surprise attack against moving or temporarily halted enemy units. It combines the advantages and characteristics of the offense with those of the defense.

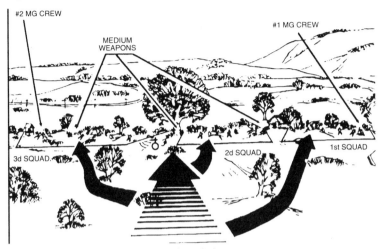

Terrain technique.

Limited-Visibility Attacks

Attacks during limited visibility surprise the enemy, cause panic in a weak and disorganized enemy, avoid heavy losses, exploit success, maintain momentum, and keep pressure on the enemy. Platoons and squads attack whenever possible during darkness, fog, heavy rain, and falling snow. Limited-visibility attacks require additional control measures to prevent fratricide and to keep the attack focused on the objective. Boundaries, restrictive fire lines, and limits of advance may assist in control.

Limited-visibility attacks require the following fundamentals:
- Well-trained squads.
- Enough natural light to employ night vision devices.
- A simple plan with sufficient control measures.
- Detailed, successful reconnaissance of the objective, routes, passage points, support-by-fire positions, and other key locations. This should be done during daylight and down to the lowest level possible. Surveillance of the objective area to report enemy repositioning or additional defensive preparation is part of the reconnaissance plan.

There will be increased difficulty in performing the following:
- Controlling individuals and squads.

- Identifying targets and controlling direct and indirect fires.
- Navigating and moving.
- Identifying friendly and enemy soldiers.
- Locating, treating, and evacuating casualties.
- Locating and bypassing or breaching enemy obstacles.

Control techniques during limited-visibility attacks include the following:

- Fire control techniques. Leaders in the assault element fire all tracers, and their soldiers fire where the tracers impact. A support element tripod mounted machine gun is positioned on the flank nearest the assault force and fires a burst of tracers every fifteen seconds to indicate the near limit of the supporting fires. All other supporting weapons keep their fire on the appropriate side of the tracers.
- No flares, grenades, or smoke should be used on the objective.
- Only certain personnel with night vision devices may engage targets on the objective.
- Use mortar or artillery rounds to orient the attacking elements.
- Place guides from the line of departure to the release points, at the entrance to the assault position, and at points along the probable line of deployment.
- Reduce intervals between soldiers and units.
- Place luminous tape on helmets.

5

Defense

The purpose of the defense is to cause the enemy attack to fail and to create conditions favorable to assuming the offense. Platoons and squads normally defend as part of a larger force to disrupt, disorganize, delay, deny an area to the enemy, or protect a flank. Leaders plan and establish the defense in order to find the enemy first, without being found; fix the enemy with obstacles and fires; locate or create a weakness in the enemy's attack plan; and maneuver to exploit that weakness with quick, violent counterattacks.

CHARACTERISTICS

Preparation
The defender arrives in the battle area before the enemy. He must take advantage of the early arrival to prepare the area and determine where best to kill the enemy. Soldiers prepare and conceal fighting positions, register weapons, mark their sectors, clear fields of fire, and learn the terrain. Leaders reconnoiter the terrain, complete fire plans, plan for resupply, and develop counterattack plans.

Security
Since the enemy determines the time and place of attack, all-around secu-

rity is posted to provide early warning. Reconnaissance and counter-reconnaissance activities include placing observation posts along likely avenues of approach and active patrolling. Positions are camouflaged and are established away from natural lines of drift or obvious terrain features, and noise and light discipline is enforced.

Disruption
Counterattacks, indirect fires, obstacles, and retention of key or decisive terrain prevent the enemy from concentrating its strength. Concentration refers to the effects of combat power, not just numbers of soldiers or weapons. To defeat the attacker, the defender must gain a local advantage at points of decision. The defender might economize in one area to gain superiority in another, by positioning units and soldiers, maneuvering, and shifting fires.

Flexibility
The defender must be agile enough to counter or avoid the attacker's blow and then strike back effectively. Flexibility results from detailed planning, reconnaissance and surveillance, organization in depth, and retention of a reserve.

CONTROL MEASURES
Control measures are used to assign responsibilities, coordinate fires and maneuver, control combat operations, and clarify the concept of the operation. Additionally, control measures ensure the distribution of fires throughout the platoon's area of responsibility and the initial positioning and subsequent maneuvering of squads. Graphic control measures used in the defense include sectors, battle positions, boundaries, contact points, coordination points, forward edge of the battle area (FEBA), strong points, target reference points (TRP), assembly areas, phase lines, passage points and lanes, release points, and engagement areas. Fire commands and control measures for individual and key weapons also constitute a type of control measure available to leaders. Weapons control measures include range cards, sectors of fire, principal direction of fire, final protective line, and final protective fires. In addition, antiarmor gunners, machine gun teams, fire teams, squads, and platoons can be given engagement priorities and fire commands.

CONDUCT OF THE DEFENSE

The standard sequence of actions that a platoon takes in defensive operations is as follows:

1. Prepare for combat.
2. Move to defensive positions.
3. Establish defensive positions.
4. Locate the enemy.
5. Fight the defense.
6. Reorganize.

Prepare for Combat

The platoon leader issues a warning order; makes a tentative plan; conducts a reconnaissance of the defensive area; inspects the soldiers for proper equipment, weapons, ammunition, rations, camouflage, and soldier's load; and moves the platoon if not already moving.

Move to Defensive Positions

As with all movement, the platoon applies the fundamentals of movement and uses covered and concealed routes; avoids likely ambush sites; enforces camouflage, noise, and light discipline; maintains all-around security; and uses formations and movement techniques based on METT-T.

Establish Defensive Positions

The platoon halts in a covered and concealed position to the rear of the defensive area, and the leaders conduct reconnaissance of assigned positions. The platoon moves forward as a whole or by squads, using guides to control movement into positions. A priority of work is established to prepare the defense. The platoon's normal priority of work is as follows:

Establish Local Security

Platoons provide their own security by patrolling, using observation posts, and detailing a percentage of the platoon to man hasty positions while the rest of the soldiers prepare the defense.

Position Weapons and Soldiers

Leaders must position antiarmor weapons, machine guns, and squads and assign sectors of fire. The positioning of soldiers and weapons is a key part of every defense. Leaders must understand the weapon, the terrain (OCOKA), and how the enemy will approach. The leader positions weapons where they have protection, avoid detection, and will surprise the enemy with accurate, lethal fire. If the platoon faces an armored threat, antiarmor weapons are positioned along the most likely avenue of approach first.

Machine guns are the platoon's main weapons and are positioned first if the enemy is a dismounted force. Leaders position machine guns to concentrate fires where they want to kill the enemy, fire across the platoon front, cover obstacles by fire, and tie in with adjacent units. They provide a high volume of lethal fire to break up and stop enemy assaults.

Each gun is given a primary and secondary sector of fire. Their sectors of fire should overlap each other and those of adjacent platoons. A gunner fires in his secondary sector only if there are no targets in his primary sector, or when ordered to do so.

Squad leaders position all other weapons to support these key weapons, cover dead space, and provide security. The platoon leader positions antiarmor weapons according to the armored threat. He selects a primary (and supplementary) position and field of fire for each antiarmor weapon. He considers fields of fire, tracking time, and minimum arming range. The antiarmor leader selects alternate positions. Each position should allow flank fire and have cover and concealment. The thermal sights are integrated into the platoon's limited visibility reconnaissance and surveillance plan.

The M203 grenade launcher is the squad's indirect-fire weapon. It is positioned to cover dead space in the squad sector, especially the dead space for the machine guns. The M203 gunner is also assigned a sector to cover with rifle fire. Each rifleman in the squad is assigned a position and sector of fire. Normally, these positions support the machine guns and antiarmor weapons. They are also positioned to cover obstacles, provide security, cover gaps between units, or provide observation.

Establish the Command Post and Wire Communications

The platoon command post (CP) is set up in a spot from where the platoon leader can best see and control his platoon. If he cannot see all of the platoon sector from one place, he sets up where he can see and control

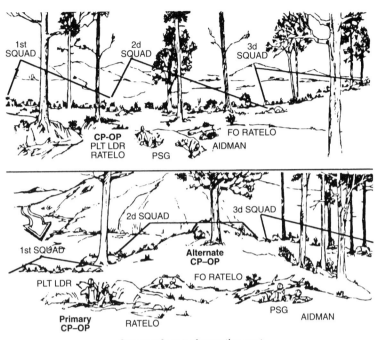

Command post, observation post.

the main effort. He then sets up an alternate CP where the platoon sergeant can see and control the rest of the platoon.

The platoon CP ties in to the company wire net with a field telephone. Wire is the primary means of communications between the platoon leader and squad leaders. The platoon has its own radio net and the platoon leader also uses messengers, visual signals, personal contact, or whistles to communicate.

Designate Final Protective Lines and Final Protective Fires

Each machine gun's primary sector includes a final protective line (FPL) or a principal direction of fire (PDF). The gun is laid on the FPL or the PDF unless engaging other targets. When final protective fires (FPF) are called for, the gunner shifts to and engages on the FPL or PDF. Where terrain allows, the platoon leader assigns a machine gun an FPL. The FPL is a line along which grazing fire is placed to stop an assault.

Grazing fire.

Grazing fire is no more than 1 meter above the ground. The FPL is fixed in elevation and direction. A soldier walks the FPL to find dead space. The gunner watches the soldier walking the line and marks spaces that cannot be grazed. The dead space is covered with obstacles, grenade launcher fire, or mines.

When the terrain does not lend itself to an FPL, the platoon leader assigns the machine gun a PDF. A PDF is a priority direction of fire assigned to cover an area that provides good fields of fire or has a likely avenue of approach. Final protective fires are a prearranged barrier of indirect fires used to defeat the assaulting enemy unit as soon as possible after it moves into its assault formation. The FPF can be anywhere between the forward position of the friendly unit and the enemy's assault position, which is normally just out of range of the platoon's organic weapons. The FPF should be fired only to stop an enemy assault. On signal, the FPF is fired continuously until the order is given to stop or the mortar or artillery unit runs out of ammunition. All other platoon weapons fire while the FPF is being fired.

Clear Fields of Fire and Prepare Range Cards and Sector Sketches

Fields of fire are cleared far enough out (40 meters) to kill the enemy before it can assault or throw hand grenades into fighting positions. Fields of fire are improved by selective clearing of grass, brush, trees, and rubble. Evidence of clearing is removed or camouflaged.

A range card is a record of the firing data required to engage prede-

**Maximum engagement
line for Dragon**

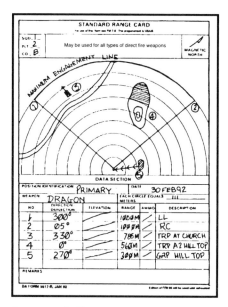

Completed range card—Dragon.

termined targets within a sector of fire during good and limited visibility. Every direct-fire weapon gunner must prepare a range card. Range cards are prepared for primary, alternate, and supplementary positions. Two copies are prepared; one stays at the position, and the other is sent to the platoon leader.

Each squad leader prepares a sector sketch to help him plan his defense and control fires. The squad leader keeps a copy and sends one copy to the platoon leader. The sector sketch shows the following:

- Squad and platoon identification.
- Date and time group.
- Magnetic north.
- The main terrain features in the sector and the ranges to them.
- Each primary fighting position.
- Alternate and supplementary positions.
- The primary and secondary sectors of fire of each position.
- Maximum engagement line.
- Machine gun FPL or PDF.

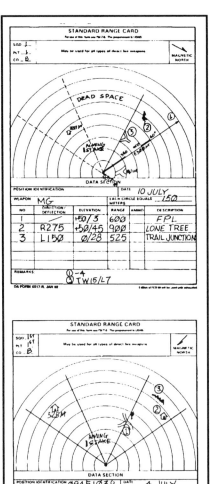

Primary sector with FPL

Primary sector with PDF

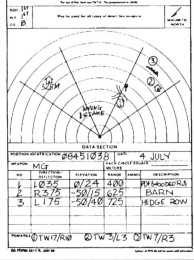

Completed range card—MG.

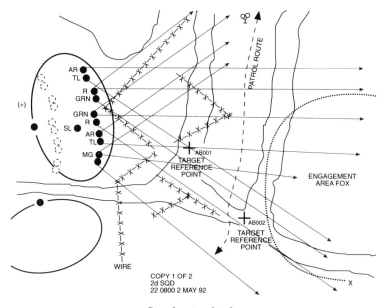

Squad sector sketch.

- Dragon (Javelin) positions with sectors of fire.
- The type of weapon in each position.
- Observation posts and the squad leader's position.
- Dead space to include coverage by grenade launchers.
- Location of night vision devices.
- Obstacles, mines, and booby traps.

The platoon leader prepares a platoon sector sketch and sends one to the company commander. The platoon leader checks squad sector sketches and range cards for gaps or other flaws in the fire plan. If he finds any dead space, he takes steps to cover it with mines, grenade launcher fire, or indirect fire. The platoon sector sketch includes all the items in the squad sketch plus indirect fires, TRPs, patrol routes, casualty collection point, and adjustments for coverage of TRPs during limited visibility.

Coordinate with Adjacent Units

Coordination between adjacent platoons and squads is normally from left

to right and from front to rear. Information exchanged includes the following:

- Location of leaders.
- Location of primary, alternate, and supplementary positions and
  sectors of fire of machine guns, antiarmor weapons, and sub-
  units.
- Route to alternate and supplementary positions.
- Location of dead space between platoons and squads and how to
  cover it.
- Location of OPs and withdrawal routes back to the platoon's or
  squad's position.
- Location and types of obstacles and how to cover them.
- Patrols to be conducted, including their size, type, times of depar-
  ture and return, and routes.
- Location, activities, and passage plans for scouts and other units
  forward of the platoon's position.
- Signals for fire, cease fire, and any others that may be observed.
- Engagement and disengagement criteria.

Fire team leaders should also coordinate to ensure that each position knows who and what weapons are to the left and right. This ensures
that all positions and all units are mutually supportive and that any gaps
between units are covered by fire, observation, patrols, or sensors.

Prepare Primary Fighting Positions

A primary position provides a soldier, weapons crew, or unit the best terrain to accomplish the mission—to observe and cover its sector of fire. It
should have observation, cover and concealment, and good fields of fire.

Emplace Obstacles and Mines

The platoon leader uses obstacles, mines, wire, and trip flares to improve
the defense. The obstacle plan must be tied into the fire and maneuver
plan. Obstacles are used to slow the enemy's advance to give the defender more time to mass fires on him, protect defending units, canalize the
enemy into places where he can more easily be engaged, separate the
tanks from infantry, and strengthen areas that are lightly defended.
Obstacles disrupt, turn, fix, or block the enemy.

There are two types of obstacles: existing and reinforcing. *Existing
obstacles* are those natural or cultural restrictions to movement that are

Ditch.

TREES FELLED TOWARD
ENEMY AT 45° ANGLE

ENEMY

75 METERS

TREES NOT DETACHED
FROM TRUNK

Abatis.

Log crib.

part of the terrain when battle planning begins, such as slopes, gullies, rivers, swamps, trees, or built-up areas. *Reinforcing obstacles* are those specifically constructed, emplaced, or detonated to tie together, strengthen, and extend existing obstacles. Reinforcing obstacles include road craters, abatis, ditches, log hurdles, cribs, rubble, or wire entanglements.

Wire is classified by its use and location.

- *Tactical wire* is sited parallel to and along the friendly side of the FPL. It breaks up the enemy attack and holds the enemy where its troops can be killed or wounded by automatic rifle fire, Claymores, hand grenades, and machine gun fire.

- *Protective wire* is located to prevent surprise assaults from points close to the defense area. It is close enough for day and night observation but far enough away (40 to 100 meters) to keep the enemy from using hand grenades. Protective wire of adjacent platoons is connected by supplementary wire; this encloses the entire defensive position. Gaps must be provided, however, to allow patrols to exit and enter the position.

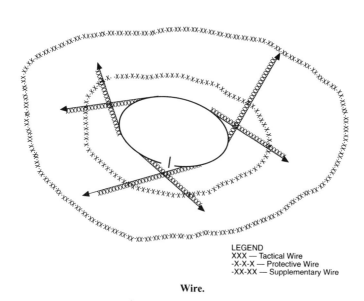

LEGEND
XXX — Tactical Wire
-X-X-X — Protective Wire
-XX-XX — Supplementary Wire

Wire.

- *Supplementary wire* is used to disguise the exact lines of the tactical wire. It prevents the enemy from locating the unit's perimeter and machine guns by following the wire.

Mines are one of the most effective tank destroyers and personnel killers on the battlefield. Minefields the infantry platoon most commonly emplaces are the hasty protective, point, and phony.

- *Hasty protective minefields* are used to supplement weapons, prevent surprise, and give early warning of enemy advance. The platoon can lay this type of minefield but only with company commander authorization. These minefields are placed across likely avenues of approach, within range of and covered by the platoon's organic weapons. The mines can be laid in a random pattern on top of the ground, if time does not permit burying them. Only metallic mines are used; booby traps are not used in a hasty protective minefield because they delay removal of the mines. The minefield location must be recorded and reported to the company commander and adjacent platoons. When the platoon leaves the area (except when forced to withdraw by enemy action), the minefield must be removed or transferred to the relieving platoon leader.

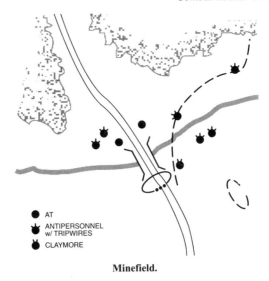

Minefield.

- *Point minefields* disorganize enemy forces and hinder their use of key areas. Point minefields are of irregular shape and size; they include all types of antitank, antipersonnel, and antihandling devices. They are used to add to the effect of existing and reinforcing obstacles or to rapidly block an enemy counterattack along a flank of approach.
- *Phony minefields* simulate live minefields and deceive the enemy. They are used to degrade enemy mobility and preserve friendly mobility. They are used when lack of time or material prevents the use of actual mines. Phony minefields may be used as gaps in live minefields. To be effective, a phony minefield must look like a live one; metallic objects must be buried or the ground made to look as though objects are buried.

Establish Target Reference Points and Other Fire Control Measures

Target reference points (TRP) are easily identifiable man-made or natural objects used to reference enemy locations. Fire control measures ensure the proper concentration and distribution of fires. Antiarmor weapons normally are part of the company or battalion plan. One leader controls all antiarmor weapons firing from a single position or into a single engagement area. Platoon leaders usually control the fires of machine guns. Squad leaders and fire team leaders control automatic rifles, grenade launchers, and rifle fire.

Sectors of fire are used to assign responsibility and ensure distribution of fires across the platoon and squad front. Sectors should always overlap with adjacent sectors.

Engagement areas are used to concentrate all available fires into an area where it is desired to kill the enemy.

Fire distribution is controlled by two methods: point fire and area fire. When firing *point fire,* the platoon's fires are directed at one target, usually marked by tracer fire or by M203 fire. When firing *area fire,* the platoon covers an area from left to right and in depth using frontal fire, cross fire, depth fire, or a combination.

Frontal fire is used when the enemy is moving perpendicular to the platoon's direction of fire. Each squad engages targets to its immediate front. As targets are destroyed, fires are shifted toward the center of the enemy.

Cross fire is used when the enemy is moving perpendicular to the platoon's direction of fire and terrain does not allow frontal fire. It is also used when the enemy is moving oblique to the platoon's direction of fire. When using cross fire, the squads engage targets from left to right or from right to left, depending on their location.

Depth fire is used when the enemy is moving parallel to the platoon's direction of fire. Squads engage targets from front to rear or from rear to front. As targets are destroyed, fires are shifted toward the center of the enemy. Depending on the situation, the platoon may use any combination of the above techniques.

Leaders use fire commands to direct fires of the unit. A fire command has six parts:

1. Alert. The leader alerts the soldiers by name or unit designation, by some type of visual or sound signal, by personal contact, or by any other practical way.
2. Direction. The leader tells the soldiers the general direction or pinpoint location of the target.
3. Description. The leader describes the target briefly but accurately. The formation of enemy soldiers is always given.
4. Range. The leader tells the range to the target in meters.

5. Method of fire. The leader designates the weapons to fire. He can also tell the type and amount of ammunition to fire and the rate of fire.

6. Command to fire. The leader tells soldiers when to fire. He can use an oral command, a sound, or a visual signal. When he wants to control the exact moment, he says, "At my command." When he wants firing to start at the completion of the command, he just says, "Fire."

Targets appear in random order at different times and locations throughout the battlefield. *Engagement priorities* allow the leader to designate which target he wants destroyed first. Engagement priorities are usually done by weapons systems. For example, Dragon gunners would first fire at the most threatening armored vehicle and then at any armored vehicle in the kill zone or primary sector. Machine guns would fire at groups of five or more in the primary sector and then at automatic weapons. Riflemen would fire in their primary and secondary sectors from nearest to farthest, starting on the flank and working toward the center. Any number of priorities can be assigned to any weapon system.

Prepare Alternate and Supplementary Positions
Soldiers prepare their primary positions first. Once both alternate and supplementary positions have been assigned, the leader decides which of the two to prepare after the primary position.

Alternate positions allow soldiers, crews, or units to cover the same sector of fire covered from the primary position. Soldiers occupy alternate positions when the primary position becomes untenable or unsuitable for carrying out their tasks. Soldiers may occupy alternate positions before an attack to rest and/or perform maintenance, or to add the element of surprise to their defense.

Supplementary positions provide the best means to accomplish a task that cannot be accomplished from the primary or alternate positions. Supplementary positions are normally located to cover additional enemy avenues of approach and to protect the flanks and rear of the platoon position.

Establish a Sleep and Rest Plan
The leader must ensure his soldiers can conduct both sustained and con-

PRIMARY
POSITION

ALTERNATE
POSITION

SUPPLEMENTARY
POSITION

Relationship of positions.

tinuous operations; to do so, it is essential that soldiers and leaders get enough rest. The work-rest-sleep plan must provide for leaders as well as soldiers to sleep. The plan should allow soldiers at least four to five hours of sleep each twenty-four hours; this will sustain performance for several days. Six to eight hours of sleep can sustain performance indefinitely.

Reconnoiter Routes
The platoon leader and squad leaders must reconnoiter routes to and from alternate and supplementary positions and routes used on a counterattack.

Rehearse Engagements, Disengagements, and Counterattack Plans
The platoon must rehearse movement to and from alternate and supplementary positions and the counterattack plan. Leaders use rehearsals to practice essential tasks, reveal weaknesses or problems in the plan, coordinate the actions of subordinate elements, and improve soldier understanding of the concept of operations.

Stockpile Ammunition, Food, and Water

The platoon requests and allocates pioneer tools, barrier material, rations, water, batteries, and ammunition. Ammunition and water resupply points are set up.

Dig Trenches to Connect Positions

Based on available time, trenches are dug to connect fighting positions so soldiers can move by covered routes. The trench should zigzag so the enemy will not be able to fire down a long section.

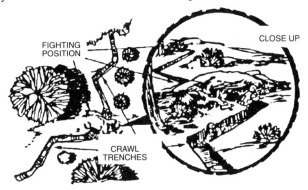

Trenches.

Improve or Adjust Positions as Required

As time allows, the platoon's positions are continually improved.

Locate the Enemy

In the defense, platoons and squads use both active and passive measures to enhance security. Active measures include patrolling, OPs, specific levels of alert, and stand-to times. Passive measures include camouflage, movement control, noise and light discipline, proper radio-telephone procedures, ground sensors, night-vision devices, and thermal sights. These measures are all designed to find the enemy before it finds you.

Fight the Defense

Forces conduct the defense aggressively, continuously seeking opportunities to take advantage of the enemy's errors or failures. Defense includes maneuver and counterattack, as well as keeping key positions secure. The battle begins when the planned signal or event for beginning fire occurs. All leaders and the FO search for indirect-fire targets. If no enemy armor appears, antiarmor weapons can fire at other enemy vehicles. Machine gunners, automatic riflemen, riflemen, and grenadiers fire at targets in their sectors as dictated by their priority of engagement. The platoon increases its rate of fire as the enemy approaches the defensive position. When tanks and infantry attack, the defenders place fire to force the tanks to button up and to separate the foot soldiers from the tanks.

If attacking formations are not broken up forward of the platoon's position and if the enemy assaults, the platoon leader calls for his FPF. Machine guns shift to their FPL or PDF. All other weapons fire until the assault has been halted. The FPF can be repeated as needed. The FPF expends a lot of ammunition, however, and should be called for only when needed to stop an enemy assault from closing on the position. If the enemy gets through the FPF, the platoon repels the troops with close combat. If the platoon is threatened from the flanks or rear, the platoon leader moves soldiers to fight from supplementary positions.

Common defensive techniques employed by the infantry platoon are reverse slope defense, perimeter defense, a defense in sector, and mutually supporting battle positions.

Reverse Slope Defense

The reverse slope defense is an alternative to defending on the forward slope. This defense takes place on the part of a hill or ridge that is masked by the crest from enemy direct fire and ground observation. The platoon must control the crest by fire. The advantages of defending from a reverse slope are as follows:

- Enemy ground observation of position is masked.
- Because of this, there is more freedom of movement in the position.
- Enemy direct-fire weapons cannot hit the position.
- Enemy indirect fire is less effective due to the lack of ground observation.
- The defender gains the element of surprise.
- If the enemy attacks over the crest, it will isolate itself from its supporting elements.

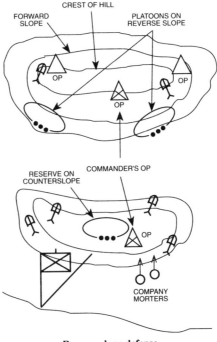

CREST OF HILL

FORWARD
SLOPE

PLATOONS ON
REVERSE SLOPE

OP

OP

OP

RESERVE ON
COUNTERSLOPE

COMMANDER'S OP

OP

COMPANY
MORTERS

Reverse slope defense.

The disadvantages are as follows:

- It is more difficult to observe the enemy. Soldiers can see no farther forward than the crest, so it is difficult to determine just
  where the enemy is as it advances. This is especially true during
  periods of limited visibility. OPs must be placed well forward of
  the crest for early warning and long-range observation.
- Moving out of the position under pressure may be more difficult.
- Fields of fire are normally short. Grazing fire may be less than
  600 meters.
- Obstacles on the forward slope can be covered only with indirect
  fire or by units on the flanks, unless some weapons are initially
  placed forward.
- If the enemy gets to the crest, it can assault down the hill. This
  may give the enemy a psychological advantage.
- If not enough OPs are put out or if they are not put in the right

positions, the enemy may suddenly appear at close range without sufficient warning.

Preparing the Reverse Slope Defense. The forward platoons are 200 to 500 meters from the crest of the hills where they can have the best fields of fire and still have the advantages of the reverse slope. If it places them in supporting distance, the overwatching platoon may be positioned on the forward slope of the next high ground to the rear (counterslope). The following are the tasks of the overwatching platoon:

- Protect the flanks and rear of the forward positions.
- Reinforce the fires of the forward elements.
- Block penetrations of the forward positions.
- Cover the withdrawal of forward units.
- Counterattack.

Platoon leaders plan indirect-fire FPFs on or short of the crest of the hill to deny that area to the enemy and to help break up the enemy's assault as it crosses the hill. OPs are positioned on or just forward of the crest to watch the entire platoon sector of fire. The OPs can vary in size from two soldiers to a squad reinforced with machine guns and antiarmor weapons. Leaders place obstacles below the crest of the hill on the friendly side. Tied in with the FPF, this can be effective in stopping or slowing an assault.

Fighting the Reverse Slope Defense. The conduct of the defense from a reverse slope is the same as from a forward slope; however, the OPs forward of the position not only warn of the enemy's advance but also delay, deceive, and disorganize the enemy by fire. OPs withdraw before they become engaged by the enemy. If machine guns are with the OPs, they withdraw first so they can occupy their primary fighting positions before the enemy reaches the crest.

As the OPs withdraw, indirect fire is placed on the forward slope and on the crest of the hill to slow the enemy's advance. Soldiers in primary positions hold their fire until the enemy crosses the crest. Then, as the enemy moves over the crest of the hill, the defenders hit the enemy with all available fire.

When the enemy assaults across the crest and is defeated, it will try to turn, bypass, or envelop the defense. To counter this, the overwatch element orients its fires to the flanks of the forward slope. Also, the defense must have appropriate supplementary positions and obstacles, as well as security elements, to warn if the enemy tries to envelop or bypass the position. Against armored, motorized, or road-bound attack, position antiarmor weapons and machine guns so their primary sectors are to the flanks of the reverse slope.

Perimeter Defense

The major advantage of the perimeter defense is the preparedness of the platoon to defend against an attack from any direction. The main disadvantage is that combat power is not concentrated at first against an enemy avenue of approach. A perimeter defense differs from other defense in the following respects:

- The trace of the platoon is circular or triangular rather than linear.
- Unoccupied areas between squads are smaller.
- The flanks of the squads are bent back to conform to the plan.
- The bulk of combat power is in the perimeter.
- The reserve is centrally located.

Perimeter defense.

Defense in Sector

Defense in sector maximizes the combat abilities of the infantry. It allows the platoon to fight throughout the depth of the sector using dispersed small-unit tactics.

Preparing to Defend in Sector. The platoon is usually assigned a sector within the company sector. The platoon leader may in turn assign sectors to individual squads to permit maximum freedom of action. (A sector is delineated by boundaries, and a unit assigned a sector can maneuver and fire within that sector without coordinating with neighboring units. A squad has no way to call for fire, and normally their movement is restricted by the platoon leader. These limitations argue against squad sectors.) Each squad conducts detailed reconnaissance of its sector (or position) and identifies all likely enemy avenues of approach, choke points, kill zones, and obstacles, as well as all tentative positions. The platoon leader confirms the selected tentative sites and incorporates them into his concept. He designates initial positions and the sequence in which successive positions are to be occupied. He gives each squad specific guidance concerning contingency plans, rally points, and other

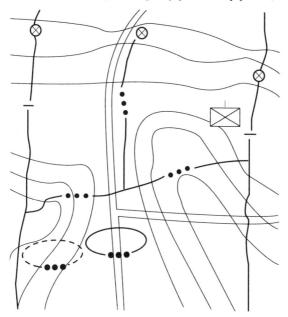

Sector defense.

coordinating instructions. Squads then prepare the defense in the sequence designated by the platoon leader. They initially prepare the primary position, then a hasty supplementary position, and finally they select an alternate position. Squads improve positions as time permits.

Fighting the Sector Defense. When security warns of approaching enemy, the squad occupies its primary positions and prepares to engage the enemy. As the enemy moves into the choke point or kill zone, the squad initiates an ambush. It engages the enemy targets only as long as squads do not become decisively engaged. Squads then move to their next position and repeat the same process. The leader must plan the disengagement. Supporting positions, the use of smoke, and rehearsals are key to effective disengagement. Casualty evacuation and resupply are difficult when defending this way.

Mutually Supporting Battle Positions

This technique concentrates firepower into a given engagement area and prevents the attacker from isolating one part of the company and concentrating its combat power in that area.

Preparing to Defend from Mutually Supporting Battle Positions. Platoons are assigned mutual supporting battle positions that cover the likely enemy avenue of approach. Each position must be supported by another position that can deliver fires into the flank or rear of the enemy attacking it. Battle positions (BP) should be positioned to achieve surprise and to allow maneuver within and between BPs. The BPs are located on terrain that provides cover and concealment and restricts vehicular movement. The fire plan includes obstacles with extensive use of mines to slow and stop the enemy in the engagement area. Aggressive counterreconnaissance by squad-size patrols provide security and confuse the enemy as to the location of the main defenses.

Fighting the Battle Position Defense. Fighting the battle position defense relies on achieving surprise from each of the BPs. If the counterreconnaissance effort has been successful in keeping the enemy from locating the BPs, when the obstacles and indirect fire trap the enemy in the engagement area, one platoon initiates fires. As the enemy orients on this platoon and begins to maneuver against it, other BPs open fire; once the original platoon is no longer receiving enemy fire, it withdraws and maneuvers to an alternate BP to continue destruction of the enemy or to a rally point.

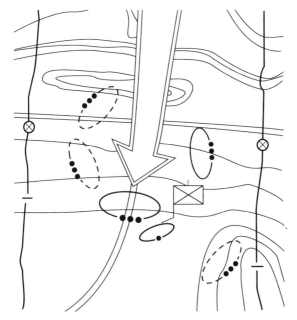

Mutually supporting battle positions.

A variation is engaging with massed fires from all BPs. A disadvantage to this technique is that if there are still uncommitted enemy forces outside the engagement area, they will know the location of the BPs and will attempt to isolate and concentrate against them.

Reorganization

Reorganization begins automatically at team and squad level during the battle to be prepared for the next battle. To prepare for the next attack, the platoon should accomplish the following:

Man Key Weapons

Replace key soldiers lost during battle, for example, ensure that crew-served weapons are manned and new team leaders are designated.

Reestablish Security

If soldiers withdrew from the OPs to their fighting positions, return them to their OPs. If some did not get back to their positions, check their status and replace casualties. As soon as possible, reestablish the sleep-alert system.

Treat and/or Evacuate Casualties
Treat casualties as far forward as possible. Return those who can continue to fight to their positions; evacuate the others.

Redistribute Ammunition and Supplies
Distribute remaining ammunition and supplies equally among the soldiers, including ammunition from the casualties.

Relocate Fighting Positions and Weapons Positions
During the assault, the enemy may have pinpointed some of the fighting and weapons positions. If certain positions are in danger, move soldiers and weapons (especially crew-served weapons) to their alternate positions.

Reestablish Communications
If a phone line was cut during the attack, soldiers on each end of the line try to find and repair the break or lay new wire. If a signal, such as a green star cluster, was used to cease fire, consider changing the signal, since its meaning may now be known by the enemy.

Repair Fighting Positions
Each soldier checks and replaces the camouflage, overhead cover, and sandbags on existing positions and camouflages new positions.

Repair and/or Replace Obstacles
Repair and/or replace damaged or breached obstacles, mines, and booby traps only if enemy soldiers are far enough away that it can be done safely. Otherwise, wait for poor visibility to do so or use smoke to hinder observation.

6

Other Tactical Operations

Other tactical operations include retrograde, relief in place, linkup, and stay-behind. Platoons participate in these operations as part of a larger force and employ the tactics and techniques discussed in other chapters. These operations require special planning and considerations in their execution.

RETROGRADE

A retrograde operation is an organized movement to the rear or away from the enemy. Forces conduct these operations to harass, exhaust, resist, delay, and destroy the enemy. Retrograde operations gain time, avoid combat under unfavorable conditions, or draw the enemy into an unfavorable position. The three types of retrograde operations are withdrawal, delay, and retirement.

Withdrawal

In a withdrawal, all or part of a deployed force voluntarily disengages from the enemy to free itself for a new mission. The mission might be

Thinning the lines.

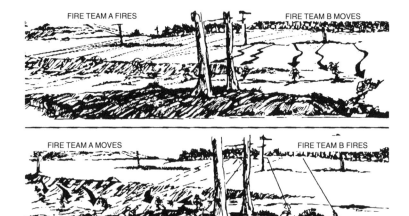

Disengagement by fire teams.

to defend another position or to attack someplace else. Units withdraw either under pressure or not under pressure. Platoons have three basic methods of disengaging from the enemy: They can thin their lines or move out either by fire team or by squad.

- To disengage by thinning the lines, squad and team leaders direct soldiers to move rearward in buddy teams, each of which covers the other as they move back in turn. Smoke must be used for concealment if the soldiers are moving across open areas.
- To disengage by fire teams, one team fires while the other one

moves, alternating roles. This method can be used if thinning the lines is not needed because enemy fire is light or teams have already moved back far enough.

· To disengage by squads, the platoon leader has each squad move back in turn, covered by the fire of the others. The platoon moves back by squads if thinning the lines or maneuver by fire teams is not needed because enemy fire is light or squads have already moved back sufficiently.

Withdrawal Not under Pressure

Withdrawal not under pressure is conducted with speed, secrecy, and deception and is best performed at night or during periods of reduced visibility. The company disengages and moves to the rear while the enemy is not attacking. The company leaves a detachment left in contact (DLIC) to cover the withdrawal by deception, fire, or maneuver. A platoon or one squad from each platoon serves as the DLIC. The composite platoon is normally the best method because there is less repositioning involved. As the DLIC, platoons perform the following:

· Reposition squads and weapons to cover the company's withdrawal.
· Reposition a squad in each of the other platoon positions to cover the most dangerous avenue of approach into the area.
· Continue the normal operating pattern of the company.
· Cover the company withdrawal by fire if the company is attacked during withdrawal.

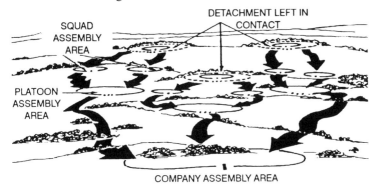

Withdrawal not under pressure.

- Withdraw once the company is at its next position. If under contact, the DLIC might have to maneuver to the rear until contact is broken, then assemble to move to the company.

Withdrawal under Pressure

The amount of enemy pressures determines how the withdrawal is conducted. If it is not possible to prepare and position the security force, the platoon conducts a fighting withdrawal. The platoon disengages from the enemy by maneuvering to the rear. Soldiers, fire teams, and squads not in contact are withdrawn first so they can provide suppressive fires to allow the soldiers, team, or squad in contact to withdraw. If enemy pressure is light enough to permit a security force, a platoon (or a composite platoon) repositions itself to fight the enemy as the rest of the company withdraws.

Delay

Units conduct delaying operations when there are too few forces to attack or defend or when the defensive plan calls for drawing the attacker into an unfavorable situation. The enemy is made to slow its movement by being forced to repeatedly deploy for the attack. Before the enemy assaults, the delaying force withdraws to a new position. The basics of a delay require the following of the delaying force:

- Have mobility equal to that of the enemy, or reduce the mobility of the enemy to a level the delaying force can contend with.
- Maintain contact with the enemy to avoid being outmaneuvered.
- Preserve the freedom to maneuver.

The squads and platoons disengage from the enemy as in a withdrawal. Once disengaged, the platoon moves to its next position and defends again, forcing the enemy to deploy. These tactics slow the advance of the enemy, causing casualties and equipment losses. The platoon can employ ambushes, snipers, obstacles, minefields, and artillery and mortar fire.

Retirement

Retirements are rearward movements conducted by units not in contact. Platoons and squads participate in a retirement as part of a larger force and move using standard movement techniques. Typically, another unit's security force covers their movement. Retiring units move at

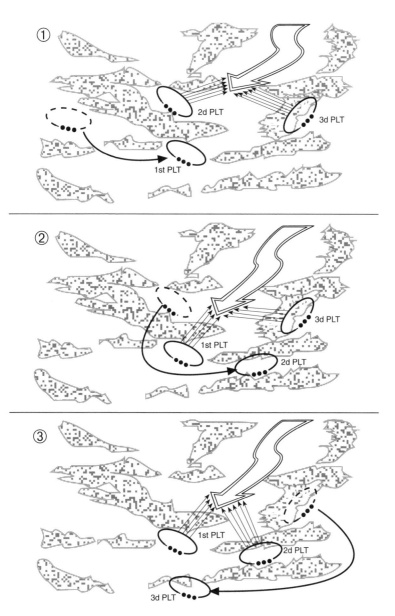

Withdrawal under pressure.

night if possible and conduct daylight movement only if the mission requires it or if the enemy is incapable of interfering. Operational security is emphasized during the entire movement.

RELIEF IN PLACE

A relief in place may be needed to maintain combat effectiveness during prolonged combat operations. A relief in place is an operation in which a platoon is replaced in combat by another platoon. The incoming platoon assumes responsibility for the combat mission and assigned sector or zone of action of the outgoing platoon.

Coordination

Platoon responsibility is usually limited to the detailed coordination between key personnel and their counterparts.

Leaders must reconnoiter different routes into and out of the position; assembly area; logistics points; primary, alternate, and supplementary positions; obstacles; immediate terrain; and when possible, patrol routes and OP locations. The outgoing leader must provide copies of the platoon sector sketch, fire plan, range cards for all weapons, barrier plan, minefield records, counterattack plans, and plans for any other tasks that the platoon may have been tasked to perform.

Both leaders must know which method and sequence of relief has been prescribed in the higher unit order and how they will execute the plan. They are responsible for the following:

- Knowing if their platoons will execute the relief by squads or as a complete platoon (method). Platoons may also execute the relief by occupying adjacent terrain or terrain in depth (to the rear) rather than by relieving soldiers in position.
- Knowing the order of relief (sequence) for platoons within the company.
- Coordinating the use of guides (outgoing unit places guides to move incoming unit to positions), signals, challenge and password, and passage of responsibility for the mission and control of the platoon (normally when the majority of the incoming platoon is in place).
- Coordinating the exchange of tripods for crew-served weapons, phones or switchboards, and emplaced munitions. Platoons do not exchange radios.

- Identifying numbers, types, and location of supplies to be left behind, including sensors, construction materiel, wire, and any supplies that might slow down the movement of the outgoing platoon.

Execution

During the execution, both leaders should co-locate at the outgoing platoon leader's CP. The leader of the outgoing platoon remains responsible for the defense of the area until the majority of the incoming platoon is in position. If the enemy attacks during the relief, the leader who has responsibility at the time is in control. The other leader assists with assets under his control as directed.

Squad leaders physically walk soldiers to positions and trade them out on a one-for-one basis. They allow time for outgoing soldiers to brief their reliefs on their position, range cards, and other pertinent information. Both the relieved and relieving platoons must maintain security to deny the enemy knowledge of the relief. The relieved platoon keeps local security elements in place. These elements are the last soldiers to be relieved. Both platoons observe strict communications security and maintain normal movement and activity. All leaders report completion of their portion of the relief as soon as possible.

LINKUP

Linkups normally occur in enemy-controlled areas and are meetings of friendly ground forces. Linkups depend on control, detailed planning, and stealth.

Site Selection

Sites must be easy to find at night, have cover and concealment, be off the natural lines of drift, be easily defensible for a short period of time, and offer access and escape routes.

Recognition Signals

Far and near recognition signals are needed to keep friendly units from firing at each other. Although units conducting a linkup exchange radio frequencies and call signs, radio is used only to ensure control and prevent fratricide. Visual and voice recognition signals are planned. A near signal could be a sign and countersign exchange, using either words or number combinations. A far signal could use flashlights, chemical lights, infrared lights, or VS-17 panels. There are also signals placed on the linkup point. Examples are stones placed in a prearranged pattern, markings on trees, and arrangements of wood or tree limbs. The first unit to the linkup point places the signal and positions the contact team to watch it. The next unit to the site then stops at the signal and initiates the far recognition signal.

Indirect Fire

Leaders plan use of indirect fires to support linkup operations. Indirect fires can mask noise, deceive the enemy of friendly intent by placing fire at other locations, and distract the enemy. Plan indirect fires along the routes and at the linkup point for support in case chance contact is made.

Contingency Plans

Contingency plans should be made for enemy contact before linkup, during linkup, and after linkup; how long to wait at the linkup point; and what to do if some elements do not make it to the linkup point. Alternate linkup points and rally points need to be designated.

Execution

The unit stops and sets up a linkup rally point about 300 meters away from the linkup point. A contact team is sent to the linkup point; it pinpoints the site and observes the area. If it is the first at the site, it clears the immediate area and marks the linkup point, using the prearranged signal. It then takes up a covered and concealed position to watch the linkup point. The next unit approaching also sets up a rally point and sends out a contact team. When this contact team arrives at the linkup point and spots the recognition signal, it then initiates the far recognition signal, which is answered by the first team, and they exchange near recognition signals. The contact teams coordinate the actions required to link up the units.

STAY-BEHIND OPERATIONS

Stay-behind operations can be used as part of defense or delay missions. If the enemy bypasses the friendly unit, this offers an opportunity to attack the enemy's weakest point (CS and CSS units). The unit that stays behind can inflict casualties on the enemy; disrupt its offensive cohesion by attacking key command, control, and communications elements; and detract from the enemy's main effort by making it necessary to allocate forces for rear area operations. The stay-behind force can furnish intelligence on the enemy in the area and call for and adjust indirect fires.

Stay-behind operations are either unplanned or deliberate. An *unplanned* stay-behind operation is one in which the platoon finds itself cut off from other friendly elements for an indefinite time without specific planning or targets. A *deliberate* stay-behind operation is one in which the platoon plans to operate in enemy-controlled areas as a separate element for a certain amount of time or until a specific event occurs. Squads and platoons conduct this type of operation as part of larger units.

Planning

Planners must pay strict attention to task organization, reconnaissance, combat service support, and a deception plan.

Task Organization

The stay-behind unit includes only the soldiers and equipment needed for the mission. It needs only minimal logistics support and provides for its own security. It must be able to hide easily and move through restrictive terrain.

Reconnaissance

Reconnaissance is conducted to locate suitable sites for patrol bases, OPs, caches, water sources, dismounted and mounted avenues of approach, kill zones, engagement areas, and covered and concealed approach routes.

Combat Service Support

Because the stay-behind unit will not be in physical contact with its supporting unit, water, rations, ammunition, radio batteries, and medical supplies are cached.

Deception Plan

Most stay-behind operations are set up covertly. The enemy must be misled during this effort to cause it to act in a manner favorable to the unit's plan.

Execution

While other friendly forces keep the enemy occupied, the unit moves its elements from defensive positions by clandestine techniques to avoid detection. The unit allows the enemy to bypass it without making contact. Once the stay-behind units are positioned and other friendly forces have withdrawn, combat operations are begun. These include reconnaissance, raids, and ambushes against targets of opportunity or against a set of priority targets assigned by higher headquarters. The stay-behind unit can either wait in place until friendly forces counterattack to their locations, or it can infiltrate small units through the enemy to friendly positions.

7

Patrolling

A patrol is a mission given to units, normally of squad, platoon, or company size. The unit organizes for a patrol, maintaining unit integrity as much as possible. For example, when a platoon is ordered to conduct a patrol, the platoon leader leads the patrol.

ORGANIZATION

A unit preparing to conduct a patrol must organize to perform the specific functions of that type of patrol.

Headquarters

The patrol headquarters consists of the leader, assistant leader, radiotelephone operators (ratelo), forward observer (FO), and any other troops required to control and support the patrol.

Elements

Elements are the subordinate organizations in the patrol unit tailored to the patrol's mission. The leader of a patrol must decide what elements and teams are needed, select men for these elements and teams, and decide what weapons and equipment to provide. He should use his unit's normal organization and chain of command (squad leaders and platoon sergeant) to conduct the patrol. For example, a platoon conducting a combat patrol requiring a headquarters, an element to perform the assault, an element to provide security, and an element to provide fire support may be organized as follows:

The platoon leader, his ratelo, the platoon sergeant, the FO, and perhaps a medic compose the *headquarters.* The first and second squads make up the *assault element.* The third squad is the *security element.* The Dragon gunners along with the machine gun teams act as the *support element.*

Elements of a patrol may be further designated as *teams* to accomplish essential tasks. The organization of each category depends on its mission.

CATEGORIES

There are two categories of patrols: reconnaissance and combat. Both can be conducted mounted or dismounted.

Reconnaissance Patrol

Reconnaissance (area or zone) patrols collect information or confirm or disprove the accuracy of information previously gained. In an *area reconnaissance,* the patrol is organized into a headquarters, a reconnaissance element, and a security element. In a *zone reconnaissance,* the patrol is organized into a headquarters and several reconnaissance elements. Reconnaissance elements may be organized into several reconnaissance teams for an area reconnaissance or organized into reconnaissance and security teams for a zone reconnaissance. Security teams are organized as required to secure the objective area.

Combat Patrol

Combat (ambush, security, or raid) patrols provide security and harass, destroy, or capture enemy troops, equipment, and installations. A combat patrol also collects and reports information as part of its mission. A combat patrol is normally organized into a headquarters, an assault element, a security element, and a support element. At times, the support element may be omitted and automatic weapons added to the assault element. Combat patrol elements may be further organized into teams as necessary to accomplish the elements' tasks. Special-purpose teams may also be organized, such as scout dog, demolition, litter, search, and prisoner teams.

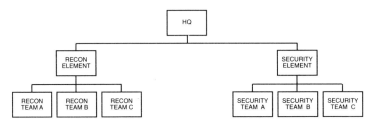

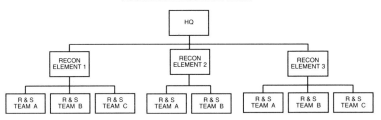

Organization of reconnaissance patrols.

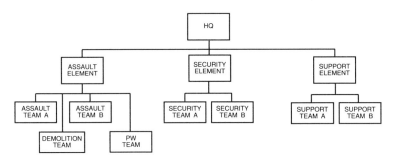

Organization of combat patrol.

A team that may be designated for either type of patrol will consist of a compass man to continually check direction, a point man to follow the directions of the compass man and provide security, and a pace man to keep a running count of his 100-meter pace to verify the distance covered.

PLANNING

When given an order to lead a patrol, the leader starts his procedures by issuing a warning order to all members of the patrol and by initiating coordination, which is continuous throughout the patrol planning and preparation. Before leaving the place where he gets his operation order, the leader coordinates what he can. This location will probably be the battalion or company command post since communications are good and key personnel located there can help him in the coordination.

The leader coordinates the following with the staff member or element designated:

- *Intelligence officer (S2).* Changes in the enemy situation. Special equipment requirements.
- *Operations and training officer (S3).* Changes in the friendly situation. Route selection, landing zone selection. Resupply (in conjunction with the S4). Signal plan, call signs, frequencies, code words, pyrotechnics, and challenges and passwords. Departure and reentry of friendly lines. Other units in the area. Attachment of specialized troops (demo teams, scout dogs, etc.). Rehearsal areas with terrain similar to the objective site.
- *Platoon FO or company FSO.* Fire support on the objective. Fire support along routes to and from the objective, including alternate routes.
- *Friendly forward unit.* The leader gives identification, size of patrol, time of departure and return, and area of the patrol's operation. The forward unit gives information on terrain, known or suspected enemy positions, likely enemy ambush sites, and latest enemy activity. It also furnishes detailed information on friendly positions, obstacle locations, fire plan, and type of support the unit can furnish, such as fire support, litter teams, guides, communications, and reaction units. The forward unit also provides the signals to be used upon reentry and the procedure to be used by the patrol and the guide during departure and reentry. Also furnished are locations of dismount point (if used), initial rally point, departure point, and reentry point.
- *Adjacent patrols.* Identification of the patrol. Mission. Route. Fire plan. Signal plan. Planned times and points for departure and reentry. Any information that either patrol may have about the enemy.

After the warning order has been given and initial coordination started, the leader completes his plan. He first assigns essential tasks to be performed by elements, teams, and men.

Tasks in the Objective Area
Essential tasks in the objective area are assigned. The leader plans how elements, teams, and men are to perform their tasks. Other tasks are assigned and planned to help the patrol reach the objective and return. These tasks can include navigation, security during movement and halts, actions at danger areas, actions on enemy contact, and water crossing.

Times of Departure and Return
Times of departure and return are based on the amount of time needed to reach the objective, to accomplish essential tasks in the objective area, and to return to a friendly area.

Time to reach the objective is determined by considering the distance, terrain, anticipated speed of movement, friendly and enemy situation, and (if applicable) the time the mission must be accomplished.

Time to accomplish essential tasks in the objective area includes the leaders' reconnaissance and movement of elements and teams into positions as well as the accomplishment of the unit mission.

Time to return to a friendly area may be difficult to determine because casualties, prisoners, and captured equipment may slow the patrol. The use of a different return route may change the time needed.

Primary and Alternate Routes
The leader selects the primary route to and from the objective. The return route should be different from the outgoing route. He also selects an alternate route that may be used either to or from the objective. The alternate route is used when the patrol has made contact with the enemy on the primary route. It also may be used when the leader knows or suspects that the patrol has been detected.

Rally Points
A rally point is a place where a patrol can reassemble and reorganize if dispersed during movement, or a place to temporarily halt to reorganize and prepare for actions at an objective, to prepare to depart from friend-

ly lines, or to prepare to reenter friendly lines. The leader should pick rally points either during the patrol or by a map study before the patrol. Those points picked from a map are tentative and will be so until confirmed on the ground.

In seeking a good rally point, the leader should look for places that meet the following requirements:

- Are large enough to allow the patrol to assemble.
- Are easily recognized.
- Have cover and concealment.
- Are defensible for a short time.
- Are away from normal routes of troop movement.

The leader must select an initial rally point (on the friendly side of a forward unit's lines), where a patrol rallies if dispersed before departing friendly lines or before reaching an en route rally point. He must also select rally points on both the near and far sides of danger areas.

In addition, the leader selects an objective rally point, where a patrol will halt to prepare for action at its objective. It is also a point to which a patrol returns after its actions at its objective. It must be near a patrol's objective, but that distance can vary. It should be far enough from the objective so that the patrol's activities will not be detected by the enemy.

Finally, the leader must select a reentry rally point on the enemy side of a forward unit's lines. A patrol halts at a reentry rally point to prepare to reenter friendly lines. It is short of friendly lines and out of sight and sound of friendly observation points.

Inspections and Rehearsals

These activities must be well planned and conducted even though the men are experienced in patrolling. Coordination is made with the commander or S3 for use of a rehearsal area resembling the objective area. Plans must provide for inspections by element and team leaders as well as by the leader of the patrol.

Inspections

Inspections determine the patrol's physical and mental state of readiness. Inspections before rehearsals ensure completeness and correctness of uniform and equipment. Men are questioned to see if they know the following:

- The plan.
- What each is to do and when he is to do it.
- What others are to do.
- Challenges and passwords, signals, codes, radio call signs, frequencies, and reporting times.

Rehearsals

It is through well-directed rehearsals that men become familiar with what they must do when on patrol. If the patrol is to be at night, it is advisable to hold both day and night rehearsals. A good way to rehearse is to have the leader walk and talk the whole patrol through each action. He describes the actions of elements, teams, and men, and he has them perform these actions. In this dry run, men take their positions in formations at reduced distances to get the "feel" of the patrol. When the different actions are clear to all concerned, a complete (normal speed) rehearsal is held with the whole patrol. This is a wet run. As many dry runs and wet runs are conducted as deemed necessary. When possible, element and team leaders rehearse their units separately before the final rehearsal of the entire patrol.

Communications

The plan must include radio call signs, primary and alternate frequencies, times to report, and codes. The challenge and password from the communications-electronic operation instructions (CEOI) should not be used beyond the forward edge of the battle area (FEBA). The leader may devise his own challenge and password system to be used beyond the FEBA. An example of this is the odd-number system. Any odd number can be used. If the leader specified 11 as the odd number, the challenge could be any number between 1 and 10. The password would be the number that, when added to the challenge, equals 11 (e.g., challenge, 8; password, 3).

The signals to be used on the patrol must be planned and rehearsed. Signals may be needed to lift or to shift supporting fire, to start an assault, to order withdrawal from the objective, to signal "all clear," and to stop and start movement of the patrol. Visual and audible signals such as arm-and-hand signals, flares, voice, whistles, radios, and infrared equipment may be used. All signals must be known by all patrol members.

Location of Leaders

The location of the leaders of the patrol is planned for all phases of the patrol—during movement, at danger areas, and at the objective. The leader plans to be where he can best control the patrol during each phase. The assistant leader may be given a special job for each phase of the patrol. He may help the leader control the patrol by being where he can best take command, if required. Some places the assistant leader may be during actions in the objective area are as follows:

- On a raid or ambush, with the support element.
- On an area reconnaissance, in the objective rally point.
- On a zone reconnaissance, with a reconnaissance element that has been directed to move to and establish the point at which all elements are to link up after reconnoitering.

ISSUE THE ORDER

The standard operation order format is used and briefed in sequence. Terrain models, sketches, or blackboards are used to illustrate the plan. Sketches to show planned actions can be drawn in dirt, sand, or snow. Personnel may make notes but should hold questions until the order is completed. This prevents interruption of the leader's train of thought. Included in the order are changes to the chain of command given in the warning order.

CONDUCT

The departure of the patrol through another unit's lines can be confusing and dangerous. The leader coordinates with the forward unit commander and checks to learn of recent enemy activity or situation changes that may require adjustment in the patrol plan. When the patrol is ready, it moves up to and halts at the initial rally point. Then a guide from the forward unit leads the patrol through the wire and other obstacles forward of the unit.

After the patrol has moved beyond the range of the friendly unit's small arms and final protective fires, it halts briefly to adjust to the sights and sounds of the battlefield. As the patrol moves along its route, the leader selects rally points or confirms points selected earlier from a map. The patrol halts as it nears its tentative objective rally point, and a reconnaissance element moves forward to see if the point is suitable as an ORP and to see that no enemy troops are near. When the patrol leader is satisfied, the rest of the patrol is brought into the ORP and sets up a perimeter for all-around security.

When the ORP is secure, the leader of the patrol, a compass man, and element leaders go on a leaders' reconnaissance. The assistant leader knows the plans for the leaders' reconnaissance and stays at the ORP with instructions about what to do if the patrol leader makes contact or fails to return. The leaders' reconnaissance is conducted to pinpoint the objective, to pick positions for the patrol's elements, and to get information to confirm or to alter the plan.

After the reconnaissance, the leaders return to the ORP to complete planning and disseminate information. One or more men may stay behind to observe the objective. On a reconnaissance patrol, if the leader gets enough information about the objective during the leaders' reconnaissance, his mission is accomplished and the patrol returns to friendly lines. If he does not get enough information, the patrol reconnoiters as planned until enough information is gained.

DANGER AREAS

Specific plans are made in advance for crossing each known danger area (an area where there is an increased chance of detection or a fight). The patrol tries to avoid danger areas. Typical danger areas include known enemy positions, roads and trails, streams, and open areas.

To cross a danger area, a patrol must designate near- and far-side rally points, secure the near side, secure the far side, and cross the area.

ACTIONS ON ENEMY CONTACT

Unless required by a mission, a patrol must strive to avoid enemy contact. If it does make unexpected contact with the enemy, it must quickly break the contact and continue its mission. Battle drills are well-rehearsed actions intended to provide fast reaction to unexpected enemy contact. As soon as any member of the patrol recognizes a situation requiring an immediate action, he initiates the appropriate drill, as follows:

Air Attack

The first man to see an aircraft shouts, "Aircraft, front (or right, left, or rear)!" If the leader sees that the aircraft is making a firing run on the patrol, he hits the ground at once and shoots at the aircraft. All men follow his example.

Chance Contact—"Freeze"

This drill is used when a patrol, not yet seen by the enemy, sees the enemy and does not have time to take any other action. All men hold still until signaled to continue or to do something else.

Chance Contact—"Hasty Ambush"

This drill is used when a patrol, not yet seen by the enemy, sees the enemy approaching and has time to take some action other than to "freeze." When the signal is given to initiate this drill, all men move on line and take concealed firing positions. The leader lets the enemy pass if his patrol is not detected. If the patrol is detected, the ambush is initiated.

Chance Contact—"Immediate Assault"

This drill is used when a patrol and an enemy element of the same size or smaller see each other at the same time and at such close range that fire and movement are not feasible. The men nearest the enemy open fire and shout, "Contact, front (or right, left, or rear)!" The patrol moves swiftly into the assault. The assault stops if the enemy withdraws and breaks contact. If the enemy stands and fights, the assault is carried through the enemy, and movement is continued until the enemy is destroyed or contact is broken.

Chance Contact—"Clock System"

This drill is used when a patrol and a larger enemy element see each other at the same time. The patrol must break contact or be destroyed. The direction in which the patrol is moving is always twelve o'clock. When contact is made, the leader shouts a direction and a distance to move—for example, "Eight o'clock, 200!" This tells the patrol to move in the direction of eight o'clock for 200 meters. If contact is broken, the patrol rallies the designated distance away and continues its mission. If contact is not broken, another direction and distance are given. This process continues until contact is broken.

Ambush

If a patrol finds itself in an enemy ambush, it must get out of the kill zone or face destruction. To do so, it must take the following battle-drill action:

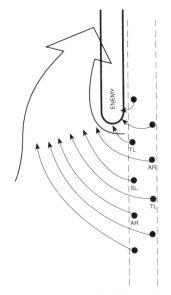

Counter-ambush drill—envelopment.

1. The men in the kill zone, without order or signal, immediately return fire and quickly move out of the kill zone by the safest way. Smoke can help conceal the men in the kill zone.
2. The men not in the kill zone fire to support the withdrawal of the others.
3. The patrol breaks contact and reorganizes in the last designated rally point.

Indirect Fire

If a patrol comes under indirect fire, the leader immediately has the patrol move out of the impact area. The men do not seek cover. By continuing to move, the patrol is more difficult to hit and the chance of being pinned down is reduced.

Sniper Fire

If a patrol comes under sniper fire, it immediately returns fire in the direction of the sniper. The patrol then conducts fire and movement to break contact with the sniper.

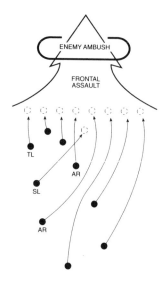

Counter-ambush drill—encounter.

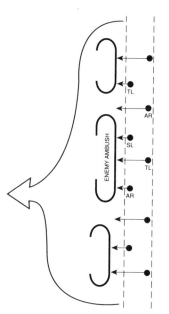

Counter-ambush drill—immediate assault.

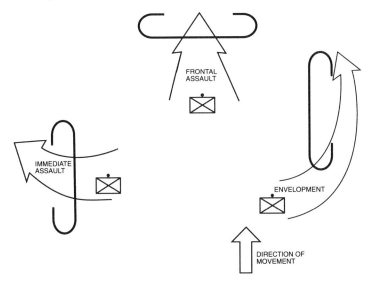

Counter-ambush drill—platoon counter-ambush against L- or U-shaped ambushes.

CASUALTIES AND PRISONERS

Patrols must have a plan for handling casualties and prisoners. The method must not jeopardize the mission.

Wounded are moved from the immediate area of a firefight before they are given first aid. Giving first aid during a firefight risks even more casualties. Dead may be handled the same way as seriously wounded, except that no one is left with the body, which is concealed for later pickup.

Prisoners are bound and gagged, and they may be blindfolded. They may then be taken under guard to a friendly area and evacuated by air, taken with the patrol, or concealed for later pickup.

REENTRY OF FRIENDLY LINES

The reentry of a patrol through another unit's lines can be confusing and dangerous if it is not well coordinated before the patrol's departure on its mission. When a patrol returns to friendly lines, it stops at the reentry rally point, out of sight and sound of friendly OPs, where the leader transmits a radio message code to tell the friendly unit that a patrol is ready to reenter.

If radio communications are not possible, one member of the patrol should contact an OP, using the challenge and password. Once contact is made, the OP can then relay a message to the unit's commander. The friendly unit then sends a guide to lead the patrol through its position.

If radio communications are established, and the friendly unit is ready to guide the patrol through the lines, the patrol moves to the reentry point. The guide and leader exchange signals to identify the patrol, and the patrol is led through the lines.

The assistant leader should stay at the reentry point and count the men going through the lines to ensure that only members of the patrol reenter friendly lines.

AMBUSH PATROLS

An ambush is a surprise attack from a concealed position on a moving or temporarily halted target. It may include an assault to close with and destroy the enemy, or the attack may be fire only. There are two types of ambush: point and area. In a *point ambush,* troops deploy to attack a single kill zone. In an *area ambush,* troops deploy as two or more related point ambushes. Ambushes are described in the following terms:

The *ambush site* is the terrain on which a point ambush is established.

The *kill zone* is the part of an ambush site where fire is concentrated to isolate, trap, and kill the enemy.

The *assault element* is the part of the ambush patrol that fires into and assaults the kill zone.

The *support element* is the part of the ambush patrol that supports the assault element by firing into and around the kill zone.

The *security element* is the part of the ambush patrol responsible for early warning and security. It secures the ORP and blocks enemy avenues of approach into and out of the ambush site.

Keys to a Successful Ambush

Surprise is a major feature that distinguishes an ambush from other forms of attack. Surprise is achieved by good planning, preparation, and execution.

Coordinated Fire

All weapons, including mines and demolitions, must be positioned, and all fire, including that of supporting artillery and mortars, must be coordinated. The goals are to isolate the kill zone, to prevent escape or reinforcement, and to deliver a large volume of highly concentrated surprise fire into the kill zone.

Control

Close control must be maintained during movement to, occupation of, and withdrawal from the ambush site. Control is most critical at the time of the enemy's approach. Control measures must provide for the following:

- Early warning of enemy approach.
- Withholding fire until the enemy has moved into the kill zone.
- Opening fire at the proper time.
- Initiation of proper action if the ambush is prematurely detected.
- Lifting or shifting of supporting fire when the attack includes assault of the target.
- Timely and orderly withdrawal of the patrol to the ORP.

Ambush Formations
Line Formation

In the line formation, the assault and support elements are deployed generally parallel to the enemy's route of movement (road, trail, stream). This subjects the enemy to flanking fire. The enemy is trapped in the kill

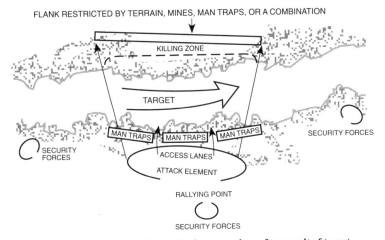

Line formation—destruction ambush—access lanes for assault of target.

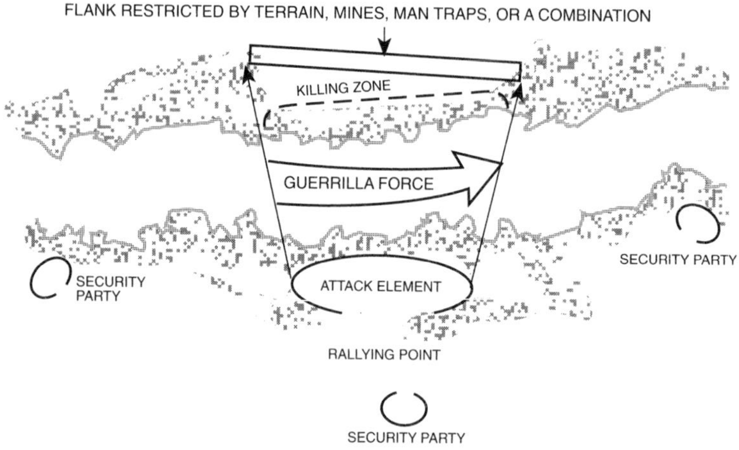

FLANK RESTRICTED BY TERRAIN, MINES, MAN TRAPS, OR A COMBINATION

KILLING ZONE

GUERRILLA FORCE

SECURITY PARTY

SECURITY PARTY

ATTACK ELEMENT

RALLYING POINT

SECURITY PARTY

Line formation—harassing or obstruction ambush.

zone by natural obstacles, mines (Claymore, antitank, antipersonnel), explosives, and direct and indirect fire. A disadvantage of the line formation is that its target may be so dispersed that it is larger than the kill zone.

The line formation is good in close terrain that restricts the enemy's movement and in open terrain where one flank is blocked by natural obstacles or can be blocked by mines or explosives. An advantage of the line formation is the relative ease by which it can be controlled under all conditions of visibility.

L Formation

The L-shaped formation is a variation of the line formation. The long leg of the L (assault element) is parallel to the kill zone, providing flanking fire. The short leg (support element) is at the end of, and at a right angle to, the kill zone. This provides enfilade fire that interlocks with fire from the other leg. This formation can be deployed on a straight stretch of trail, road, or stream, or at a sharp bend.

Squad Antiarmor Ambush

The purpose of an antiarmor ambush is to destroy armored vehicles. A squad can conduct a dismounted antiarmor ambush, organizing into an

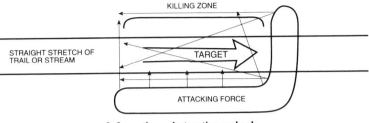

L formation—destruction ambush.

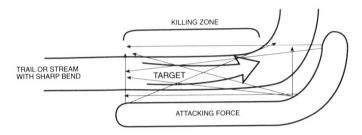

L formation—destruction ambush—bend of trail or stream.

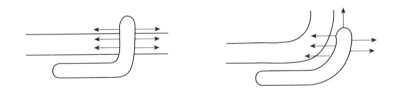

L formation—short leg prevents escape or reinforcement.

armor-killer team and a support-and-security team. The armor-killer team fires into the kill zone. Normally, the Dragon is the main weapon of this team. Where fields of fire are less than 100 meters, light antitank weapons (LAWs) may be the main antiarmor weapon. In that case, the armor-killer team must mass LAW fires into the kill zone to make sure the enemy vehicle is destroyed. The support-and-security team provides security and should be positioned where it can cover the withdrawal of the armor-killer team.

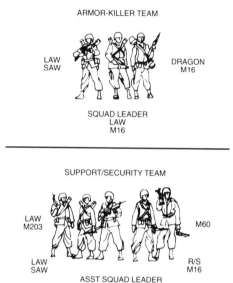

ARMOR-KILLER TEAM

LAW
SAW

DRAGON
M16

SQUAD LEADER
LAW
M16

SUPPORT/SECURITY TEAM

LAW
M203

M60

LAW
SAW

R/S
M16

ASST SQUAD LEADER
M203

Squad antiarmor ambush.

At the Ambush Site

When the squad arrives at the ambush site, the leader reconnoiters and picks the kill zone. Good positions have the following attributes:

- Good fields of fire.
- Cover and concealment.
- An obstacle between the teams and the kill zone.
- Covered and concealed withdrawal routes.

Establishing an Antiarmor Ambush

Position a support-and-security team first and provide security on both flanks. Position the Dragon and then the machine gun so they can cover the kill zone.

The leader initiates the ambush when the enemy enters the kill zone. A command-detonated antiarmor mine is an excellent means of initiating the ambush. The Dragon may be used to initiate the ambush, but it has a slow rate of fire, gives off a signature, and may not hit the target. When possible, the first and last vehicles of a column should be destroyed to keep other vehicles from escaping.

The rest of the squad opens fire when the ambush is initiated. Indirect fires should fall into the kill zone as soon as possible. If the kill zone is in range, squad members fire a LAW.

If enemy dismounted troops precede the armored vehicles, the squad leader must decide whether they pose a threat to the ambush. If they can outflank his squad before the enemy armor can be hit, he may decide to withdraw and set up another ambush somewhere else.

TRACKING PATROL

Platoons and squads may receive the mission to follow the trail of an enemy unit. Even while tracking, they still gather information about the enemy, the route, and surrounding terrain.

Training

Soldiers must be trained to move stealthily and well trained in tracking techniques. Training is essential to develop and maintain tracking skills. Once soldiers are deployed into an area of operations, training continues so that the platoon can learn about local soil, climate, vegetation, animals, vehicles, footwear, and other factors.

Organization

When the platoon receives the mission to conduct a tracking patrol, it assigns the task of tracking to only one squad. The remaining squads and attachments provide security.

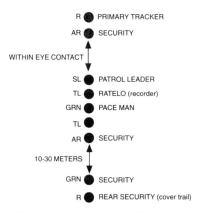

Tracking organization and formation.

Trail Signs

Men, machines, and animals leave signs of their presence as they move through an area. These signs can be as subtle as an odor or as obvious as a well-worn path. All soldiers can read obvious signs such as roads, worn trails, or tracks in sand and snow; however, attention to detail, common sense, alertness, logic, and knowledge of the environment and enemy habits enable soldiers to obtain better information from signs they find in the battle area.

Trail and Sign Analysis

Once the first sign is discovered, it must not be disturbed or covered and should be analyzed carefully before the patrol follows the enemy. If the sign is found at the site of enemy activity, the exact occurrence can often be reconstructed. If a trail is the first sign found, the tracker can still determine such facts as the size and composition of the groups being tracked, their direction, and their general condition. The tracker must determine as much as possible about the enemy before following them, and his knowledge of the enemy continues to grow as he finds additional sign.

Finding the Trail

Finding the trail is the first task of the tracking team. The tracking team can reconnoiter around a known location of enemy activity when the trail cannot be found in the immediate area. There are two ways to hunt for a trail:

1. The tracking team can locate and follow the enemy's trail from a specific area or location where the enemy has been seen. This can be a camp or base, or the site of an enemy attack or enemy contact.

2. The route of a friendly unit may cross a trail left by an enemy group. This can be by chance, or the team can deliberately take a route it believes will cut across one or more probable enemy routes.

Regaining a Lost Trail

If the tracker loses the trail, he immediately stops. The tracking team then retraces its path to the last enemy sign and marks this point. The team studies the sign and the area around it for any clue as to where the enemy went. It looks for signs that the enemy scattered, backtracked,

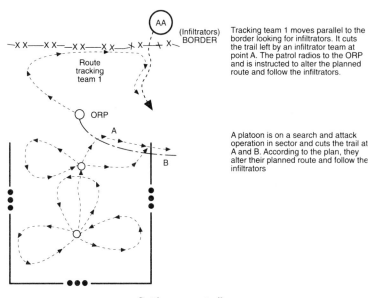

Tracking team 1 moves parallel to the border looking for infiltrators. It cuts the trail left by an infiltrator team at point A. The patrol radios to the ORP and is instructed to alter the planned route and follow the infiltrators.

A platoon is on a search and attack operation in sector and cuts the trail at A and B. According to the plan, they alter their planned route and follow the infiltrators

Cutting enemy trail.

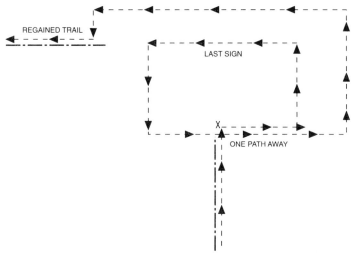

Boxing technique.

doglegged, or used any other countertracking method. If the trail still cannot be found, the team establishes security in a spot that avoids destroying any sign. Then the tracker and an assistant look for the trail by "boxing" the area around the last sign. The tracking team always returns to the same path, away from the last sign, to create as few trails as possible.

PATROL BASES

A patrol base is a position set up when a squad or platoon conducting a patrol halts for an extended period. When the unit must halt for a long time in a place not protected by friendly troops, it takes both active and passive security measures. Patrol bases should be occupied no longer than twenty-four hours, and the same patrol base is never used twice. Patrol bases are used for the following purposes:

- To avoid detection by stopping all movement.
- For hiding during a long, detailed reconnaissance of an objective area.
- To eat, clean weapons and equipment, and rest.
- To plan and issue orders.
- To reorganize after infiltrating an enemy area.
- As a base from which to conduct several consecutive or concurrent operations such as ambush, raid, reconnaissance, or security.

Site Selection

A tentative site is normally selected from a map or by aerial reconnaissance. Its suitability must be confirmed before occupation. An alternate site is selected in the event the first site is unsuitable or must be evacuated unexpectedly. The site should be on terrain of little tactical value to the enemy, off natural lines of drift, difficult for foot movement, near a source of water, offering cover and concealment, and defensible for a short period of time.

Occupation of the Patrol Base

The area is reconnoitered, and when determined secure, the patrol enters from a 90-degree turn. The platoon sergeant and the last fire team get rid of any tracks from the turn. A two-man OP is left at the turn. The platoon moves into the position with squad leaders moving to the left

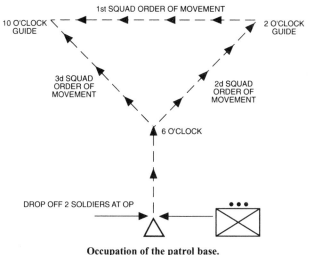

Occupation of the patrol base.

flank of their squad sector. The platoon leader checks the position, starting at six o'clock and moving in a clockwise direction. He meets each squad leader at the squad's left flank, adjusts the perimeter as needed, and repositions machine guns if he finds better locations.

When the perimeter is secure, the platoon leader directs each squad to conduct a reconnaissance to the front of its sector. Each squad sends out a team from the left flank of the squad sector, which moves a distance away from the position as directed by the platoon leader (200 to 400 meters depending on terrain and vegetation). It then moves clockwise and reenters the patrol base at the right flank of the squad sector. The team looks for enemy, water, built-up areas, human habitat, roads, or trails. The platoon leader gathers information from the reconnaissance teams and determines the suitability of the area as a patrol base.

Patrol Base Activities

The considerations for a perimeter defense apply to establishing a patrol base. The leader assigns a priority of work including the following:

Security

Each squad establishes an OP, and the soldiers quietly dig hasty fighting positions. Priorities of work can be accomplished by two-man positions, with one soldier on guard while the other soldier digs, conducts personal hygiene and maintenance, and eats. Noise and light discipline is enforced. Claymores are put out. Sector sketches and range cards are prepared. Soldiers should use only one point of entry and exit.

Alert Plan
The platoon leader states the alert posture (for example, 50 percent or 33 percent awake) and stand-to time for day and night. He prepares a roster for periodic checks of fighting positions and OPs, and ensures that OPs are relieved periodically and that at least one leader is awake at all times. No more than half of the platoon eats at one time.

Withdrawal Plan
The platoon prepares a contingency plan for enemy contact, including a signal (for example, star cluster) to withdraw, order of withdrawal (squads not in contact move out first), and rendezvous point.

Maintenance
Leaders ensure that weapons and equipment are cleaned and maintained. Machine guns, radios, and night-vision devices are not broken down at the same time. Weapons are not disassembled at night.

Field Sanitation and Personal Hygiene
Latrines are dug and trash points designated. Soldiers shave, wash, and brush teeth daily. A water party is organized to fill all canteens. No trash is left behind, and the position is sterilized upon departure.

8

Air Assault and Airborne Operations

AIR ASSAULT OPERATIONS

Air assault operations are those in which assault forces using the fire-power and mobility of helicopters maneuver on the battlefield to engage and destroy enemy forces or to seize and hold key terrain. They are deliberate and precisely planned combat operations designed to allow friendly forces to strike over extended distances and terrain barriers.

Ground Tactical Plan

The foundation of an air assault operation is the commander's ground tactical plan, around which subsequent planning is based. The ground tactical plan for an air assault operation contains essentially the same elements as any other infantry attack but differs in that it is prepared to capitalize on speed and mobility in order to achieve surprise. Assault echelons are placed on or near the objective and organized so as to be capable of immediate seizure of objectives and rapid consolidation for subsequent operations. The plan depends on the commander's evaluation of METT-T, including, in particular, the availability of landing zones (LZ) in the area. The plan should include the following:

- Missions of all subordinate elements and methods for employment.
- Zones of attack, sectors, or area of operations with graphic control measures.
- Task organization, to include command relationships.
- Location and size of reserves.
- Fire support.
- Combat service support.

It is important that air crews know the ground tactical plan and the ground commander's intent.

Landing Plan

The landing plan must support the ground tactical plan. This plan sequences elements into the area of operations, ensuring that elements arrive at designated locations and times and are prepared to execute the tactical plan. The following considerations should be taken into account in the landing plan:

- The availability, location, and size of potential LZs are overriding factors.
- The company is most vulnerable during landing.
- Elements must land with tactical integrity.
- Troops are easily disoriented if the landing direction changes and they are not kept informed.
- The company must be prepared to fight in any direction after landing, since there may be no other friendly troops in the area.
- The landing plan should offer flexibility so that a variety of options is available in developing a scheme of maneuver.
- Supporting fires (artillery, attack helicopters, close air support, naval gunfire) must be planned in and around each LZ.
- Although the objective may be beyond the range of supporting artillery fire, artillery or mortars can be brought into the LZs early to provide fire support for maneuver troops.
- Resupply and medical evacuation by air must be provided for.

Selection of Landing Zones

Each landing zone is selected using the following criteria:

- *Location.* It can be located on, near, or away from the objective, depending on METT-T.
- *Capacity.* The size determines how much combat power can be landed at one time. Size also determines the need for additional LZs or separation between serials.
- *Alternates.* An alternate LZ should be planned for each primary LZ to ensure flexibility.
- *Enemy disposition and capabilities.* Enemy troop concentrations, air defenses, and their capability to react are considered when selecting an LZ.
- *Cover and concealment.* Landing zones are selected that deny enemy observation and acquisition of friendly ground and air elements while they are en route to and/or from (and in) the LZ. Depending on METT-T, the LZ and approaches should be masked from the enemy by terrain features.
- *Obstacles.* If possible, the company should land on the enemy side of obstacles when attacking, and at other times use the obstacles to protect LZs from the enemy. Landing zones must be free of obstacles. Engineers must be part of the task organization for contingency breaching of obstacles.
- *Identification from the air.* LZs should be easily identifiable from the air. If pathfinder support or friendly reconnaissance units are present, they should mark the LZ with chemical lights, preferably of the infrared type, if the assault troops wear night-vision goggles.
- *Approach and departure routes.* Approach and departure routes should avoid continued flank exposure of aircraft to the enemy.
- *Weather.* Reduced visibility or strong winds may preclude or limit the use of marginal LZs.

Single versus Multiple Landing Zones

In addition to deciding where to land in relation to the objective, consideration is given to the use of a single LZ or multiple LZs.

The following are the advantages of using a single LZ:

- Allows concentration of combat power.

- Facilitates control of the operation.
- Concentrates supporting fire.
- Provides better ground security for subsequent lifts.
- Requires fewer attack helicopters for security.
- Makes it more difficult for the enemy to detect the operation by the reduced number of flight routes in the operation area.
- Centralizes any required resupply efforts.
- Concentrates efforts of limited LZ control personnel and engineers on one LZ.
- Requires less planning and rehearsal time.

The following are the advantages of using multiple LZs:
- Avoids grouping assets in one location and creating a lucrative target for enemy fire.
- Allows rapid dispersal of ground elements to accomplish tasks in separate areas.
- Reduces the enemy's ability to detect and react to the initial lift.
- Forces the enemy to fight in more than one direction.
- Reduces the troop and aircraft congestion that can occur on one LZ.
- Makes it difficult for the enemy to determine the size of the air assault force and the location of supporting weapons.

Air Movement Plan

The air movement plan is based on the ground tactical and landing plans. It specifies the schedule and provides instruction for air movement of troops, equipment, and supplies from PZ (pickup zone) to LZ. It also provides coordinating instructions regarding air routes, air control points, and aircraft speeds, altitudes, and formations.

Loading Plan

The loading plan is based on the air movement plan. It ensures that troops, equipment, and supplies are loaded on the correct aircraft. Unit integrity is maintained when aircraft loads are planned; however, assault forces and equipment may be cross-loaded so that command and control personnel, all types of combat power, and a mix of weapons arrive at the LZ ready to fight. Aircraft loads are also planned in priority to establish a bump plan. A bump plan ensures that essential troops and equipment are loaded ahead of less critical loads in case of aircraft breakdown or other problems.

Planning must cover the organization and operation of the PZ, including load positions, day and night markings, and communications. The loading plan is most important when mixing aircraft types. Ground and aviation unit movement to the PZ is scheduled so that only the troops to load and the helicopter to be loaded arrive at the PZ at the same time. To coordinate movement of units to the PZ, assembly areas, holding areas, and routes of movement are selected.

At company and lower levels, each man and major items of equipment or supplies are assigned to specific aircraft by an airloading table. The airloading table is an accountability tool, a loading manifest for each aircraft. When time is limited, the table can be a sheet of paper from the squad leader's notebook. These lists are left with a specified person in the PZ. This procedure ensures that if an aircraft is lost, a list of personnel and equipment on board is available.

During load planning, unit leaders attempt to maintain the following:

- Tactical integrity of units. Fire teams and squads are loaded intact on the same aircraft, and platoons in the same serial. This ensures integrity as a fighting unit upon landing.
- Self-sufficiency of loads. Each load should be functional by itself whenever possible. Every towed item is accompanied by its prime mover. Crews are loaded with their vehicle or weapon. Ammunition is carried with the weapon. Component parts accompany the major items of equipment. Sufficient personnel are on board to unload the cargo.
- Tactical cross-loading. Loads should be planned so that all leaders, or all crew-served weapons, are not loaded on the same aircraft. Thus if an aircraft is lost, the mission is not seriously hampered.

Aircraft Bump Plan

Each aircraft load has a bump sequence designated on its airloading table. Bump priority ensures that the most essential personnel and equipment arrive at the objective area first. It specifies personnel and equipment that may be bumped and delivered later. If all personnel within the load cannot be lifted, individuals must know who is to offload and in what sequence. This ensures that key personnel are not bumped arbitrarily.

Also, bump sequence is designated for aircraft within each serial or flight. This ensures that key aircraft loads are not left in the PZ. When an aircraft within a serial or flight cannot lift off and key personnel are on board, they offload and reboard another aircraft that has priority. A PZ bump and straggler collection point is established to account for, regroup, and reschedule these personnel and/or loads for later delivery.

Lifts, Serials, and Loads
To maximize operational control, aviation assets are designated as lifts, serials, or loads.

A *lift* is one sortie of all utility and cargo aircraft assigned to a mission. Each time all assigned aircraft pick up troops and/or equipment and set them down on the LZ, one lift is completed. The second lift is completed when all lift aircraft place their second loads on the LZ.

When a lift is too large to fly in one formation, it is organized into a number of *serials.* A serial is a tactical grouping of two or more aircraft under the control of a serial commander and separated from other tactical groupings within the lift by time or space. Serials also may be organized when the capacity of available PZs or LZs is limited or to take advantage of available flight routes.

A *load* is personnel or equipment designated to be moved by a specific aircraft. Each aircraft within the lift is termed a load. For example, within a lift of ten, there are aircraft loads one through ten.

Staging Plan
The staging plan is based on the loading plan and prescribes the arrival time of ground units (troops, equipment, and supplies) at the PZ in the proper order for movement. Loads must be ready before aircraft arrive at the PZ; usually, ground units are expected to be in PZ posture fifteen minutes before aircraft arrive.

Helicopters
Several types of helicopters may be used in air assault operations: observation, utility, cargo, and attack.

Observation Helicopters (OHs)

The OHs are organic to aviation units found within the division. The OHs are used to provide command and control, aerial observation and reconnaissance, and aerial target acquisition.

Utility Helicopters (UHs)

The UHs are the most versatile of all helicopters, performing a variety of tasks, and as such they are available in almost every unit possessing helicopters. UHs are used to conduct combat assaults and provide transportation, command and control, and resupply. When rigged with special equipment, they also may be used to provide aeromedical evacuations, conduct radiological surveys, and dispense scatterable mines.

Cargo Helicopters (CHs)

These aircraft are organic to corps aviation units. They normally provide transportation, resupply, and recovery of downed aircraft.

Attack Helicopters (AHs)

AHs are organized in groups varying in size from company to battalion and can also be task organized to meet mission needs. They are used to provide overwatch, destroy point targets, provide security, and suppress air defense weapons.

Capabilities

Under normal conditions, helicopters can ascend and descend at relatively steep angles; this enables them to operate from confined and unimproved areas. Troops and their combat equipment can be unloaded from a helicopter hovering a short distance above the ground with troop ladders and rappelling means, or if the helicopter can hover low enough, the troops may jump to the ground. The troop ladder can also be used to load personnel when the helicopter cannot land. Cargo can be transported as an external load and delivered to areas inaccessible to other types of aircraft or to ground transportation.

Because of a wide speed range and high maneuverability at slow speeds, helicopters can fly safely and efficiently at low altitudes, using terrain and trees for cover and concealment. Because of their ability to fly at high or low altitudes, decelerate rapidly, maintain slow forward speed, and land nearly vertically helicopters can operate under marginal weather conditions.

Helicopters can land on the objective area in a tactical formation, LZ(s) permitting. Night and/or limited-visibility landings and liftoffs can be made with a minimum of light. Helicopters flying at low levels are capable of achieving surprise, deceiving the enemy at the LZ(s), and employing shock effect through the use of suppressive fires. Engine and rotor noise may deceive the enemy as to the direction of approach and intended flight path.

Limitations

The high fuel consumption of helicopters imposes limitations on range and allowable cargo load (ACL). Helicopters may reduce fuel loads to permit an increased ACL, but reducing the fuel load also reduces the range and flexibility. The load-carrying capability of helicopters decreases with increases of altitude, humidity, and temperature. This limitation may be compensated for through reduction of fuel load. Weight and balance affect flight control. Loads must be properly distributed to keep the center of gravity within allowable limits.

Hail, sleet, icing, heavy rains, and gusty winds (30 knots or more) will limit or preclude use of helicopters. Crosswind velocities above 15 knots for utility helicopters and 10 knots for cargo helicopters, and downwind velocities above 5 knots for either type of helicopter, will affect the selection of the direction of landing and liftoff.

Engine and rotor noise may compromise secrecy. Aviator fatigue requires greater consideration in the operation of rotary-wing aircraft than in the operation of fixed-wing aircraft.

Loads

The type-load method is the most efficient method used in the conduct of air assault operations and in operational planning. Army aviation units are frequently required to support numerous major units operating over expansive tactical zones. Standardization of type loads within the theater of operations ensures responsive and effective air mobility with a minimum of time required for planning.

The use of type loads does not limit the flexibility of a ground tactical unit to be airlifted. The type-load method is very useful at battalion and company levels to plan and conduct air assault operations.

Sample Type Loads

UH-1. Maximum ACL for the UH-1 is 2,000 pounds. As fuel is reduced following the initial airlift, the troop load may be increased to eight or nine for subsequent liftoffs.

Cargo	Weight	Total
1) 7 personnel	1,680	1,680
2) Bulk cargo	2,000	2,000
3) 1 ea mule (slingload)	900	
Load on mule	1,000	1,900
4) 1 ea ¼-ton trailer	565	
Load on trailer (external load)	500	1,065

UH-60. Maximum ACL is 11 to 13 troops, depending on seating configuration.

Cargo	Weight	Total
1) 11 personnel	2,640	
1 ea ¼-ton truck w/trailer (external)	3,500	6,140
2) 7 personnel	1,680	
1 ea M102 howitzer	3,195	
40 rds ammo (A-22)	2,400	7,275
3) 1 ea M99B (HMMWV-loaded) (external)	7,700	7,700

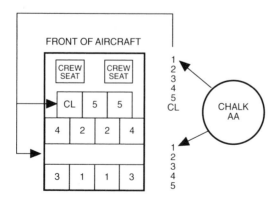

UH-60 loading diagram.

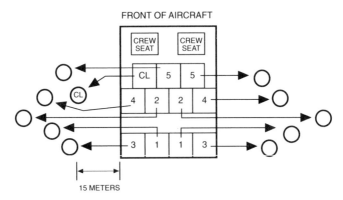

UH-60 unloading diagram.

CH-47. Type-load data is based on an aircraft maximum gross weight of 33,000 pounds on a standard day at mean sea level. As density altitude increases, or when the aircraft is required to operate at higher altitudes, the payload is reduced accordingly.

Cargo	Weight	Total
1) 20 personnel	4,800	
1 ea A-22 container (slingload)	3,000	7,800
2) 8 personnel	1,920	
Mules loaded	6,000	7,920
3) 22 personnel	5,280	
3 ea 81-mm mortars	282	
150 rds ammo (slingload)	2,250	7,812
4) 16 personnel	3,840	
2 ea mortars, 4.2-in.	1,200	
100 rds ammo (slingload)	3,000	8,040
5) 5 personnel	1,200	
1 ea M998 (loaded) (slinghold)	7,700	8,900
6) 3 personnel	720	
1 M101A1 howitzer	4,680	
with sec equip		
40 rds ammo	2,400	7,800
7) 1 M102 howitzer	3,195	
60 rds 105-mm ammo	3,600	
Equip	430	7,225
8) 33 personnel	7,920	7,920

CH-54. Type-load data based on an aircraft maximum gross weight of 38,000 pounds on a standard day at mean sea level. As density increases, or when the aircraft is required to operate at higher altitudes, the payload is reduced accordingly.

Sample pod loads	Weight
1) Mixed cargo	10,000
2) 1¼-ton truck with trailer	8,000
3) 150 rds 105-mm ammo (boxed)	17,000
4) 67 troops at 240 lbs ea	16,080

Sample 4-point slingloads	Weight
1) 2½-ton truck	13,000
2) Road grader (front sec)	9,000
3) Road grader (rear sec)	14,000
4) HD6 bulldozer	16,000
5) APC, M113	18,000

Sample single-point slingloads	Weight
1) 4 ea 500-gal fuel bags	13,200
2) CH-47 helicopter minus engines and blades	16,000
3) 155-mm howitzer	14,000
4) 100 rds 155-mm ammo	14,000

Seats-out Operation

With the UH-60, if the troop seats are removed, twenty-two combat-loaded soldiers and their rucksacks can be loaded. Conducting combat operations with seats out reduces the number of aircraft needed for each mission. The aircraft can be loaded from either or both sides. Loading is quicker if both sides are used. Before the soldiers enter the aircraft, each soldier's rucksack is placed on the floor of the aircraft where the soldier will sit. Once all rucksacks are loaded, the soldiers are loaded from rear to front. Soldiers in the aircraft help by pulling the others in tightly until they are all loaded and the doors are closed. The aircraft doors should be opened as the helicopter approaches the LZ. Soldiers hold on to each other until time to unload. They should unload from both sides if the ground slope permits. (*Caution:* The seats-out technique is used in combat only—never in training.)

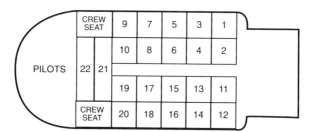

UH-60 seats-out loading diagram.

AIRBORNE OPERATIONS

Airborne forces may be strategically, operationally, or tactically deployed on short notice to drop zones (DZ) anywhere in the world. The primary advantages of airborne operations are their abilities to respond quickly on short notice, to bypass all land or sea obstacles, to surprise, and to mass rapidly on critical targets.

Missions

Airborne forces execute parachute assaults to destroy the enemy and to seize and hold important objectives until linkup is accomplished.

Strategic Missions

Simply alerting airborne forces for employment is a show of force that is politically significant in a strategic context. Airborne forces have strategic mobility and can move from distant bases to strike at important targets deep in enemy-held territory with little warning.

Operational Missions

Airborne forces can be employed anywhere in the theater of war. They attack deep to achieve operational-level objectives.

Tactical Missions

Airborne forces assault in the rear or to the flank of the enemy, preferably where few fixed defenses exist and where well-organized enemy combat units are not initially present.

Fundamentals

Airborne forces require specially selected, trained, and highly disciplined soldiers and leaders. Airborne operations must capitalize on surprise, and they require centralized, detailed planning and aggressive, decentralized execution. The ground tactical plan must drive all other plans through the reverse-planning process.

Echelons

Army combat forces within an airborne force are organized into three echelons: the assault, the follow-on, and the rear.

Assault Echelon

The assault echelon consists of those forces required to seize the assault objectives and the initial airhead, reserves, and supporting units.

Follow-on Echelon

The follow-on echelon consists of forces required for subsequent operations. It enters the objective area by air or surface movement when required.

Rear Echelon

The rear echelon consists of administrative and service elements that remain in the departure area. These elements may be brought forward to support the airhead, as required.

Phases

An airborne operation is conducted in four closely related phases: marshaling, air movement, landing, and ground tactical.

Marshaling Phase

The marshaling phase begins with the receipt of the warning order and ends when the transport aircraft departs.

Air Movement Phase

The air movement phase begins with aircraft takeoff and ends with unit delivery to the DZ or LZ.

Landing Phase

The landing phase begins when paratroopers and equipment exit the aircraft by parachute or are airlanded and ends when all elements of the relevant echelons are delivered to the objective area.

Ground Tactical Phase

The ground tactical phase begins with the landing of units and extends through the seizure and consolidation of the initial objectives. It ends when the mission is completed or the airborne force is extracted or relieved.

Reverse-Planning Process

The reverse-planning process is accomplished as follows:

Ground Tactical Plan

The ground tactical operation phase of an airborne operation can include, but is not limited to, raids, linkup, relief, withdrawal, exfiltration, recovery, and/or airfield seizure. As with air assault operations, the ground tactical plan is the basis for development of all other plans. Special consideration is given to the reassembly and reorganization of the assault forces and to the decentralized nature of initial operations in the objective area. The ground tactical plan includes the following:

  • Assault objectives and airhead line. The initial goal of airborne operations is the establishment of an airhead and its subsequent defense. An appropriate assault objective is one that the force must control early in the assault to accomplish the mission or enhance security of the airborne unit during the establishment of the airhead. The airborne unit is vulnerable from the time it lands until follow-on forces can be delivered to the airhead. A mobile enemy unit attacking the airhead during these early moments can completely disrupt the operations; therefore, the commander selects as assault objectives places where high-speed enemy avenues of approach enter the airhead. These are secured before the defense is set up in the airhead line. The airhead is then cleared of organized enemy resistance and forces are positioned to secure the airhead line.

  • Reconnaissance and security forces to include OPs. Security in all directions is an overriding consideration early in any airborne operation, since an airhead is essentially a perimeter defense. Security forces are landed early in the assault echelon. The reconnaissance and security line is established immediately 4 to 6 kilometers from the airhead to afford security to the airborne force during its landing and reorganization. The security force includes scouts, AT weapons, engineers, Army aviation, and (sometimes) light armor.

- Boundaries. Boundaries assign sectors of responsibility to combat elements. Each unit should be able to clear its assigned area of enemy forces. Boundaries should be selected that can serve during the assault and later operations.
- Task organization. Once commanders have determined the scheme of maneuver and fire support features of the ground plan, they task-organize units (e.g., group different types of units) to execute assigned missions. Infantry units usually form the nucleus of the tactical groupings. Attachments are made before the move to or on arrival in the marshaling area. Units are organized into assault, follow-on, and rear echelons. Infantry platoons are normally in the assault echelon.
- Designation of reserve. The employment of the reserve elements follows the normal employment of a reserve unit in ground operations. At battalion level, a platoon is normally assigned a reserve mission and enters the airhead with the assault echelon.
- Supply. There are three supply phases: accompanying, follow-on, and routine. *Accompanying* supplies are taken into the airhead by assault forces. They are issued to units before marshaling. At platoon level they include each soldier's combat load, basic loads of ammunition, and other supplies. *Follow-on* supplies include all classes of supply. They are air-delivered after the assault to help the unit operate until normal supply procedures can be set up. *Routine* supplies are requested and delivered by normal procedures, depending on the tactical situation.

Landing Plan

The landing plan links the air movement plan to the ground tactical plan. The landing plan includes the following:

- Locations and descriptions of drop zone (DZ), landing zone (LZ), and/or extraction zone (EZ). Drop zones and/or landing zones can be on top of the objective, near the objective, or at a distance from the objective. Single or multiple drop zones can be used. Factors such as surprise, strength of enemy force, complexity of the objective area, and time are considered in selecting DZs and/or LZs. Extraction zones support low-altitude parachute extraction system (LAPES) delivery of supplies. In this system, a parachute is deployed behind the aircraft and attached to a platform that is extracted from the aircraft. Using LAPES, loads up to 37,175 pounds can be delivered into a small EZ. The impact and slide-out zone should be clear of obstructions and relatively flat.

- Sequence of delivery. The sequence of delivery is based on the ground commander's priorities and not on the allocation or availability of aircraft.
- Method of delivery. Personnel can arrive by parachute drop or can be airlanded. Equipment and supplies can be airlanded or delivered by free drop; high-velocity drop; low-velocity drop; high-altitude, low-opening (HALO); or LAPES.
- Place of delivery. At higher echelons, zones are assigned in broad general terms. At lower levels, locations must be described more specifically and only after a detailed analysis. Factors to be considered are ease of identification, straight-line approach, keeping out of range of enemy suppressive fires, proximity to the objective, weather and terrain, mutual support, and configuration.
- Time of delivery. The timing varies with each operation; however, the airborne force will try to conduct assaults during limited visibility to protect the force and to surprise the enemy. If the airborne assault is a supporting attack, it can be committed in advance of, during, or after the main effort.
- Assembly plan. The sooner soldiers assemble and reorganize as squads and platoons, the sooner they can de-rig their equipment and start fighting as cohesive units. Cross-loading of key personnel, weapons, and equipment is important in rapid assembly. The assault force may assemble on the objective (if it is lightly defended or the enemy can be suppressed); on the DZ when the DZ will not be used by follow-on forces, speed is not essential, and dismounted avenues of approach from the DZ to the objective are available; or adjacent to the DZ when the DZ is to be used by follow-on forces or is compromised during the airborne assault. Units both assemble and leave the assembly area (AA) as quickly as possible. They stay in the AA only long enough to establish CPs and communications, organize into combat groupings, and determine their status.

Movement Plan

The air movement plan provides the information required to move the airborne force from the departure airfields to the objective area. The air movement plan includes departure airfields, aircraft by serial, parking diagram, aircraft mission (air movement tables and routes), and unit providing the aircraft.

The air component commander is responsible for execution of the air movement phase, but the planning is done jointly. It ensures the efficient loading and delivery of units to the objective area. Army planners consider tactical integrity, cross-loading, and self-sufficiency of each load.

- Tactical integrity. Squads are kept together on the same aircraft if possible; fire teams are never split. Fire support teams and their ratelos are on the same aircraft with the commander they support. Platoon leaders (and platoon sergeant on a different aircraft) should have their FO, ratelo, and at least one machine gun crew and one Dragon (Javelin) gunner on the same aircraft.
- Cross-loading. Cross-loading distributes leaders, key weapons, and key equipment among the aircraft of the formation to preclude total loss of command and control or unit effectiveness if an aircraft is lost.
- Self-sufficiency. Each aircraft load should be self-sufficient so its personnel can operate effectively by themselves if any other aircraft misses the DZ. A weapons system should have the complete crew for the system on the same aircraft, along with sufficient ammunition. Squads and/or fire teams should jump both aircraft doors to reduce the amount of separation on the DZ.

Marshaling Plan

The marshaling plan provides the needed information and procedures for units of the airborne force to prepare for combat, move to departure airfields, and load aircraft. It includes movement to the marshaling area, passive defensive measures, dispersal procedures, departure airfields, marshaling camp operations, briefback schedule, preparation for combat (inspection, supervision, rehearsal, and rest), and communications.

The marshaling plan is developed by higher headquarters and includes all the details to move the platoon and get it loaded onto aircraft. During this phase, leaders brief pesonnel, inspect, prepare airdrop containers, issue rations and ammunition, rehearse, perform maintenance, and store unneeded items.

9

Operations in Special Environments

The infantry platoon can be expected to operate in all types of environments. This chapter describes the characteristics, tactics, techniques, and special considerations of operations in built-up areas, jungles, deserts, and mountains. Remember, however, that the principles and fundamentals of combat do not change in different environments. Priorities may alter, techniques may vary, but fit and trained soldiers and units can quickly adjust to different conditions.

OPERATIONS IN BUILT-UP AREAS
Urban growth in all parts of the world has changed the face of the battlefield. Built-up areas include all man-made features, cities, towns, and villages, as well as some natural terrain. Combat in built-up areas focuses on fighting for and in cities, towns, and villages.

Characteristics
Built-up areas consist mainly of man-made features, such as buildings.

Buildings provide cover and concealment, limit fields of observation and fire, and block movement of troops. Thick-walled buildings provide ready-made, fortified positions.

Streets are usually avenues of approach. Forces moving along streets are often canalized by the buildings, however, and have little space for off-road maneuver. Thus, obstacles on streets in towns are usually more effective than those on roads in open terrain.

Subterranean systems found in some built-up areas, including subways, sewers, cellars, and utility systems, are easily overlooked but can be important to the outcome of operations.

Built-up areas are classified into four categories.

1. Large cities: population in the millions; with associated urban sprawl, cover hundreds of square kilometers.
2. Towns or small cities: population up to 1 million and not part of a major urban complex.
3. Villages: population of 3,000 or less.
4. Strip areas built along roads connecting towns or cities.

Special Considerations
Target Engagement
In the city, the ranges of observation and fields of fire are reduced by structures. Targets are usually briefly exposed at ranges of 100 meters or less. Fighting in built-up areas consists mostly of close, violent combat. Infantry troops will use mostly light antitank weapons, automatic rifles, machine guns, and hand grenades. Antitank guided missiles are seldom used because of the short ranges involved and the many obstructions that interfere with missile flight.

Small-Unit Battles
Units fighting in built-up areas often become isolated, making combat a series of small-unit battles. The defender has tactical advantages over the attacker, occupying strong positions, whereas the attacker must be exposed in order to advance. Greatly reduced line-of-sight ranges, built-in obstacles, and compartmented terrain require the commitment of more troops for a given frontage. The troop density for both an attack and a defense can be three to five times greater than for an attack or defense in open areas.

Munitions and Special Equipment

Because of the short engagement ranges and limited visibility, large quantities of ammunition are needed. Platoons also must have special equipment such as grappling hooks, rope, snaplinks, collapsible pole ladders, rope ladders, construction material, axes, and sandbags.

Communications

Wire is the primary means of communications for units in defending in built-up areas. Radio communications sometimes encounter problems because of tall structures and electrical power lines. Visual signals are limited to fields of observation. Messengers can be used as a means of communications.

Stress

Continuous close combat, intense pressure, high casualties, fleeting targets, and concealed enemy fire produce psychological strain and physical fatigue for soldiers.

Offensive Operations

The offense takes the form of either a hasty attack or a deliberate attack.

Hasty Attacks

Hasty attacks occur as a result of a movement to contact or a meeting engagement. A hasty attack in a built-up area is different from a hasty attack in an open terrain, because the close nature of the built-up area makes command, control, and communications difficult. Also, massing fires to suppress the enemy may be difficult.

Deliberate Attacks

Deliberate attacks are fully coordinated operations that employ all assets against the enemy's defense. Attacking the enemy's main strength is avoided, and combat power is focused on the weakest point of its defense. A deliberate attack is usually conducted in the following phases:

1. Reconnoiter the objective.
2. Move to the objective.
3. Isolate the objective. This involves seizing terrain that dominates the area so the enemy cannot supply or reinforce the defenders.

4. Secure a foothold. This involves seizing an intermediate objective that provides cover from enemy fire and a place from which attacking troops can enter the built-up area.
5. Clear a built-up area. A clearing unit must enter, search, and clear each building in its zone. A single building may be an objective for a squad or, if the building is large, for a platoon.

Attack of a Building

The most common platoon offensive mission is the attack of a building. The platoon must kill the defenders and secure the building. The assault has three steps:

1. Isolate the building.
2. Enter the building.
3. Clear the building methodically, room by room and floor by floor.

Attack of a building.

Technique for looking around a corner.

An attacking platoon is organized with an assault element, a support element, and a security element. Close coordination is required between the assault and support elements, and all means of communications are used between them.

The attack involves isolating the building to prevent the escape or reinforcement of its defenders, suppressing the defenders with supporting direct and indirect fires, entering the building at the least defended point, and clearing the building. To clear it, troops normally go quickly to the top floor and clear from the top down. The clearing is performed by the rifle squads, which pass successively through each other (leapfrogging) as rooms and floors are secured. Platoons should be supported by engineers to help with demolition clearing.

Defensive Operations

A defender can inflict heavy losses on a larger attacking force by taking advantage of the abundant cover and concealment, using the terrain, and fighting from well-prepared and mutually supporting fighting positions.

Defensive Area

The defense of a built-up area should be organized around key terrain features, buildings, and areas that provide cover and concealment, fields of fire and observation, and impediments to the enemy attack. Likely avenues of approach should be blocked by obstacles and covered by fire. A platoon is normally tasked to defend a building, part of a building, or a group of small buildings. The platoon should be organized into a series of firing positions, located to cover avenues of approach and obstacles, and to provide mutual support. Snipers may be placed on the upper floors.

Considerations in Preparing the Defense

- Dispersion. It is better to have defensive positions in two mutually supporting buildings than in one building that can be bypassed.
- Concealment. City buildings provide excellent concealment. Obvious positions, especially at the edge of a built-up area, should be avoided, since they are the most likely to receive the heaviest enemy fire.
- Fields of fire. Positions should have good fields of fire in all directions. Broad streets and open areas, such as parks, offer excellent fields of fire.
- Observation. Select buildings that permit observation into the adjacent sectors. The higher stories offer the best observation but attract enemy fire.
- Covered routes. Routes for movement of personnel and supplies should go through or behind buildings.
- Fire hazards. Buildings that burn easily should be avoided.
- Time. Buildings that need extensive preparation are undesirable when time is a factor.

JUNGLE OPERATIONS

The jungle environment includes densely forested areas, grasslands, cultivated areas, and swamps. Jungles in their various forms are common in tropical areas of the world, mainly Southeast Asia, Africa, and Latin America. Jungles are classified as primary or secondary jungles based on the terrain and vegetation.

Primary Jungles

Primary jungles are the tropical forests. Depending on the type of trees growing in these forests, primary jungles are further classified as either tropical rain forests or deciduous forests.

Tropical Rain Forests

Tropical rain forests consist mostly of large trees whose branches spread and lock together to form canopies. These canopies, which can exist at two or three different levels, may form as low as 10 meters from the ground. The canopies prevent sunlight from reaching the ground, causing a lack of undergrowth on the jungle floor. Extensive above-ground root systems and hanging vines are common. These conditions, combined with a wet, soggy surface, make vehicular traffic difficult, although foot movement is easier in tropical rain forests than in other types of jungle. Observation from the air is nearly impossible, and ground observation is generally limited to about 50 meters.

Deciduous Forests

Deciduous forests are found in semitropical zones where there are both wet and dry seasons. In the wet season, trees are fully leaved; in the dry season, much of the foliage dies. Trees are generally less dense than in rain forests, allowing more rain and sunlight to filter to the ground; this produces thick undergrowth. In the wet season, when the trees are in full leaf, observation from the air and on the ground is limited and movement is more difficult than in rain forests. In the dry season, however, both observation and trafficability improve.

Secondary Jungles

Secondary jungles are found at the edges of rain forests and of decidu-ous forests and in areas where jungles have been cleared and aban-doned. Secondary jungles appear when the ground has been repeatedly exposed to sunlight. These areas are typically overgrown with weeds, grasses, thorns, ferns, canes, and shrubs. Foot movement is extremely slow and difficult. Vegetation may reach a height of 2 meters, limiting observation to the front to a few meters.

Characteristics of Jungle Operations

Jungle battles are most often ambushes, raids, and meeting engage-ments; battles are not fought for high ground as frequently as conven-tional battles. Orientation is on the enemy rather than on the terrain. Hills in the jungle are often too thickly vegetated to permit observation and fire. In the jungle, roads, rivers and streams, fording sites, and land-ing zones are more likely to be key terrain features. The following lim-itations may restrict fire and movement:

- Lack of line of sight and clearance may prevent visual contact between units, interlocking fires, and the use of optically tracked, wire-guided missiles or Dragon missiles.
- Tree limbs may block mortars, flame weapons, 40-millimeter grenades, and hand grenades.
- Machine guns may not be able to attain grazing fire.
- Adjustment of indirect fire support is difficult due to limited visibility and may have to be accomplished by sound.
- Sounds do not carry as far in the jungle as on the conventional battlefield because of the amount of foliage.
- Movement through the heat, thick vegetation, and rugged terrain will tire soldiers rapidly, and a lack of roads will hinder resupply and evacuation.
- Command and control is difficult because, with the dense foliage, leaders can see and control only a portion of their units.
- Thick foliage and heavy monsoon rains often weaken radio communications.

Jungle Movement

Map and aerial reconnaissance should be conducted before making a move in the jungle. Leaders should consider the following:

- Lines of drift, such as ridgelines, are easy to guide on because they avoid streams and gullies and because they are usually less vegetated.
- Danger areas, such as streambeds and draws, are usually more thickly vegetated. They offer excellent concealment, but travel along them is slow and difficult.
- Roads and trails should be avoided. Although they are easy to move on, they offer little concealment and are most likely to be under enemy observation, are easily ambushed, and may well be mined or boobytrapped.

Jungle Movement Technique

The jungle movement technique is basically a formation of mutually supporting multiple columns. This technique should be used only by platoons and is most effective during daylight. The lead fire team is always in a wedge (modified). Each squad maintains an azimuth and a pace. Support elements may move with the headquarters element or be

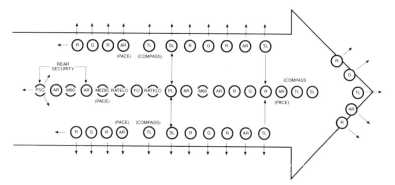

Jungle movement formation.

attached to a squad or squads. Traveling overwatch and bounding over-watch may be used when necessary. The file formation should be avoided in all but the most thickly vegetated areas.

Halts
Halts should be planned on terrain that lends itself to all-around defense. During short halts, soldiers drop to one knee and face outward, their weapons at the ready. If halted at a trail crossing, security elements should be sent out along the trail. During longer halts, a perimeter defense should be established; run security patrols around the position and emplace Claymore mines and early-warning devices. Before an overnight halt, stop while there is still enough daylight to establish a secure perimeter defense, prepare ambushes, and dispatch patrols, as necessary.

Night Movement
The following points can be of assistance during a night movement:
- Attach two luminous tape strips, about the size of a lieutenant's bar, side by side to the back of each soldier's headgear. Having two strips aids depth perception and reduces the hypnotic effect that one strip can cause.
- Reduce distance between soldiers. When necessary, each soldier should hold on to the belt or pack of the man in front of him.
- The leading man should carry a long stick to probe for sudden drop-offs or obstacles.

- Listening may become more important to security than observing. When a strange noise is heard, halt and listen for at least one minute. If the noise is repeated or cannot be identified, send out patrols to investigate. Smells likewise can be an indication of enemy presence in an area.
- All available night-vision devices should be used.

Lost or Disoriented Soldiers
Few soldiers have ever been permanently lost in the jungle, although many have taken longer to reach their destination than they should have. Disoriented soldiers should ask themselves the following questions:
- What was the last known location?
- Did we go too far and pass the objective? (Compare estimates of time and distance traveled.)
- Does the terrain look the way it should? (Compare the surroundings with the map.)
- What features in the area will help to fix your location? (Try to find these features.)

If still unable to determine location, the leader can call for an air or artillery orienting round. (This may cause a loss of security.) An Army or Air Force aircraft can be contacted and guided to the general location by radio and the pilot then signaled by a mirror, smoke, or panels. The pilot will determine and report your location. (This also causes a loss of security and should only be a last resort.)

DESERT OPERATIONS
Deserts are arid, barren regions of the earth incapable of supporting normal life due to a lack of water. Temperatures vary according to latitude and season, from 136° Fahrenheit and above in Mexico and Libya to the bitter cold winter of the Gobi in East Asia. There are three types of deserts: mountain, rocky plateau, and sandy or dune deserts.

Mountain Deserts
Mountain deserts are characterized by scattered ranges or areas of barren hills or mountains, separated by dry, flat basins. High ground may rise gradually or abruptly from flat areas to several thousand feet above sea level. The deserts of Yemen are examples of mountain deserts.

Rocky Plateau Deserts

Rocky plateau deserts have a relatively slight relief interspersed by extensive flat areas, with quantities of solid or broken rock at or near the surface. They may be cut or dry, steep-walled eroded valleys, known as wadis in the Middle East and arroyos or canyons in the United States and Mexico. The Golan Heights is an example of rocky plateau desert.

Sandy or Dune Deserts

Sandy or dune deserts are extensive flat areas covered with sand or gravel, the products of ancient deposits or of modern wind erosion. Flat is relative in this case, as some areas may contain sand dunes that are more than 300 meters high and 6 to 10 kilometers long. Other areas, however, may be totally flat for distances of 3,000 meters or more. Areas of California, New Mexico, and the western Sahara are examples of dune deserts.

Man-made Features in Deserts

Roads and Trails

Roads and trails are scarce in the open desert. Some surfaces, such as lava beds or salt marsh, may preclude any form of routine vehicular movement. Ground transportation often can travel in any direction necessary, but speed of movement varies depending on surface texture. Rudimentary trails exist in many deserts for use by minor caravans and nomadic tribesmen, with wells or oases approximately every 12 to 20 kilometers, although there are some waterless stretches of over 60 kilometers.

Structures

Apart from nomadic tribesmen who live in tents, desert inhabitants live in thick-walled structures with small windows, usually built of masonry or a mud and straw mixture (adobe). The ruins of earlier civilizations are scattered across the deserts. Ancient posts and forts, usually in ruins, invariably command important avenues of approach and frequently dominate the only available passes in difficult terrain.

Mineral Extraction

Exploration for and exploitation of minerals, of which oil is the best known, occurs in many desert areas, especially in the Middle East. Wells, pipelines, refineries, quarrying, and crushing plants may be of strategic and tactical importance. Pipelines are often raised 1 meter off the ground and can inhibit movement.

Agriculture

Many desert areas are fertile when irrigated, and a number of desert villages depend on irrigation canals. Agriculture in these areas has little effect on military operations except that canals may hamper surface mobility.

Environmental Effects on Personnel

The desert is essentially neutral, affecting both sides equally; the side whose personnel are best prepared for desert operations has a distinct advantage. Desert operations need to take into account the following:

- Acclimatization to heat is necessary to permit the body to reach and maintain efficiency in its cooling process. A period of approximately two weeks should be allowed for acclimatization, with progressive degrees of heat exposure and physical exertion. Situations may arise in which it is not possible for men to become fully acclimatized before being required to do heavy labor; then, heavy activity should be limited to cooler hours and soldiers should be allowed to rest more frequently than normal.
- The sun's rays, either direct or reflected off the ground, affect the skin and can also produce eyestrain and temporarily impaired vision. Overexposure will cause sunburn. Soldiers should acquire a suntan in gradual stages, in the early morning or late afternoon, to gain some protection against sunburn. In all operational conditions, soldiers should be fully clothed in loose garments.
- The combination of wind and dust or sand can cause extreme irritation to the mucous membranes and chap the lips and other exposed skin surfaces. Irritative conjunctivitis, caused by fine particles entering the eyes, is a frequent complaint of vehicle crews, even if wearing goggles.
- Climatic stress on the human body in the hot desert can be caused by any combination of air temperature, humidity, air movement, and radiant heat. The body is also adversely affected by such factors as a lack of acclimatization, overweight, dehydration, alcoholic excess, lack of sleep, old age, and poor health.

- Sandstorms can be extremely painful on bare skin, one reason why soldiers must always be fully clothed. When visibility is reduced by sandstorms to the extent that military operations are impossible, soldiers should not be allowed to leave their group unless secured by a line for recovery.

Tactical Operations
The desert environment and its effects on personnel and equipment require some modification to tactics, techniques, and procedures.

Objective
The objective of unit operations in desert warfare is destruction of the enemy. Because key terrain features are scarce in many desert areas (although they do exist in some, such as the passes of Sinai), units are seldom tasked to seize or retain specific terrain features. It may be necessary to secure terrain for water sources, routes, or communication sites, or to control positions that permit observation even though they may be only a few meters higher than the surrounding area.

Mobility
Most deserts permit movement by ground troops. Speed of execution is essential and requires self-contained all-mechanized or air assault forces with excellent communications. Dismounted infantry is used in areas where vehicular movement is limited, such as mountains, and sometimes is also used to establish strong points and blocking positions.

Observation and Field of Fire
The normally flat desert terrain permits direct-fire weapons to be used out to their maximum range. The desert is not absolutely flat, however, so weapons are sited to provide mutual support. When preparing defensive positions it is important to inspect the positions from the enemy side to ensure that available cover and concealment are maximized. Observation of fires, especially direct fires, may be difficult. Considerable dust clouds can be thrown up by high-velocity, direct-fire weapons. Use flank observers to report elevation and azimuth errors.

Maneuver
Small units move using proper movement techniques and whatever cover

is available. To surprise the enemy, it is almost always necessary to maneuver in conditions that preclude observation—at night, behind smoke, or during dust- or sandstorms.

Reconnaissance and Security

Aggressive and continuous reconnaissance and constant all-around security are required because of the almost complete freedom of maneuver on desert terrain, together with the ability to observe great distances. Many desert maps are inaccurate, making up-to-date terrain reconnaissance necessary. Observation posts should be sited in pairs, as far apart as possible to permit accurate resection, and at different heights to avoid the possibility of dust clouds blocking the vision of both simultaneously. Patrols most often perform mounted, dismounting only when necessary to accomplish a mission.

Cover and Concealment

When moving in the desert, cover can only be achieved by terrain masking, because of the lack of heavy vegetation or man-made objects. Total concealment is rarely attained, but camouflage properly used can make it difficult for the enemy to perceive what an object is. Any form of desert movement creates dust; in order to reduce dust clouds, movement should be on the hardest ground available. Light and noise at night may be seen or heard from miles away, so strict discipline in those areas is necessary.

Special Operations

Because of the wide areas involved in desert operations, gaps can almost always be found in enemy defenses. Small units can slip through to conduct raids, sabotage installations and pipelines, gather intelligence, and effect liaison with friendly irregular forces.

MOUNTAIN OPERATIONS

As in other unique environments, units operating in mountainous terrain will find it necessary to apply different planning considerations than in less restrictive terrain. Mountain ranges are grouped for military purposes into three basic categories: alpine, interior, and coastal ranges.

Alpine Ranges

Alpine ranges have high, rugged peaks and meadows or plateaus that extend well above the regional snowline. Frequently, glacial ice and snow remain on the ground throughout the year. Abrupt slopes, sharp peaks and ridges, exposed bedrock, numerous lakes, and large masses of rock and gravel deposited by glaciers are common. Valleys, separated by almost impenetrable masses of high, steep cliffs, generally rise to narrow passes that allow lines of communications. These passes are often closed by snow during the winter, however. The battle is fought along these valleys and on the terrain that allows access to the passes. The intervening highlands can fragment major units. Alpine ranges are typified by the Alps of central Europe.

Interior Ranges

Interior or inland ranges are less formidable than alpine systems and may cover large areas. They are normally complex and incorporate a variety of land forms. They may include large upland plains as well as regions of high peaks that rise above the snowline. The valleys in interior ranges are generally below the timberline, and in some ranges they have historically served as invasion routes. Above the timberline are steep slopes and vertical cliffs. Valleys and upland meadows are usually covered with vegetation. During winter, valleys and mountain slopes may be blanketed with snow, making movement difficult. During spring thaws or heavy rains, the rivers and streams may become deep and swift. Roads are few and normally follow the valleys. Units in interior ranges may be fragmented in many cases by rugged terrain on the heights separating natural communication corridors. Examples of interior ranges are the Appalachian Mountains of the United States, the Harz Mountains of central Germany, and the Pyrenees of Spain.

Coastal Ranges

Coastal ranges border expanses of water and have been sculpted by erosion of glaciers, wind, and water. Most peaks do not rise above the timberline, but many slopes are devoid of vegetation because of their steepness and rocky surfaces. Roads are normally limited, and during the winter, there may be sufficient snowfall to close the few that exist. Examples include the fjords of Norway and the mountains of southern Alaska, British Columbia, southern Chile, and the Pacific Northwest.

Mountain Characteristics

Certain characteristics apply to most mountain ranges.
- There is normally a temperature drop of 3° to 6° Fahrenheit for each 300-meter gain in elevation.
- In higher elevations, there may be a 40° to 50° Fahrenheit difference between the temperature in the shade and in the sun.
- Fog generally occurs more frequently in mountainous terrain than at lower elevations.
- On clear days, the temperature rises quickly after sunrise and falls quickly after sunset.

Effects on Weapons

Although mountainous terrain generally permits excellent long-range observation and fields of fire, steep slopes and rugged terrain frequently produce significant areas hidden from observation. To reduce the amount of dead space and to prevent low-hanging clouds from adding to the visibility problem, observation posts can be echeloned in depth and in height.

To provide fire into dead space, alternate firing positions for direct-fire weapons are prepared and indirect fire is planned in these areas. A great amount of dead space gives added importance to weapons with a high angle of fire, as well as to hand grenades and grenade launchers. Grenade launchers are useful for covering close-in dead space and supplementing indirect fires. Machine guns and automatic weapons provide long-range fire along avenues of approach. Grazing fire can rarely be achieved because of the radical changes in elevation.

The slopes of the terrain affect range estimation. An observer looking down from a height tends to underestimate the range, while someone looking upward from low ground is likely to overestimate the range. The steepness of the slope and irregularities of the terrain limit the extent of grazing fire from automatic weapons. The difficulties of ammunition resupply make it necessary to enforce strict fire control and discipline. Terrain features may separate adjacent units, precluding mutual support.

The effectiveness of rifle fire is increased by splintering and ricocheting effects when a bullet impacts on rock. Expert marksmen should be identified to take advantage of opportunities to engage targets to the maximum effective range of weapons. Soldiers have a tendency to shoot high when firing downhill and low when firing uphill.

LAW, Flash, and recoilless rifles are ideally suited for direct fire against enemy weapon emplacement. The 90-millimeter recoilless rifle is more effective than the LAW or M202 Flash against bunkers and dismounted infantry.

Antitank guided missiles are manportable but may be a hindrance in dismounted operations because of bulk and weight. Their employment may be limited by a lack of armored avenues of approach and suitable targets.

Mortars are suitable for supporting dismounted infantry because of their high angle of fire and rapidity of fire. The 60-millimeter mortar is an ideal weapon because of its portability, its ease of concealment, and the light weight of its ammunition, which eases resupply. The 81-millimeter mortar provides longer range and delivers more explosives. The 4.2-inch mortar (107-millimeter) can fire either WP or HE at greater ranges than smaller mortars. The weight of this mortar and its ammunition may necessitate employing fewer mortars and using the extra gun crews to transport ammunition.

Movement

In mountain operations, platoons can use any of the three movement techniques based on the situation, keeping in mind the following considerations:

- When moving from one ridge to another (cross-compartment), use bounding overwatch with the lead element securing the high ground before the rest of the unit crosses the low ground.
- When moving along a compartment, move on the high ground (not on a ridge) or place an element there to secure the flanks.
- Because of the narrow routes, squads and fire team wedges may be compressed to files.
- When the danger of rockslides or avalanches exists, the distances between soldiers and units should be increased.
- Movement in the mountains is slow. A good estimate of the ground distance is the map distance plus one-third.
- While existing roads and trails offer the easiest routes for foot movement, the tactical situation may require that other routes be used. The enemy knows that the roads and trails exist and will be

watching them. (In 1982, the Israeli Defense Force consistently moved on single-lane mountain roads in eastern Lebanon with tanks and armored personnel carriers. Time after time, they were ambushed by Syrian antitank gunners and infantrymen.) Infantry must secure the high ground controlling trails.

10

Combat Support and Combat Service Support

Combat support is any external support provided by the battalion anti-tank (AT) and mortar platoons, field artillery (FA), close air support (CAS), air defense artillery (ADA), military intelligence (MI), and combat engineers.

INDIRECT FIRE

Normally, the company plans most of the indirect fires and assigns platoons specific responsibilities. The platoon is limited by its ability to observe and initiate fires.

Field Artillery

FA can provide indirect fires to suppress, neutralize, or destroy enemy targets. Because it can mass fire quickly, FA produces more devastating effects on targets than mortars do.

Mortars

Mortars are organic to the battalion and the company and at times may be attached to or in direct support of platoons. They provide responsive fire against closer and smaller targets. Mortars can be used to do the following:

- To attack infantry in the open.
- To attack infantry in positions without overhead cover (using VT fuzes) or with light overhead cover (using delay fuzes).
- To suppress enemy positions and armored vehicles.
- To obscure the enemy's vision (using white phosphorus).
- To engage enemy on reverse slopes and in gullies, ditches, built-up areas, and other defilade areas.
- To provide continuous battlefield illumination.
- To provide obscuring smoke (smoke on the enemy positions) or screening smoke (smoke between the enemy and friendly units).
- To mark enemy locations for direct fire or CAS.

DIRECT FIRE

Direct-fire support can be provided by tanks and antitank weapons (TOW, Dragon/Javelin, MK19). Leaders can direct tank or antitank and MK19 fires by radio, by phone, or face-to-face. They can identify the target location by TRP or tracer fire, or give the direction, description, and range. Another technique uses the gun barrel or TOW launcher with the clock method as a baseline for direction—for example, "Enemy tank, ten o'clock, 1,200 meters." The gun barrel is at twelve o'clock when pointing directly forward from the vehicle or launcher, and it is at six o'clock when pointing directly to the rear.

Attack Helicopters

Attack helicopters are mainly antiarmor weapons, but they do have anti-personnel ability with rockets. Aeroscouts usually arrive ahead of the attack aircraft and set up communication with the ground force.

Close Air Support

The USAF provides CAS on a preplanned or immediate-need basis. A forward air controller (FAC), on the ground or in the air, acts as a link between the ground force and the aircraft. Friendly positions must always be marked during close air strikes. Smoke grenades, flares, signal mirrors, strobe lights, vehicle lights, and thermal sources are commonly used as markers.

AIR DEFENSE ARTILLERY

Divisional air defense weapons may support and be positioned with infantry units. All ADA fires are controlled by orders and procedures established by higher headquarters.

MILITARY INTELLIGENCE

Ground surveillance radar and remote sensor teams from the division MI battalion may be attached to or support infantry units.

COMBAT ENGINEERS

Engineers are a valuable asset, and higher commanders determine their priority. Engineers can help the infantry prepare obstacles or positions by providing technical advice or the skills to do work beyond the ability of infantry units.

COMBAT SERVICE SUPPORT
AT PLATOON LEVEL

Combat service support (CSS) operations at platoon level consist of supply, personnel, and health service functions. At platoon level, the platoon sergeant is the key CSS operator. He consolidates information from the squad leaders, requests support from the XO or 1SG, and assigns responsibilities to squads.

Resupply Operations

Squad leaders must know the status of ammunition, water, rations, clothing, and equipment for each member of the squad. As supplies and materials are used, he requests resupply through the platoon sergeant. Platoon resupply is mainly a "push" system. A standard package of supplies is received based on past usage factors. Three resupply techniques are used for platoons and squads: the in-position, out-of-position, and pre-position techniques.

In-Position Technique

The in-position technique is used during contact or when contact is imminent. Supplies and equipment are brought forward by the company to individual fighting positions.

Out-of-Position Technique
To use the out-of-position technique, soldiers must leave their fighting positions. Entire squads, parts of squads, or certain squad members may be selected to move to a company or platoon resupply point, conduct resupply, and then return to their positions.

Pre-Position Technique
In the pre-position technique, the company places supplies and equipment beforehand along a route to or at a platoon's destination.

Aerial Resupply
Aerial resupply is not a resupply technique, but it is often used to get supplies and equipment to the platoon. Helicopters are usually more precise than fixed-wing aircraft in delivering supplies, and they are used to deliver supplies and equipment to LZs, while fixed-wing aircraft are used for DZs.

Backhauling
During each resupply operation, the platoon plans for backhauling of excess items. Backhauling is a technique used to remove residue, casualties, damaged equipment, or excess ammunition to the rear.

Personnel Service Support
Personnel service support functions include strength accounting, casualty reporting, handling enemy prisoners of war (EPWs), and other services.

Strength Accounting
Leaders use battle rosters to keep up-to-date records of their soldiers and to provide reports to the company at specific intervals. During combat, leaders also provide hasty strength reports upon request or when important strength changes occur.

Casualty Reporting
During lulls in the battle, platoons give by-name (roster line number)

casualty information to the company. Forms are completed to report KIAs who were not recovered, as well as missing or captured soldiers. A separate form is used to report KIAs who have been recovered and soldiers who have been wounded.

Handling Enemy Prisoners of War

EPWs are treated in accordance with international law. They are allowed to keep personal protective equipment, are not physically or mentally abused, and are treated humanely. If they cannot be evacuated within a reasonable time, they are given food, water, and if necessary, first aid.

Other Services

Other personnel service support functions include awards, leaves, mail, financial matters, legal assistance, rest and recreation, and other services related to the morale and welfare of soldiers.

Health Service Support

Health service support consists of the prevention, treatment, and evacuation of casualties.

Prevention

Prevention is emphasized; soldiers can lose their combat effectiveness because of nonhostile injuries or disease. Observing field hygiene and sanitation, preventing weather-related injuries, and considering the soldier's overall condition can cut back on the number of casualties.

Treatment and Evacuation

Casualties are treated where they fall (or under nearby cover and concealment) by the individual himself, a buddy, an aidman, or a combat lifesaver. Casualties are collected at the platoon casualty collection point and separated into treatment and evacuation categories. The casualties' weapons and equipment may be retained and redistributed as necessary or backhauled to the field trains. Machine guns, M203s, and other special weapons are never evacuated but are reassigned to other soldiers. At least one soldier in each squad must be trained as a combat lifesaver to help the aidman treat and evacuate casualties.

ARMORED VEHICLE SUPPORT

Armored units and mechanized infantry units can support infantry units in combat operations. In operations in which dismounted infantry forces predominate, dismounted infantry forces lead the combined arms attack, while all other arms support the infantry. Infantry helps armored forces by finding and breaching or marking antitank obstacles and by providing security for armored vehicles. They detect and destroy or suppress antitank weapons, designate targets for tank main gun fire, and spot the impact of tank rounds for the gunner. Heavy forces help infantry by leading them in open terrain; providing them a protected, fast-moving assault weapons system; suppressing and destroying enemy weapons, bunkers, and tanks by fire and maneuver; and providing transport for the infantry when the situation permits.

Tanks

Tank platoons use the wingman concept: The platoon leader with his wingman and the platoon sergeant with his wingman operate as a four-vehicle platoon. Tank organization tables do not break the organization down further than a platoon. Tanks and infantry must work closely, however. In most operations where they work together, infantrymen must establish direct contact with individual tanks. They will not have time to designate targets or direct fires through the platoon chain of command. Infantrymen and tankers must know how to communicate by radio, phone, and visual signals.

Mechanized Infantry

Mechanized infantry combines the protection, firepower, and mobility of armored forces with the security and close-combat capability of infantry forces. Infantry may work together or in synchronization with mechanized forces to clear a way through obstacles before an armored attack, hold a strongpoint while mechanized infantry maneuvers around it, or conduct MOUT missions.

Infantry Riding on Armored Vehicles

Soldiers routinely ride on the outside of armored vehicles. As long as they are moving in the same direction and contact is not likely, soldiers should always ride on tanks. When mounting or riding an armored vehicle, remember the following:

- Before mounting an armored vehicle, always approach the vehicle from the front to get permission from the vehicle commander to mount. Mount the side of the vehicle away from the coaxial machine gun and in view of the driver.
- Ensure that the vehicle gun stabilization system is off before the vehicle moves.
- Infantry should not ride on the lead tank, so that if necessary this tank can immediately traverse and engage enemy while the infantry dismounts from follow-on tanks. Infantry must dismount as soon as possible if tanks come under fire or if targets appear that require the tank gunner to traverse the turret quickly to fire. If enemy contact is made, the tank should stop in a covered and concealed position to allow the infantry to dismount and move away from the tank.
- Be alert for obstacles that can cause the tank to turn suddenly and for trees that can knock riders off the tank.
- The rear deck of an M1 tank is unsafe for riders because of the high engine temperature. One squad can ride on the turret, with soldiers sitting on its sides and rear, facing out. Everyone must be to the rear of the smoke grenade launchers.
- The infantry should not ride with anything more than their combat gear.

Working in Restricted Terrain

Tanks are more likely to work directly with infantry in highly restrictive terrain. When armored vehicles are buttoned up, crew vision is impaired; dismounted infantry must work near the tanks to provide mutual close protection. At terrain features such as narrow passes or defiles, the dismounted infantry platoon secures the edges using bounding overwatch while the armored vehicles overwatch. The infantry looks for mines, antitank missile systems, and enemy armored vehicles.

Movement and Offensive Operations

Lack of visibility, limited fields of fire, and inability to traverse to targets because of nearby trees are common problems in wooded and jungle terrain. These factors, along with the enemy's antitank capability, determine the lead element in movement.

Armored vehicles lead in open terrain if the antitank threat is light or if fields of fire are too short for wire-guided missiles. Armored vehicles can scan treelines and other vegetated areas with thermal viewers to provide the infantry with early warning of impending contact and possible bypass routes. Armored vehicles are the first to make contact. They then continue forward to destroy the enemy or to provide a base of fire so that the dismounted infantry can maneuver to destroy or bypass the enemy.

If the antitank threat is medium or heavy, the infantry leads and tanks move from one overwatch position to the next.

Defensive Operations

Armored vehicles provide the infantry with great firepower, but their inability to move quietly may be a disadvantage. Tanks can be positioned at first to provide early warning using thermal viewers. Tanks cover mounted avenues of approach, while infantry covers dismounted avenues of approach. Dismounted infantry support must be placed forward to provide local security for forward tank positions. Tank range finders accurately determine locations of target reference points (TRPs) and other range card data.

Part Two
SOLDIER COMBAT SKILLS

11

Call for Fire

A *call for fire* is a message prepared by an observer and containing the information needed by an artillery fire direction center (FDC) to have the target hit as requested. It is normally sent as the three following parts, consisting of six elements, with a break and readback after each part:
- Observer identification and warning order.
- Target location.
- Target description, method of engagement, and method of fire and control.

OBSERVER IDENTIFICATION
Despite the availability of artillery FISTs, infantrymen are often in the best location to call for and adjust fire. Calls for fire will be accepted from untrained personnel acting as observers. FDC personnel will help the untrained observer in the call for fire. They will ask leading questions to determine the following:
- The observer's location.
- The target's location.
- The target's identity.
- The target's nearness to friendly troops.
- The target's location in relation to the observer's and other known locations.

- The direction from the observer to the target. (This may be given in mils, degrees, or as a cardinal direction.)

Target Location
The target's location may be given in any manner clearly understandable to both the observer and the FDC:

Polar
In a polar plot mission, the word "polar" alerts the FDC that the target will be located with respect to the observer's position. (The observer's location must be known to the FDC.) The observer sends the direction to the nearest 10 mils and the distance to the nearest 100 meters.

Grid
In a grid mission, six-place grids normally are sent.

Shift
In a shift from a known position, the point from which the shift will be made is sent. The point must be known to both the FDC and the observer. The observer then sends the observer-target (OT) direction.

Normally, direction to the target will be sent to the nearest 10 mils; however, FDCs can use mils, degrees, or cardinal directions, as specified by the observer. Next to be sent are the lateral shift (how far to the left or right the target is from the known point, to the nearest 10 meters); the range shift (how much farther [add] or closer [drop] the target is in relation to the known point, to the nearest 100 meters); and the vertical

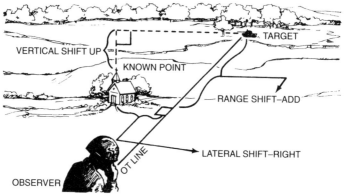

Shift from a known point.

shift (how much the target is above [up] or below [down] the altitude of the known point, to the nearest 5 meters). The vertical shift is ignored unless it exceeds 30 meters.

Target Description
The observer must describe the target in sufficient detail to enable the FDC to determine the amount and type of ammunition to use—for example, a platoon of troops in bunkers with overhead cover.

METHOD OF ENGAGEMENT
The method of engagement consists of the type of adjustment, trajectory, ammunition, and distribution. (The term "danger close" is included in the method of engagement when the predicted impact is within 600 meters of friendly troops.)

Type of Adjustment
Two types of adjustment may be employed: area or precision. Unless precision fire is requested, area fire will be used.

Trajectory
Low-angle fire is standard for artillery. If high-angle fire is desired, it is requested. If mortars fire the mission, only high-angle fire is used.

Ammunition
Shell high explosive (HE) is normally used, although any type of ammunition may be requested by the observer. If a different type of shell or fuse is desired, the observer requests it.

Projectile
Examples of requests for other than HE projectiles are "illumination," "ICM," and "smoke."

Fuse
Most missions are fired with fuse quick.

Distribution
The observer may control the pattern of bursts, called a sheaf, in the target area. A converged sheaf places all rounds on a specific point. An open sheaf separates the bursts by the maximum effective burst width

of the shell fired. Unless otherwise specified, the FDC assumes a circular target with 100-meter radius and determines the bursts for best coverage. Special sheafs of any length and width may be requested.

METHOD OF FIRE AND CONTROL

The method of fire and control element indicates the desired manner of attacking the target, whether or not the observer wants to control the time of delivery of fire and whether or not he can observe the target. If the observer wants to control the time of delivery of fire, he includes "At my command" in the method of control.

Example:

Identification and warning order:	A78, this is A79. Adjust fire. Polar.
Target location:	Direction 5420. Distance 2400.
Description of target:	Company assembly area in woods, radius 200.
Method of engagement and method of fire control:	At my command.

FIRE FOR EFFECT IN INITIAL DATA

When an observer can locate the target accurately, he requests "Fire for effect" in his initial call for fire.

ADJUSTING FIRE

All corrections are made in relation to the OT line. The observer must spot the first and each successive adjusting round and send deviation (left or right) and range (short or over), as required, back to the FDC until fire hits the target. Corrections are given in the following order: The lateral deviation, in meters, between the burst center with respect to the OT line; then the desired range change in hundreds of meters.

Normally, the observer uses range changes of 100, 200, 400, or 800 meters to make bracketing the target easier. The observer successively splits the bracket until he is sure of being within 50 meters of the target. The observer fires for effect when he is sure that rounds will impact within 50 meters of the target.

END OF MISSION

The observer concludes the firing by announcing "End of mission" and reports the results of the firing on the enemy target

12

Camouflage

Camouflage is anything you use to keep yourself, your equipment, and your position from looking like what they are. Both natural and man-made material can be used for camouflage. Change and improve your camouflage often. Natural camouflage will often die or fade, and man-made camouflage may wear off or fade. When this happens, you may no longer blend with your surroundings.

CAMOUFLAGE CONSIDERATIONS

Keep in mind the following camouflage considerations:

- Movement draws attention and can be seen by the naked eye at long ranges. In the defense, stay low and move only when necessary. In the offense, move only on covered and concealed routes.
- Positions should not be built where the enemy would expect to find them. Build on the side of a hill, away from road junctions or lone buildings, and in covered and concealed places. Avoid open areas.
- Outlines and shadows may reveal your position or equipment to air or ground observers. The shape of a human body and the outline of a helmet are easily recognized. Use camouflage and concealment to break up outlines and shadows and blend them with

Camouflage.

their surroundings. When moving, stay in the shadows as much as possible.

- Shine may also attract the enemy's attention. In the dark the problem may be a light such as a burning cigarette or flashlight. In daylight it can be light reflected from a polished surface, such as metal mess gear, a windshield, a watch crystal and band, or exposed skin. To reduce shine, cover your skin with clothing and/or camouflage paint. Dull the surfaces of equipment and vehicles with paint, mud, or some natural camouflage material.

- The color of your skin, uniform, and equipment may help the enemy detect you if the colors contrast with the background. For example, a green uniform will contrast with snow-covered terrain. Camouflage yourself and your equipment to blend with the surroundings.

- Dispersion is the spreading of men, vehicles, and equipment over a wide area. It is usually easier for the enemy to detect soldiers when they are bunched, so spread out. Distances will normally be set by unit leaders and a unit SOP.

CAMOUFLAGE STICKS

A loam and light green camouflage stick is for use in areas with green vegetation. A sand and light green stick is for use in areas lacking green vegetation. Loam and white is for use in snow-covered terrain.

When applying a camouflage stick to your skin, work with a buddy and help each other. Apply a two-color combination of camouflage stick in an irregular pattern. Paint shiny areas—forehead, cheekbones, nose, ears, and chin—with a dark color. Paint shadow areas—around the eyes, under the nose, and under the chin—with a light color. In addition to the face, paint the exposed skin on the back of the neck, arms, and hands. When camouflage sticks are not available, use burnt cork, bark, charcoal, or light-colored mud.

13

Land Navigation and Map Reading

COMPASS

Compasses are the primary tools to use when moving in an outdoor world where there is no other way to find directions. The lensatic compass is the most common and simplest instrument for measuring direction. The lensatic compass consists of the following major parts:

- The *cover* protects the floating dial. It contains a sighting wire and two luminous sighting slots or dots used for night navigation.

- The *base* or body of the compass contains a thumb loop and moving parts that include the floating dial, which is mounted on a pivot and rotates freely when the compass is held level. Printed on the dial in luminous figures are an arrow and the letters E and W. The arrow always points to magnetic north, and the letters rest at east (90 degrees) and west (270 degrees). There are two scales, the outer denoting mils and the inner (normally in red) denoting degrees. Encasing the floating dial is a glass containing a fixed, black index line.

- The *bezel ring* is a ratchet device that clicks when turned. It will make 120 clicks when rotated fully; each click is equal to 3 degrees. A short, luminous line that is used in conjunction with the north-seeking arrow is contained in the glass face of the bezel ring.
- The *lens* is used to read the dial. It contains the rear-sight slot used in conjunction with the front sight for sighting on objects. The rear sight must be opened more than 45 degrees to allow the dial to float freely.

Handling the Compass

The compass is a delicate instrument and should be closed and in its case when not being used. Metal objects and electricity can affect the performance of a compass. Nonmagnetic metals and alloys do not affect the compass. To ensure its proper functioning, observe these suggested safe distances:

High-tension power lines	55 meters
Field gun, truck, or tank	18 meters
Telegraph or telephone wires and barbed wire	10 meters
Machine gun	2 meters
Steel helmet or rifle	½ meter

Using the Compass

The compass must always be held level and firm when sighting on an object. Some of the techniques are as follows:

Centerhold

Open the compass to its fullest so that the cover forms a straight edge with the base. Place your thumb through the thumb loop, form a steady base with your third and fourth fingers, and extend your index finger along the side of the compass. Place the thumb of the other hand between the lens (rear sight) and the bezel ring; extend the index finger along the other side of the compass and the remaining fingers around the fingers of the other hand. Pull your elbows in firmly to your sides—this places the compass between your chin and belt. To measure an azimuth, simply turn your entire body toward the object, pointing the compass cover directly at the object. Then look down and read the azimuth from beneath the fixed, black index line.

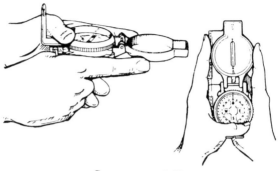

Compass centerhold.

Compass-to-Cheek

Open the cover of the compass containing the sighting wire to a vertical position, and fold the rear sight slightly forward. Look through the rear-sight slot, and align the front-sight hairline with the desired object in the distance. Then glance down at the dial through the eye lens to read the azimuth.

Presetting a Compass

In Daylight or with a Light Source

Hold the compass level in the palm of the hand. Rotate it until the desired azimuth falls under the fixed, black index line. Turn the bezel ring until the luminous line is aligned with the north-seeking arrow. The compass is now preset.

To follow the azimuth, assume the centerhold technique and turn your body until the north-seeking arrow is aligned with the luminous line. Then proceed forward in the direction of the front cover's sighting wire, which is aligned with the fixed, black index line.

In Darkness or Limited Visibility

Set the azimuth by the click method (each click equals a 3-degree interval). Rotate the bezel ring until the luminous line is over the fixed, black index line. Find the desired azimuth and divide it by three. The result is the number of clicks that you have to rotate the bezel ring. If the desired azimuth is smaller than 180 degrees, the number of clicks on the bezel ring should be counted in a counterclockwise direction. If the desired azimuth is larger than 180 degrees, subtract the number of degrees from

Compass-to-cheek.

360 degrees and divide by three to obtain the number of clicks. Count them in a clockwise direction. For example, if the desired azimuth is 330 degrees, then 360 − 330 = 30 divided by 3 = 10 clicks clockwise.

With the compass preset, assume a centerhold technique and rotate your body until the north-seeking arrow is aligned with the luminous line on the bezel. Then proceed forward in the direction of the front cover's luminous dots, which are aligned with the fixed, black index line.

Offset

A deliberate offset is a planned magnetic deviation to the right or left of an azimuth to an objective. It is used when the objective is located along or in the vicinity of a linear feature such as a road or stream. Because of errors in reading the compass or map, you may reach the linear feature without knowing whether the objective lies to the right or left. A deliberate offset by a known number of degrees in a known direction compensates for possible errors and ensures that upon reaching the linear feature you will know whether to go left or right.

Orienting Compass and Map

Place the compass on the map so that the cover of the compass is pointing toward the top of the map. Align the sighting wire or the straight edge of the compass over a north-south grid line, and rotate the map and compass together until the north arrow of the compass points in the same direction and number of degrees as shown in the current, updated grid-magnetic angle.

DETERMINING DIRECTIONS WITHOUT A COMPASS

Using the Sun

The sun is a natural source of direction. Weather permitting, you can determine true north by using the sun and an accurate but time-consuming emergency method called *equal shadow.* The *watch method* can be used to determine approximate true north and true south. This method can be in error, however, especially in the lower latitudes. The best improvised method is called *shadow tip*—it is simple and accurate, and can also be used to find the approximate time of day. Another method of finding the approximate time of day is the *shortest shadow.*

Equal Shadow Method

The shadow of a vertical rod at two hours before midday is the same length as the shadow from the same object two hours after midday. Place a stick upright into the ground in direct sunlight. In the morning, draw a circle with the base of the stick as center and the length of the shadow as radius. Mark the point where the tip of the shadow falls. As the sun rises, the shadow will get shorter. In the afternoon, the shadow lengthens. When it again touches the circle, mark again. The halfway point between the two marks will be due north of the stick.

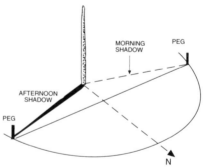

Equal shadow method.

The Watch Method

This method is well known but often inaccurate, except near the North and South Poles. With your watch running on Standard Time, lay it flat on the ground. Place a match or twig upright against the rim. Turn the

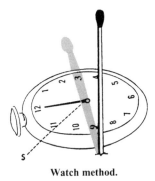

Watch method.

watch until the hour hand points along the shadow toward the sun. South lies about halfway between the hour hand and twelve o'clock.

Shadow-Tip Method

This method requires only ten to fifteen minutes in sunlight and is much more accurate than the watch method. Mark the tip of the shadow cast from a 3-foot stick. Mark the tip again after about ten minutes. A straight line through the two marks is an approximate east-west line from which any desired direction of travel can be obtained. Draw a north-south line at right angles to the east-west line at any point to assist in orienting yourself.

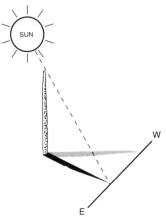

Shadow-tip method to find direction.

Shadow-tip method (continued).

If you are ever uncertain which is east and which is west, observe this simple rule: The sun rises in the east and sets in the west. The shadow tip moves just the opposite. Therefore, the first shadow tip mark is always toward the west and the second mark is always to its east—everywhere on earth.

Shadow-Tip Method of Finding Time

The approximate time of day can also be found by means of the shadow tip. The time is local "sun time." Determine the east-west line as described, then draw a noon line at right angles to the east-west line at any point. Move the stick to where these lines intersect, and set it vertical. The shadow is now an hour hand on your twenty-four-hour "shadow clock"; 6 A.M. is west and 6 P.M. is east. Divide the half circle into twelve equal arcs. Each arc represents one hour. In the example shown, the time is about 8:30 A.M.

Shortest Shadow Method

The sun is at its highest at noon; therefore, shadows are then at their shortest. Put up a stick or rod as nearly vertical as possible in a level place. Check its vertical alignment by sighting along the line of a makeshift plumb bob. Sometime before midday, begin marking the position of the end of the stick's shadow. Continue marking until the shadow definitely

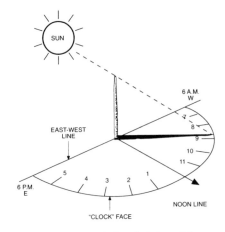

Shadow-tip method to find time of day.

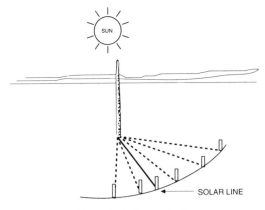

Shortest shadow method.

lengthens. The time of the shortest shadow is when the sun passed the local meridian at solar noon.

Using the Stars

Of approximately five thousand stars visible to the eye, less than sixty are used by navigators. The night sky changes with the seasons as the earth journeys around the sun, and also changes from hour to hour

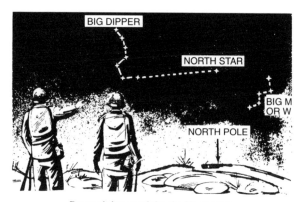

Determining north by the North Star.

Determining south from the Southern Cross.

because of the earth's rotation. But there is one star that is in almost the same place all night long every night: the North Star, also known as the Polar Star or Polaris. The North Star is less than one degree off true north and does not move from its place, because the axis of the earth is pointed toward it. Because the North Star can be seen only in the northern hemisphere, however, it cannot serve as a guide south of the equator. There, the Southern Cross is the main constellation used as a guide.

MAP READING

To be in the right place at the right time is essential on the battlefield, so map-reading and land-navigation skills are important for every soldier.

Military Grid System

A military grid system is a network of squares formed by north-south and east-west grid lines placed on a map. The distance between grid lines represents 1,000 or 10,000 meters, depending on the scale of the map. A grid system enables the map reader to locate a point on a map quickly and accurately.

A grid line is identified by a specific number printed in the margin directly opposite the line it indicates. Any point on a map can be identified by coordinates. Following are rules for reading grid coordinates:

1. Large, bold-faced numbers in the margin label each grid line.
2. Starting at the lower left-hand corner of the map, read right and up.
3. Write the coordinates as a continuous series of numbers. The first half of the total number of the digits represents the "right" reading; the last half represents the "up" reading.

Examples (using a map with 1,000-meter grid squares):

- Location of a point within a 1,000-meter grid square is used to designate an object that is easily identifiable within a large area. Identify the grid square by using the numbers of the two grid lines intersecting at the lower left-hand corner, e.g., 9176.

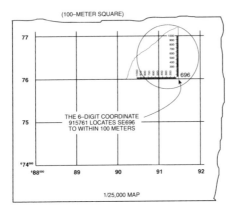

The six-digit coordinate.

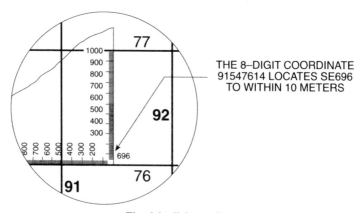

The eight-digit coordinate.

- Location of a point within 100 meters. Use the appropriate corner of a coordinate scale that breaks the 1,000-meter square into ten equal parts along each side. (Hundred-meter segments are indicated by longer lines on the coordinate scale.) Place the coordinate scale along the east-west grid at the lower left-hand corner of the grid square, then slide it eastward to the center of the object. Location is expressed as a six-digit coordinate. The third digit is the longer line nearest grid line 91, and the sixth digit is the longer line nearest the spot elevation (SE), e.g., 915761.
- Location of a point within 10 meters. The short lines divide 100-meter segments into 20-meter segments. To read to the nearest 10 meters, interpolate along the scale. The coordinate will be an eight-digit coordinate, e.g., 91547614.

Scale

Scale is defined as the fixed relationship between map distance and the corresponding ground distance. It is expressed as a representative fraction (RF):

$$RF = \frac{MD \text{ (Map Distance)}}{GD \text{ (Ground Distance)}}$$

The RF appears in the margin of the map as $\frac{1}{25,000}$, 1/25,000, or 1:25,000, each of which means that one unit of measure on the map represents twenty-five thousand similar units of measure on the ground.

Graphic Scale

The graphic scale is printed in the margin as a special ruler and is used to measure ground distances on a map. Military maps normally have three graphic scales, expressed in miles, meters, and yards.

Direction

Direction is defined as an imaginary straight line on the map or ground and is expressed as an azimuth.

Azimuth

An azimuth is a horizontal angle measured clockwise from a base direction. All directions originate from the center of an imaginary circle called the azimuth circle. This circle is divided into 360 equal units of measurement, called degrees. The degrees are numbered in a clockwise direction, with east at 90 degrees, south at 180 degrees, west at 270 degrees, and north at 360 degrees or 0 degrees. Distance has no effect on azimuth.

Back Azimuth

The back azimuth of a line differs from its azimuth by exactly 180 degrees. The rules for determining back azimuth are as follows:
- If the azimuth is less than 180 degrees, the back azimuth is the value of the azimuth *plus* 180.
- If the azimuth is more than 180 degrees, the back azimuth is the value of the azimuth *minus* 180.
- If the azimuth is 180 degrees, the back azimuth is 0 degrees or 360 degrees.

Measuring Azimuths on a Map

Map azimuths are measured with a protractor. The issue protractor (MR-1) is graduated in two scales—0 degrees to 180 degrees, and 180 degrees to 360 degrees—to represent the complete azimuth circle.

To read a map azimuth between any two points:
- Draw a line connecting the two points.
- Place index at the point from which you are measuring, ensuring that the base line of the protractor is on or parallel to a north-south grid line.
- Read the azimuth at the point where the line intersects the scale.

To plot an azimuth on a map:
- Place the protractor on the map with index at the initial point and base line parallel to a north-south grid line.
- Place dot on the map at desired azimuth reading.
- Remove the protractor; connect the initial point and the dot with a line.

Base Direction
There are three base directions: true north, grid north, and magnetic north.

True North
Direction to the north pole. The symbol is a star.

Grid North
Direction of the north-south grid lines. The symbol is GN.

Magnetic North
Direction in which the magnetic arrow of a compass points. The symbol is a half arrow.

The angular relationships among these three directions are shown by a declination diagram in the margin of a map.

Grid-Magnetic Angle
To understand the grid-magnetic (G-M) angle, you must know the meaning of azimuth. Map readers are concerned with two base directions: grid north, from which we read grid azimuths (protractor and map), and magnetic north, from which we read magnetic azimuths (compass and ground).

Grid azimuth is a horizontal angle measured clockwise from grid north. *Magnetic azimuth* is a horizontal angle measured clockwise from magnetic north. *G-M angle* is the angular difference between grid north and magnetic north, measured from grid north.

To use a grid azimuth in the field with a compass, you must first change it to a magnetic azimuth. To plot a magnetic azimuth on a map, you must first change it to a grid azimuth. To make either of these changes, you must use a G-M angle diagram: Draw the current G-M angle. From its base, draw a line to the right; this line represents any azimuth.

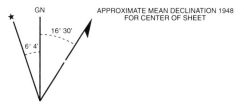

Draw this current G-M angle.

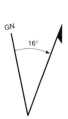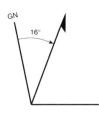

From the base of G-M angle draw a line to the right; this line represents any azimuth.

To use the G-M angle diagram in working with a map having an east G-M angle:

a. Convert magnetic azimuth to grid azimuth.

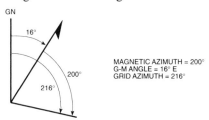

MAGNETIC AZIMUTH = 200°
G-M ANGLE = 16° E
GRID AZIMUTH = 216°

b. Convert grid azimuth to magnetic azimuth.

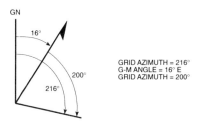

GRID AZIMUTH = 216°
G-M ANGLE = 16° E
GRID AZIMUTH = 200°

c. When working with a map having a west G-M angle convert magnetic azimuth to grid azimuth.

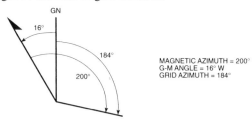

MAGNETIC AZIMUTH = 200°
G-M ANGLE = 16° W
GRID AZIMUTH = 184°

d. Then convert grid azimuth to magnetic azimuth.

To use the G-M angle diagram in working with a map having an east G-M angle:

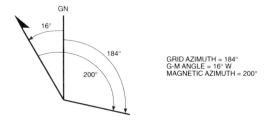

GRID AZIMUTH = 184°
G-M ANGLE = 16° W
MAGNETIC AZIMUTH = 200°

• Convert magnetic azimuth to grid azimuth.
• Convert grid azimuth to magnetic azimuth.
When working with a map having a west G-M angle:
• Convert magnetic azimuth to grid azimuth.
• Then convert grid azimuth to magnetic azimuth.

You should construct and use the G-M angle diagram *each time* conversion of azimuths is required. As a time-saving procedure when working frequently with the same map, construct a G-M angle conversion table on the margin. The following is an example, using a map having a G-M angle of 16 degrees east:

G-M angle = 16 degrees east
For Conversion of:

Magnetic azimuth to grid azimuth: Add 16 degrees
Grid azimuth to magnetic azimuth: Subtract 16 degrees

Intersection

Distant or inaccessible objects can be located on a map by intersecting lines from two known points. For example, a magnetic azimuth from a known OP to a distant point is converted to a grid azimuth and drawn on the map. Another magnetic azimuth from another OP to the same distant point is converted to a grid azimuth and drawn on the same map. The intersection of the two lines on the map is the location of the known point.

Resection

The resection method lets you locate your position on a map. Take magnetic azimuths to two distant points on the ground that can be identified on the map. Change these azimuths to back azimuths, convert to grid azimuths, and draw the *converted* azimuths from the known points on the map. Your location is where these two lines intersect. To verify and make a final determination of your position, compare ground features with those shown on the map.

Modified Resection

The modified resection is a method of locating your position on a map when you are on a road, stream, or other linear feature identified on the map. Take a magnetic azimuth to a distant point that can be identified both on the ground and on the map. Change this to a back azimuth, and convert to a grid azimuth. Draw this *converted* azimuth on the map from the known point. Your position is where the azimuth line on the map crosses or intersects the linear feature.

Elevation and Relief

Elevation is height expressed in feet or meters above or below mean sea level. *Relief* is the variation in the height and shape of the earth's surface. Elevation and relief may be shown on a map by hachures (short, broken lines used to show mountain ranges, peaks, and plateaus), layer tinting, or contour lines. On large-scale maps, contour lines are used.

Contour lines are imaginary lines on the ground connecting points of equal elevation. On a map they are shown in brown or gray. The *contour interval*—the vertical distance between contours—is stated as marginal information. Normally every fifth contour is printed more heavily than the others and is numbered to show the height above or below mean sea level. These lines are known as *index contours*. Following are some characteristics of contours:

- Contours are smooth curves that always close to form irregular circles.
- When crossing a valley or a stream, contours form Us or Vs, with the base of the U or V pointing toward higher ground (or upstream).
- When crossing ridges, contour lines form Us or Vs with the base of the U or V pointing away from high ground.
- Contours far apart indicate a gentle slope; contours close together indicate a steep slope.
- On uniform slopes, contours are evenly spaced; on irregular slopes, they are unevenly spaced.
- The last (inmost) closed contour indicates a hilltop.
- Movement parallel to contours is relatively level; movement across contours is up- or downslope.

Terrain Features

All ground forms may be classified as one of the following primary terrain features: hilltop, ridge, valley, saddle, or depression. Contour lines are used to indicate these ground forms on a map.

The relationship between contour lines and actual ground forms is illustrated as follows. To determine the elevation of a point that falls between two adjacent contours, estimate the point's relative distance between the two contours, and add the same proportion to the elevation of the lowest-valued contour line. For example, a point located seven-tenths of the distance between the 70-foot contour and the 80-foot contour would have an elevation of 77 feet.

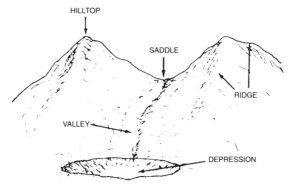

Terrain features.

HILLTOP

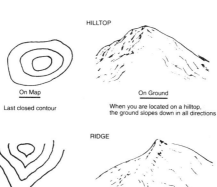

On Map

Last closed contour

On Ground

When you are located on a hilltop,
the ground slopes down in all directions

RIDGE

On Map

U- or V-shaped contours with
the base of the U or V
pointing away from higher ground

On Ground

When you are located on a ridge,
the ground slopes down in three
directions and up in one direction

DEPRESSION

On Ground

When you are located in a
depression, there is higher
ground in all directions

On Map

Indicated by depression
contours

Terrain features.

VALLEY

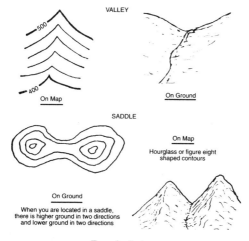

500

400

On Map

On Ground

SADDLE

On Map

Hourglass or figure eight
shaped contours

On Ground

When you are located in a saddle,
there is higher ground in two directions
and lower ground in two directions

Terrain features.

A rule of thumb to determine the elevation of a hilltop is to take the elevation of the last closed contour line and add to it one-half the contour interval. To determine the elevation of a depression, subtract one-half the contour interval from the last depression contour line.

Use of a Map in the Field

To determine your location on the map and on the ground, use the following procedures:

Orient the map to the north. Inspect the surrounding area or ground to determine all distinct terrain features. On the map, look for an area having the same types of features in the same relative positions as those observed on the ground. Through comparing the map to the ground and using a process of elimination, isolate the terrain feature on which you are located. Confirm this terrain feature by assuring that the direction to, distance from, and difference in elevation from all adjacent terrain features are identical on the map and on the ground. Determine your exact location on the isolated terrain feature by a detailed analysis of all the immediate terrain features.

GROUND NAVIGATION

Ground navigation is movement between two points in which an individual, using terrain features to guide upon, knows both his map and ground location throughout the movement. Ground navigation demands a thorough knowledge of terrain features as they appear on the map and on the ground. Since terrain features are used to guide upon during movement, the use of the compass for movement is minimal. Two basic rules must always be applied:

1. Begin from a known location on both the map and the ground.
2. Then orient the map to the ground and keep it oriented throughout the movement.

With the basic rules established, the following steps outline the ground (land) navigation procedure:

1. Through a map study of the terrain, determine the most practical route to your destination, and select terrain features along this route to guide your movement.
2. Determine the general direction of movement.
3. Begin movement, considering the horizontal and the vertical distances between terrain features along the route.

4. Confirm your location at selected terrain features (checkpoints) along the route.
5. Upon arrival at the final destination, confirm your location by a detailed comparative analysis between the ground position and the plotted map position.

Mounted Navigation

With the addition of more combat vehicles into the Army, your chances of having to navigate while mounted are increasing. The major difference between navigating while mounted and while dismounted is the speed at which you travel. When moving mounted, it is important to designate a navigator who makes sure that the correct distance and direction are followed and recorded, beginning with the leg from the start point to the first prominent feature and then to subsequent easily identifiable features on the ground. The navigator prepares a log to record azimuths and distances for each leg of the movement. During movement, the navigator must face in the direction of travel to keep his map oriented and to identify terrain features.

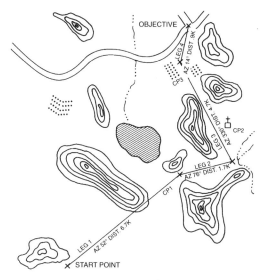

NOTE: All azimuths in this figure are grid.

Mounted movement.

Mounted navigation with a compass requires determination of the amount of deviation caused by the vehicle. This can be done in the following manner:

1. The navigator dismounts and moves 50 meters in front of the vehicle.
2. The navigator determines an azimuth from his position to a fixed object at least 50 meters to his front.
3. The driver moves the vehicle forward, keeping it centered on the navigator, and stops as close to him as safely possible.
4. The navigator then gets back into the vehicle and measures the azimuth to the fixed object from the vehicle. The vehicle engine must be running. The difference between the two azimuths is the deviation. The deviation is logged and added to or subtracted from the azimuth to be followed. This procedure should be followed for any change of direction of 10 degrees or more.

Be aware that distance measured on a vehicle's odometer during mounted movement may be greater than that measured on the map, since the map measurements do not take into consideration the rise and fall of the land.

How to Fold a Map

Use the following steps to fold a map:

1. Lay the map flat, face up, north at the top. Fold it in half, turning the bottom edge up to the top.
2. Crease map into three equal parts parallel to the center fold just made.
3. Open map completely, face up. Turn so east is at the top.
4. Repeat the folding procedures of steps 1 and 2.
5. Open map again, face up, placing north at the top. With a sharp blade, neatly cut map as shown in Sketch 1, along heavy lines.
6. Grasp as in Sketch 2, drawing paper up at crease. Fold over toward top edge.
7. Repeat step 6 with second crease from the bottom, folding to meet the top edge of the map. Fold up remaining flap. Edge view of the map should look like Sketch 3.
8. From center V, open map to center section without unfolding remainder. Turn map so east is at the top.
9. Follow same creasing and folding procedures as in steps 6 and 7.

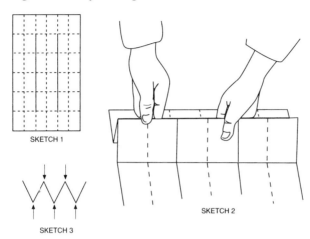

SKETCH 1

SKETCH 3

SKETCH 2

Folding a map sheet.

10. Again open map at center V without unfolding the rest, exposing center section.
11. Without unfolding the map, carefully glue or tape together the eight places where edges you have cut come together.
12. You now have three sections, each of which may be used like a bookmap. You may fold entire map so that only the desired "book" is exposed for use.

14

Fighting Positions

While it is desirable for a fighting position to give maximum protection to personnel and equipment, primary consideration is always given to effective weapon use. In the offense, weapons are sited wherever natural or existing positions are available or where weapons emplacement may be made with minimal digging.

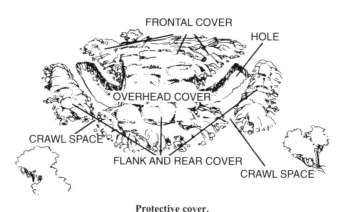

Protective cover.

TYPES OF COVER

Protection against direct and indirect fires is of primary concern for position design. Protection design for one type of enemy fire is not necessarily effective against another. The following three types of cover—frontal, overhead, and flank and rear—will have a direct bearing on designing and constructing positions. Ideally, protection is provided by natural cover. In its absence, a parapet is constructed as time permits. A position's cover should be such that when the position comes under frontal fire, the troops can move behind the frontal cover and shoot to the oblique.

Frontal Cover

Frontal cover must be thick enough (at least 18 inches of dirt) to stop small-arms fire, high enough to cover the heads of men shooting from it, and far enough in front of the hole to allow room for elbow rests and sector stakes so that the men can fire to the oblique. It must be long enough to give the soldier cover and to hide the muzzle blast of his rifle when he fires to the oblique.

Overhead Cover

Overhead cover provides protection from indirect-fire fragmentation. Soldiers are at least ten times more protected if they are in a hole with overhead cover.

Flank and Rear Cover

Flank and rear cover ensures complete protection for the soldiers from the effects of indirect fire to the flanks or rear of the position and from the effects of friendly weapons in the rear.

VARIATIONS IN FIGHTING POSITIONS

Hasty Fighting Position

A hasty fighting position is prepared when there is insufficient time to prepare a deliberate fighting position. It is put behind whatever cover is available. It should give frontal protection from direct fire and still allow shooting to the front and oblique. For protection from indirect fire, it should be in a small depression or in a hole at least 18 inches deep.

Hasty fighting position.

One-Man Fighting Position

A one-man fighting position allows flexibility in the use of cover because the hole only has to be long enough for one man and his gear. It must let a soldier shoot to the front or to the oblique from behind frontal cover.

One-man fighting position.

Two-Man Fighting Position

A two-man fighting position provides better security than a one-man fighting position. It should give frontal protection from direct fire and allow shooting to the front and oblique.

Two-man fighting position.

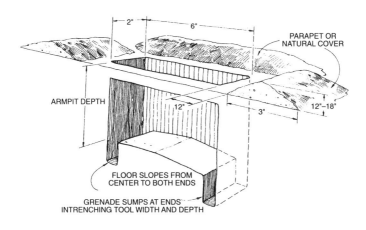

Cutaway view of two-man position.

Modified Two-Man Fighting Position

A modified two-man fighting position may be prepared in close terrain, where grazing fire and mutual support extend no farther than to an adjacent position, or prepared to cover dead space just in front of the position. This is done by extending one or both ends of the hole around the sides of the frontal cover.

Modified two-man position.

Positions on Steep Terrain

On a steep slope, a soldier in a hole behind frontal cover cannot shoot attackers without standing up and exposing himself. To overcome this, the hole is dug and firing ports are dug out at each end of the hole. The ground between the firing ports then serves as frontal cover for the position.

Steep terrain position.

PREPARING FIGHTING POSITIONS

Dig the hole armpit deep to lower the profile of the soldiers and still let them shoot. Elbow holes can be dug between the hole and the frontal cover to stabilize the shooter's arms and lower his profile. Trenches can be dug for the bipod legs of an automatic rifle, to get down closer to ground level.

Aiming stakes help a soldier fire his rifle on dangerous approaches at night. Use sector stakes, right and left, to define the sector of fire and prevent accidental shooting into adjacent positions.

Position depth.

To be able to see and shoot into your sector of fire, you may have to clear vegetation and other obstructions. This is called clearing a field of fire. When clearing a field of fire, keep in mind the following considerations:

- Do not disclose your position by careless or too much clearing.
- Leave a thin screen of natural vegetation to hide your position.
- Cut off lower branches of large, scattered trees in sparsely wooded areas.
- Clear underbrush only where it blocks your view.
- Remove cut brush, limbs, and weeds so that the enemy will not spot them.
- Cover cuts on trees and bushes forward of your position with mud, dirt, or snow.

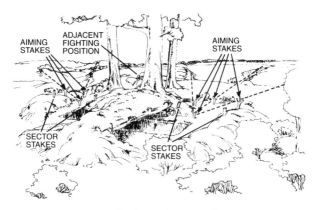

Aiming and sector stakes.

- Leave no trails as clues for the enemy.
- A field of fire to the front is needed out to the range of your weapon.

Shape the floor of the hole so that it slopes toward the grenade sumps. Water will run into the sumps, and grenades will tend to roll into them. Dig two trench-shaped hand-grenade sumps at each end of the position. The trenches should be dug as wide as the blade of an intrenching tool, at least as deep as the intrenching tool, and as long as the position is wide.

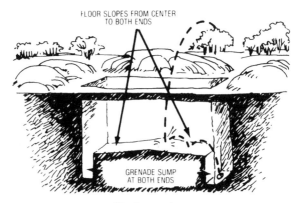

Hand-grenade sump.

PREPARING A MACHINE GUN POSITION

The primary sector of fire is usually to the oblique so that the gun can fire across the platoon's front. The tripod is used on the side with the primary sector of fire, and the bipod legs are used on the side with the secondary sector. When changing from primary to secondary sectors, the machine gun is moved but the tripod is left in place. Dig a trench for the bipod legs in the secondary sector. After the platoon leader positions the gun and assigns sectors of fire, mark the position of the tripod legs and the limits of the sector of fire. Then trace the outline of the hole and the frontal cover.

The gun is lowered by digging down the firing platforms where the gun will be placed. The platforms must not be so low that the gun cannot be traversed across the sector of fire. Lowering the gun reduces the profile of the gunner when he is shooting and reduces the height of the frontal cover needed. Dig the firing platform first, to lessen the gunner's exposure in case firing is required before the position is completed.

After the firing platforms have been dug, dig the hole, placing the dirt first where frontal cover is needed. The hole is dug deep enough to provide protection and still let the gunner shoot, usually about armpit deep. When the frontal cover is high and thick enough, the rest of the dirt is used to build the flank and rear cover. Three trench-shaped grenade sumps are dug at various points so that grenades can be kicked into them.

TRACING OUTLINE

Machine-gun position preparation.

Machine-gun position (continued).

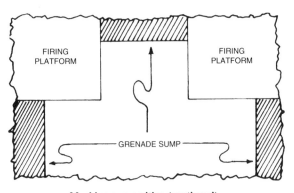

Machine-gun position (continued).

PREPARING A DRAGON POSITION

The Dragon has a primary fighting position and one or more alternate firing positions to cover its primary sector of fire. Additionally, each Dragon may have supplementary firing positions for coverage of other sectors of fire.

The backblast and the muzzle blast must be considered when employing the weapon. When the weapon is fired from an improved position, the muzzle end of the launcher must extend 6 inches beyond

Dragon position.

Position preparation.

the front of the hole. The rear of the launcher must extend out over the rear of the hole. As the missile leaves the launcher, stabilizing fins unfold that require at least 6 inches of clearance above the ground. The position is only waist deep so that the gunner can move while firing. A trench for the bipod is dug 6 inches in front of the hole.

The position should be protected to the front by a parapet or some natural or man-made cover. The ground in front of and behind the position should be free of rocks, sand, and debris to prevent a dust cloud caused by the firing from obscuring the gunner's vision.

When the Dragon is to fire in only one direction, a one-man fight-

Two-man Dragon position.

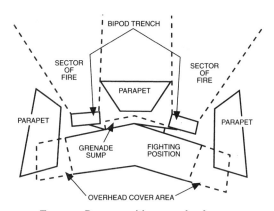

Two-man Dragon position—overhead cover.

ing position can be prepared. The Dragon should be positioned to fire to the oblique so that its position can be protected from frontal fire while the target is being engaged.

The two-man fighting position is triangular-shaped. It is best suited for use when more than one sector of fire can be covered from a single position. The design of the position gives the gunner frontal protection and allows targets to be engaged from the oblique or flank.

Overhead cover is placed on the flanks of the one- or two-man Dragon position.

MORTARS

The standard dug-in mortar position has three stages of construction:

1. The mortar pit.
2. Personnel shelters.
3. The ammunition bunker.

A dug-in position for the 81-millimeter or 60-millimeter mortars is the same as that for the 4.2-inch mortar, with only slight changes in dimensions. The standard mortar position should be constructed on a reasonably flat area of ground. It can be constructed totally below, partially above, or completely above ground, depending on the time and material available and the composition of the ground.

Stage 1. After the general location is selected, the exact baseplate position is marked and construction of the mortar pit is begun.

Stage 2. As soon as the mortar pit is completed and as time allows, construct personnel shelters with overhead cover. Firing ports should be built into the personnel shelter and positioned as determined by assigned sectors of fire. There should be a blast barrier at least two sandbags in thickness separating the personnel shelters from the mortar pit.

Stage 3. If time and resources permit, ammunition bunkers are constructed. Each bunker is divided into four sections for each type of

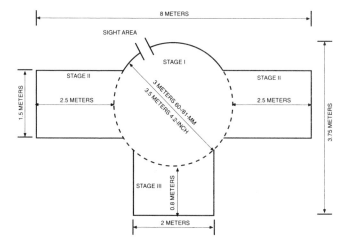

Mortar position. Three stages of construction: I, mortar pit; II, personnel shelters; III, ammunition bunker.

ammunition: white phosphorus (WP), illumination, final protective fires (FPF), and high explosive (HE).

Camouflaging the position is done in conjunction with construction through all stages.

VEHICLE POSITIONS

The deliberate position is constructed in four parts: hull defilade, concealed access ramp or route, hide location, and turret defilade. The access ramp from the hide location to the hull defilade usually provides turret defilade for a vehicle at some point on the ramp. This location is marked to allow the driver to drive to it during daylight and darkness.

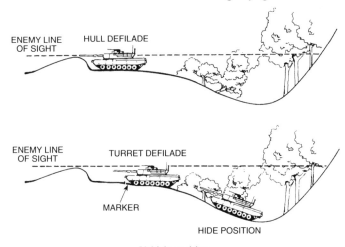

Vehicle position.

15

First Aid

Your first-aid skills could save your life or the life of your buddy.

LIFESAVING MEASURES

Clear the Airway

Check and restore breathing and heartbeat as necessary: Kneel at the injured person's head, turn his head to one side, and clear mucus and debris from his mouth. Give mouth-to-mouth or mouth-to-nose resuscitation if necessary. If heartbeat stops, give closed-chest heart massage.

Stop the Bleeding

Uncontrolled bleeding causes shock and finally death. Use pressure dressing or digital pressure. A tourniquet should not be used unless the pressure dressing fails to stop the bleeding or an arm or leg has been cut off. If left in place too long, a tourniquet can cause the loss of a leg or arm.

Prevent Shock

Shock can result from any type of injury. The warning signs of shock are restlessness, thirst, pale skin, and rapid heartbeat. To control shock,

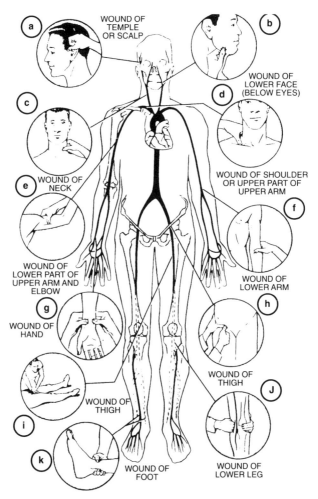

Pressure points for temporary control of arterial bleeding.

maintain adequate respiration and heartbeat, control bleeding, loosen clothing, reassure the casualty, splint all fractures, and place him on his back with his feet elevated; if he is unconscious, turn his head to the side. Keep him as warm as possible.

Dress and Bandage the Wound

ARTIFICIAL RESPIRATION

The approved method of artificial respiration in a clean atmosphere is the mouth-to-mouth method or one of its variations. When correctly applied, the mouth-to-mouth method and its variations permit more air to enter the casualty's lungs than any other known method.

AIRWAY
CLOSED
BY TONGUE

AIRWAY OPENED
BY EXTENDING
NECK

Shoulder raised and head tilted back in chin-up position

Artificial respiration.

Mouth-to-Mouth (Thumb Jaw Lift) Method

The mouth-to-mouth (thumb jaw lift) method is the preferred method in a clean atmosphere. Place casualty on his back. Clear his mouth of any foreign matter with your fingers. If available, use a blanket or some similar material under the shoulders. Tilt his head back so that the neck is stretched and the head is in the "chin-up" position. Place thumb in corner of patient's mouth and grasp his lower jaw firmly. Lift the lower jaw forward to pull the tongue forward out of the air passage. With the other hand, pinch the patient's nose shut in order to prevent air leakage. Take a deep breath and open your mouth wide. Seal your mouth around the patient's mouth and your thumb, and blow air forcefully into his mouth until you see his chest rise. When the chest rises, stop blowing and quickly remove your mouth. When exhalation is completed, again blow in a deep breath.

The first five to ten breaths must be deep and given at a rapid rate. Continue forced breathing at a rate of twelve to twenty times a minute until the patient begins to breathe normally.

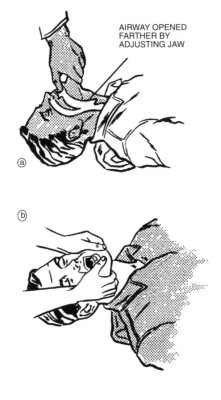

Methods for adjusting lower jaw to jutting out position.
a. Thumb jaw lift.   b. Two-hands jaw lift.

Mouth-to-Mouth (Two-Hands Jaw Lift) Method

The mouth-to-mouth (two-hands jaw lift) method is an alternate used in a clean atmosphere when the patient's jaws are so tightly closed your thumb cannot be inserted. Place the patient on his back, clear mouth if possible, and place head in a "chin-up" position. Grasp the angles of his lower jaw with both hands just below the ear lobes, and lift the jaw forcibly forward to pull the tongue forward out of the air passage. If his lips are closed, push the lower lip toward his chin with your thumbs. Take a deep breath and open your mouth wide. Seal your mouth over the patient's mouth, press your cheek against his nose to prevent air leakage, and blow air forcefully into his mouth until his chest rises. Continue as described above in the preferred method.

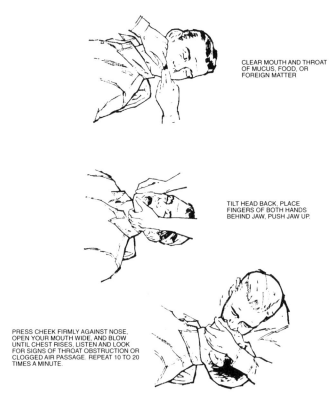

CLEAR MOUTH AND THROAT OF MUCUS, FOOD, OR FOREIGN MATTER

TILT HEAD BACK, PLACE FINGERS OF BOTH HANDS BEHIND JAW, PUSH JAW UP.

PRESS CHEEK FIRMLY AGAINST NOSE, OPEN YOUR MOUTH WIDE, AND BLOW UNTIL CHEST RISES, LISTEN AND LOOK FOR SIGNS OF THROAT OBSTRUCTION OR CLOGGED AIR PASSAGE. REPEAT 10 TO 20 TIMES A MINUTE.

Mouth-to-mouth (two-hands jaw lift) method.

Mouth-to-Nose Method

The mouth-to-nose method is an alternate used in a clean atmosphere when neither of the methods above can be used—for example, with patients having severe jaw spasm or jaw or mouth wounds or injuries. Place patient on his back, clear the mouth if possible, and put his head in the "chin-up," position. Grasp the angle of his lower jaw with one hand just below the ear lobe, and lift the jaw forcibly forward to pull the tongue out of the air passage. Seal your other hand over the patient's mouth to prevent air leakage. Take a deep breath and open your mouth wide. Seal your mouth around the patient's nose, and blow forcefully until you see his chest rise. Continue as described above.

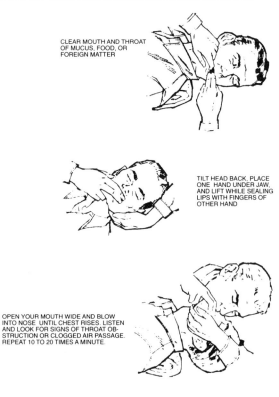

CLEAR MOUTH AND THROAT OF MUCUS, FOOD, OR FOREIGN MATTER

TILT HEAD BACK, PLACE ONE HAND UNDER JAW, AND LIFT WHILE SEALING LIPS WITH FINGERS OF OTHER HAND

OPEN YOUR MOUTH WIDE AND BLOW INTO NOSE UNTIL CHEST RISES. LISTEN AND LOOK FOR SIGNS OF THROAT OB- STRUCTION OR CLOGGED AIR PASSAGE. REPEAT 10 TO 20 TIMES A MINUTE.

Mouth-to-nose method.

BURNS

Minor burns (no charring or blistering) of small skin areas should be covered with a first-aid packet or other dry, sterile dressing. Otherwise, leave uncovered. If burn is severe (blistered or charred or covers large area of body), infection and shock must be prevented. Cover burned area with a dry, sterile dressing. Do not touch burn with anything but sterile dressings except in case of mass casualties. Then cover with clean sheets, T-shirts, etc. Leave uncovered only as a last resort. Do not place the dressing over the face or genital area. Do not pull clothes over burned area, try to remove pieces of cloth sticking to skin, try to clean burned area, break burn blister, or put grease, Vaseline, or ointment on burn.

Prevent shock by placing head and shoulders lower than rest of body and by replacing body fluids. If casualty is conscious, is not vomiting, and has no belly wound, give small amounts of cool or cold water. Give a few sips every few minutes; increase amounts until one-third of a canteen cupful is drunk every hour. If casualty vomits or acts as if he might, do not give him any more water. Do not use warm water, which can cause vomiting.

FOREIGN BODY IN THE EYE

Do not rub eye. Tears will frequently flush out the particle. If not, pull eyelid up or down and attempt to remove the particle with moist, clean corner of handkerchief. If unsuccessful, or if the foreign body is glass or metal, blindfold both eyes and evacuate to medical facilities.

FOREIGN BODY IN THE EAR, NOSE, OR THROAT

Never probe for a foreign object in ear or nose. A live insect in the ear may be removed by attracting it with a flashlight or by pouring water into ear to drown it and flush it out. Do not attempt to flush a foreign object out of the ear with water if the object will swell when wet.

Remove foreign objects from nose by blowing.

Coughing will frequently dislodge a foreign object from the throat. If this fails and the object can be reached, try to remove it with the fingers, but be careful not to push it deeper down the throat.

FRACTURES

Signs of a broken bone include tenderness over the injury with pain upon movement, inability to move the injured part, unnatural shape, swelling, and discoloration of the skin. All these signs may or may not be present with a fracture; if you are not sure, give the patient the benefit of the doubt and treat it as a fracture.

Handle with care. Prevent shock and further injury. Broken ends of bone can cut nerves, blood vessels, and so on. Do not move the patient unless necessary. If he must be moved, splint the fracture first.

If there is a wound, apply dressing as for any other wound. If there is bleeding, it must be stopped. If a tourniquet is necessary, do not place it over the site of the fracture. If time permits, improvise splints (sticks, blankets, poncho, etc.); if a weapon is used for a splint, unload it first. Pad splints well with soft material to prevent pressure and rubbing. The splint should extend from above the joint above the fracture to below the joint below the fracture. Bind splints securely at several points, but not so tightly as to interfere with blood flow (check pulse).

One of the quickest ways to splint a broken leg is by tying it to the uninjured leg (do not use narrow materials such as wire). Use padding between the legs, and tie at several points above and below the break. Tie the feet together.

Support a fracture of the arm or shoulder with a sling (do not try to bend injured elbow if it is straight).

BROKEN BACK

Any back injury is suspect, especially if the casualty has no feeling in his legs or cannot move them. The sharp fragments of broken bone can cut or damage the spinal cord and cause permanent paralysis.

Do place a low roll, such as bath towel or clothing, under the middle of the back to arch and support it; lift the casualty, if he must be moved, onto a litter or board without bending his spine—it is best to have at least four men for this job; if the casualty is in face-down position, carry him face-down on a blanket; keep body alignment straight and natural at all times, and keep the air passage free. Caution the casualty not to move.

Do not move casualty unless absolutely necessary; raise head, even for a drink of water; twist neck or back; or carry in a blanket face-up.

BROKEN NECK

A broken neck is an extremely dangerous injury; bone fragments may cut the spinal cord, as with a broken back. Keep the casualty's head straight and still, with the neck slightly arched. Caution him not to move (motion may cause his death).

Place a rolled bath towel or a roll of clothing about the same bulk as a bath towel under the neck for support and padding (roll should be thick enough to arch neck only slightly). Raise the shoulders in order to place the roll under the neck—do not bend neck or head forward. Do not twist or raise the head. Place roll so that when the casualty is lying flat, the back of his head touches the ground. To keep his head motionless after the roll is in place, put a large padded rock or pack at each side of the head.

If the casualty must be moved, get help. One person should support the head and keep it straight while others lift the casualty. Transport him on a hard litter or board. Never turn over a casualty who has a broken neck! If the casualty is found with his neck in an abnormal position, do not try to straighten head and neck; immobilize the head in the position found.

HEAT INJURIES

Heat injuries are disabling to varying degrees and can be fatal. They occur when water and salt lost in sweat, while soldiers work in heat, are not replaced. They are especially liable to occur in individuals who are not acclimatized (accustomed) to the heat and in those who are overweight, have fevers (sunburn, infection, reaction to immunizations), or are already dehydrated (have insufficient water in their bodies) because of diarrhea, alcohol consumption, or simply not having drunk enough water.

Sweating

The evaporation of sweat is the only way the body can cool itself when the temperature is above 95° Fahrenheit; evaporation is less and more water intake is required in the humid jungle than in the dry desert. Sweat contains salt and water, both of which must be replaced in order to prevent heat injury. More than 3 gallons of sweat may be lost and need to be replaced by soldiers working hard in the heat.

Water

It's best to replace water as it is lost—soldiers should drink when thirsty. There is no benefit in withholding water until later. It is impossible to train soldiers to get by on less water than the amount required to replace that lost in sweat. Water requirements can be reduced only if sweating is reduced by working during the cooler hours of evening, night, and early morning.

Salt

Extra salt is required when soldiers are sweating heavily. Salt tablets should *not* be used to prevent heat injury. Usually, eating field rations or liberal salting of garrison diet will provide enough salt to replace what is lost through sweating in hot weather.

Cause of Heat Injuries

Lack of acclimatization (adjustment of the body to heat) is the most common underlying cause of heat injury. Acclimatization requires two weeks; the greatest acclimatization occurs during the first five to seven days. Troops newly arrived in hot climates should be exposed gradually to increasing amounts of work during increasingly hotter parts of the day until they are acclimatized.

Heat Cramps

Heat cramps are cramps of the muscles of the belly, arms, or legs. They occur when a person has sweated a lot and has not taken extra water.

Heat Exhaustion

The victim of heat exhaustion may have a headache and be dizzy, faint, and weak. He has cool, pale (gray), moist (sweaty) skin and loss of appetite. Move him to a shady area or improvise shade and have him lie down. Loosen or remove clothing and boots, pour water on him, and fan him if it is a very hot day. Elevate his legs, and have him slowly drink at least one canteen full of water. The patient should not participate in further strenuous activity and should be evacuated if symptoms persist.

Heatstroke

Heatstroke is a medical emergency and can be fatal if not treated promptly and correctly. It is caused by failure of the body's cooling mechanisms. Inadequate sweating is a factor. The casualty's skin is flushed, hot, and dry. He may experience dizziness, confusion, headaches, seizures, and nausea, and his respiration and pulse may be weak. Cool the casualty immediately by moving him to a shaded area; remove outer clothing, pour water on him or immerse him in water, and fan him to permit the cooling effect of evaporation. Massage his skin, elevate his legs, and have him slowly drink water. Get him to a medical facility as soon as possible.

COLD INJURIES

Cold injuries are caused when the body loses heat. They can cause the loss of toes, fingers, feet, ears, and so on.

Frostbite

If the body heat is lost quickly and the tissues actually freeze, the injury is called frostbite. Frostbite is the actual freezing of a part of the body (usually the face, hands, or feet). There may be no pain. Frostbitten parts of the body become grayish or white and lose feeling. Use a buddy system to keep watch on one another for signs of frostbite.

Treat frostbite by removing clothing (boots, gloves, socks) and thawing the area by placing it next to a warm part of his, your own, or somebody else's body. Warm (not hot) water may be used. Remove constrictive clothing that interferes with circulation. Do not rewarm by walking, massage, exposure to open fire, cold water, or rubbing with snow. After the part has been warmed, protect it from further injury by covering it lightly with a blanket or any dry clothing. Do not use ointments or other medications.

Trenchfoot (Immersion Foot)

If body heat is lost slowly, because the body is wet, the injury is called trenchfoot or immersion foot.

Prevention of Cold Injuries

Cold injuries can be prevented by proper leadership and by training in conserving body heat.

Leadership—command interest—is essential. Cold injuries are prevented when officers and noncommissioned officers do their jobs properly. Personnel must be taught how to prevent cold injuries. Reduce their exposure to cold, wet, and wind when possible. Rotate individuals and units to warming tents. Provide changes of dry clothing, hot food, and drinks.

The individual can take the following steps:

- Do not stand in wet positions—build them up with branches, and so on.
- Carry extra, dry socks, and change after marching or standing.
- Remove cold and wet boots and socks before going to sleep.
- Sleep back to back with a buddy to prevent loss of body heat.
- Massage the feet several times daily, especially when changing socks.
- Do not touch bare metal with bare skin.

Dress Properly—Remember C-O-L-D

C: Keep It *Clean.* Dirty clothing has less insulating quality.

O: Avoid *Overheating.* Overheating causes sweating; clothing wet from sweat causes cold injury.

L: Wear It *Loose and in Layers.* Warm air is trapped between layers and acts as insulation. Tight clothing, boots, and gloves leave no room for a warm air layer or for the exercise of fingers and toes, and may act as a tourniquet to shut off circulation.

D: Keep It *Dry.* Dry clothing retains heat; wet clothing conducts heat from the body.

SNAKE BITES

Keep the bitten person quiet, and do not let him walk or run. Kill the snake if possible, and keep it for identification and proper serum. If the bite is on an extremity, do not elevate the limb; keep it level with the body. If the bite is on an arm or leg, place a constricting band (narrow gauze bandage) one to two finger widths above and below the bite. If the bite is on a hand or foot, place the band above the wrist or ankle.

The band should be tight enough to stop the flow of blood near the skin, but not so tight as to interfere with circulation. It should not have a tourniquetlike effect. Get the casualty to medical treatment as soon as possible.

UNCONSCIOUSNESS

If you can determine the cause (bleeding, heatstroke, head injury, etc.), give first aid. It is often impossible to determine the cause of unconsciousness. If the casualty has merely fainted, he will regain consciousness in a few minutes. Take off his equipment, and loosen his clothing. Do not pour liquids into the mouth of an unconscious person. Remove from the mouth or throat false teeth, chewing gum, or other objects that might choke him. If the individual is about to faint while sitting up, lower his head between the knees so that blood may flow to the head; hold him so that he does not fall and hurt himself.

WOUNDS

Apply lifesaving steps, as appropriate.

Belly Wounds

Position the casualty on his back with his knees up to prevent further exposure of bowels. Cover the wound and protruding intestines with dry, sterile dressings. Pick up any organs that may be on the ground with a clean, dry dressing or with the cleanest material available, and place them on top of the casualty's stomach.

Chest Wounds

Locate the wound, and examine it to see if there is an entry and/or exit wound. Perform the same procedures for both wounds. Air leaking into the chest cavity may cause the lungs to collapse. Use the plastic wrapper with the field dressing to create an airtight seal over the wound. Apply the dressing to the wound. Use additional material if necessary to create enough pressure to make it airtight. Position the casualty on his injured side or in a sitting position, whichever makes breathing easier.

Head Wounds

Suspect a head wound if the casualty is or has been unconscious, has blood or other fluid escaping from nose or ears, has slow pulse or headache, is vomiting, has had convulsions, or is breathing very slowly. Do not give morphine, and do not place in shock position with the head lower than the rest of the body.

Place in position with the head slightly elevated. Do not elevate the head if fluids are accumulating in the patient's throat. When there is bleeding from the mouth and throat, the casualty must be positioned on his side or face so the blood can drain out of the mouth and not down into the windpipe. If he is unconscious, remove false teeth and other objects from the mouth.

Jaw Wounds
Before applying a bandage to a casualty's jaw, remove all foreign material from the mouth. If the casualty is unconscious, check for obstructions in the airway. When applying the bandage, allow the jaw enough freedom to permit passage of air and drainage from the mouth. If the casualty is unconscious, place him on his belly or side with the head lower than the body and turned slightly to one side.

FOOT CARE

Socks
Wash and dry socks daily. Start each day with a fresh pair. After crossing a wet area, dry your feet, put on foot powder, and change socks if the situation permits. Avoid worn or tight-fitting socks. Carry an extra pair in a pack or inside the shirt.

Blisters
Wash the area, open the blister, drain, cover with adhesive tape.

Athlete's Foot
Keep feet clean and dry. Use foot powder.

16

Reporting Enemy Information

Commanders get information about the enemy from many sources, but the individual soldier is their best source. You can collect information from the following other sources:
- Prisoners of war.
- Captured documents.
- Enemy activity.
- Local civilians.

WHAT TO REPORT

Report all information about the enemy to your leader quickly, accurately, and completely. Such reports should answer the questions WHO, WHAT, WHERE, and WHEN. It is best to use the SALUTE format (size, activity, location, unit, time, and equipment) when reporting. Use notes and draw sketches as aids in remembering details.

Size

Report the number of soldiers and vehicles you saw. For example, report: "ten enemy infantrymen" (not "a rifle squad") or "three enemy tanks" (not "an enemy tank platoon").

Activity

Report what you saw the enemy doing—for example, "emplacing mines in the road."

Location

Report where you saw the enemy. If you have a map, try to give a six-digit coordinate, such as "GL567345." If you do not have a map, relate the location to some key terrain feature, such as "on the Hann Road, about 300 meters south of the Kelly River bridge."

Unit

If the enemy's unit is not known, report any distinctive features, such as bumper markings on trucks or type of headgear. Some armies have distinctive uniforms and headgear, or colored tabs on their uniform, to identify types of units. A unit's action may also indicate its type. The kind of equipment observed may be peculiar to a certain type of unit. For example, a BRDM* may indicate a reconnaissance unit.

Time

Report the time you saw the enemy activity, not the time you report it. Always report local or Zulu times.

Equipment

Report all of the equipment the enemy is wearing or using. If you do not recognize an item of equipment or a type of vehicle, sketch it and submit the sketch with the report.

The following is an example of a SALUTE report:

"Combat OP sighted four enemy tanks moving west along secondary road at grid NB612297 at 241730Z. Tanks traveling at approximately 5 KPH. Hatches were open, and visible enemy personnel were wearing protective masks."

* A Russian vehicle used by reconnaissance units.

PRISONERS OF WAR (PW) AND CAPTURED DOCUMENTS

PWs are a good source of information. They must be handled without breaking international law and without losing a chance to gain intelligence. Treat PWs humanely. Do not harm them either physically or mentally. Do not give them candy, cigarettes, or other comfort items. PWs who receive favors or are mistreated are poor interrogation subjects. In handling PWs, follow the five Ss:

- *Search PWs* as soon as they are captured. Take their weapons and papers, except identification papers and their protective masks. Give them a written receipt for any personal property and documents taken. When searching a PW, have one man guard him while another searches him. A searcher must not get between the guard and a PW. To search a PW, have him spread-eagle against a tree or wall, or get him into a push-up position with his knee on the ground.
- *Segregate PWs* into groups by sex and into subgroups such as officers, enlisted, civilians, and political figures. This keeps the leaders from promoting escape efforts.
- *Silence PWs* and do not let them talk to each other. This keeps them from planning escapes and cautioning each other on security. Report anything a PW says or does.
- *Speed PWs* to the rear. Turn them over to your leader. He will assemble them and move them to the rear for questioning by the S2.
- *Safeguard PWs* when taking them to the rear. Do not let anyone abuse them. Watch out for escape attempts. Do not let PWs bunch up, spread out too far, or start diversions.

Identification
Before evacuating a PW, attach a tag to him showing the date and time of capture, place, capturing unit, and circumstances.

Handling Captured Documents and Equipment
Enemy documents and equipment are good sources of information. Documents may be official (maps, orders, records, photos) or personal (letters, diaries).

If such items are not handled properly, the information in them may become outdated. Give them to your leader quickly. Tag each item with information on when and where it was captured; if it was found on a PW, include the PW's name on the tag.

17

Individual Movement and Security

Use proper movement techniques and security measures to avoid contact with the enemy when you are not prepared for contact.

MOVEMENT SKILLS

Observe the following practices during movement:

- Camouflage yourself and your equipment.
- Tape your dog tags to each other and to the chain to prevent rattle. Tape or pad loose parts of your weapon and equipment so they do not rattle or get snagged. Jump up and down—listen for rattles.
- Do not carry unnecessary equipment.
- Stop, look, and listen before moving. Be especially alert when birds or animals are alarmed (the enemy may be nearby). Look for your next position before leaving a position. Look for covered and concealed routes on which to move.
- Change direction from time to time when moving through tall grass.
- Use battlefield noises to conceal your movement noises.

- Cross roads and trails at places that have the most cover and concealment (large culverts, low spots, curves, or bridges).
- Avoid steep slopes and places with loose dirt or stones.
- Avoid cleared, open areas and tops of hills and ridges.

MOVEMENT METHODS

Low Crawl

The low crawl gives you the lowest silhouette. Use it to cross places where the concealment is very low and enemy observation prevents you from getting up. Keep your body flat against the ground. Grasp your weapon at the upper sling swivel with your firing hand. Let the front handguard rest on your forearm and the weapon butt drag on the ground. Push your arms forward, and pull your firing-side leg forward. Then pull with your arms and push with your leg.

High Crawl

The high crawl lets you move faster and still gives you a low silhouette. Use it when there is good concealment but enemy fire prevents you from getting up. Keep your body off the ground and resting on your forearms and lower legs. Cradle your weapon in your arms, and keep its muzzle off the ground. Alternately advance your right elbow and left knee, then your left elbow and right knee.

Rush

The rush is the fastest way to move from one position to another. Rushes are kept short to keep enemy machine gunners or riflemen from tracking you. Each rush should last from three to five seconds, but don't hit the ground just because five seconds have passed—always have cover picked out before moving for your next rush, and get behind it. If you have been firing from one position, the enemy may have spotted you and may be waiting for you to come up from cover. So before rushing, roll or crawl a short distance from your position.

STEALTH

To move with stealth, use the following procedures:

1. Hold your rifle at port arms (ready position).
2. While stepping, make your footing sure and solid by keeping your body's weight on the leading foot.
3. Raise the moving leg high to clear brush or grass.

4. Gently let the moving foot down toe first, with your body's weight on the rear leg.
5. Lower the heel of the moving foot after the toe is in a solid place.
6. Shift your body's weight and balance to the forward foot before moving the rear foot.
7. Take short steps to help maintain balance.

NIGHT MOVEMENT

When moving through dense vegetation, avoid making noise. Hold your weapon in one hand and keep the other hand forward, feeling for obstructions.

When going into the prone position:
1. Hold your rifle with one hand, and crouch slowly.
2. Feel the ground with your free hand to make sure it is clear of mines, tripwires, or other hazards.
3. Lower your knees one at a time, until your body's weight is on both knees and your free hand.
4. Shift your weight to your free hand and opposite knee.
5. Raise your free leg up and back, and lower it gently to that side.
6. Roll quietly into a prone position.

When crawling at night:
1. Crawl on your hands and knees.
2. Hold your rifle in your firing hand.
3. Use your nonfiring hand to feel for and make clear spots for your hands and knees to move to.
4. Move your hands and knees to those spots, and put them down softly.

FLARES

If you are caught in the light of a ground flare, move quickly out of the lighted area. The enemy knows where the flare is and will be ready to fire into that area. Move well away from the lighted area, and look for other team members. If you hear the firing of an aerial flare while you are moving, hit the ground (behind cover, if possible) while the flare is rising and before it illuminates the area.

The sudden light of a flare may temporarily blind both you and the enemy. To protect your night vision, close one eye while the flare is burning.

If you are caught in the light of an aerial flare and you can easily blend with the background (in a forest), freeze in place until the flare burns out. If caught in the open, immediately crouch low or lie down.

SECURITY MEASURES

The enemy must not get information about your operations. This means that you and your fellow soldiers must do the following:
- Practice camouflage principles and techniques.
- Practice noise and light discipline.
- Practice field sanitation.
- Use proper radiotelephone procedures.
- Use the challenge and password properly.
- Not take personal letters or pictures into combat areas.
- Not keep diaries in combat areas.
- Be careful when discussing military affairs.
- Use only authorized codes.
- Abide by the Code of Conduct.
- Report any soldier or civilian who is believed to be serving or sympathetic with the enemy.
- Report anyone who tries to get information about U.S. operations.
- Destroy all maps or important documents if capture is imminent.

SURVIVAL

Continuous operations and fast-moving battles increase your chances of becoming separated from your unit. Your mission is to rejoin your unit. Survival is the action of staying alive in the field with limited resources. You must survive when you become separated from your unit, are evading the enemy, or are a prisoner.

Evasion

Evasion is the action you take to stay out of the hands of the enemy. There are several courses of action you may take:
- You may stay in your current position and wait for friendly troops to find you. This may be a good course of action if you are sure that friendly troops will continue to operate in the area, and if there are a lot of enemy units in the area.

- You may break out to a friendly area. This may be a good course of action if you know where a friendly area is, and if the enemy is widely dispersed.
- You may move farther into enemy territory to temporarily conduct guerrilla-type operations. This is a short-term course of action to be taken only when other courses of action are not feasible. This may be a good course of action when the enemy area is known to be lightly held or when there is a good chance of linking up with friendly guerrillas.
- You may combine two or more of the above. For example, you may stay in your current area until the enemy moves out of the area and then break out to a friendly area.

Enemy

There may be times when you will have to kill, stun, or capture an enemy soldier without alerting other enemy in the area. At such times, a rifle or pistol makes too much noise, and you will need a silent weapon. Some silent weapons are the bayonet, the garotte (a choke wire or cord with handles), and improvised clubs.

RESISTANCE

The Code of Conduct* is an expression of the ideals and principles that traditionally have guided and strengthened American fighting men. It prescribes the manner in which every soldier of the United States armed forces must conduct himself when captured or faced with the possibility of capture. You should never surrender of your own free will. Likewise, a leader should never surrender the soldiers under his command while they still have the means to resist. If captured, you must continue to resist in every way you can, remembering the following:

- Make every effort to escape and help others to escape.
- Do not accept special favors from the enemy.
- Do not give your word not to escape.
- Do nothing that will harm a fellow prisoner.
- Give no information except name, rank, social security number, and date of birth.
- Do not answer any questions other than those concerning your name, rank, social security number, and date of birth.

* See page 241

ESCAPE

Escape is the action you take to get away from the enemy if you are captured. The best time for you to escape is right after you are captured. You will probably be in your best physical condition at that time. The following are other reasons for making an early escape:

- Friendly fire or air strikes may cause enough confusion and disorder to provide a chance of escape.
- The first guards you have probably will not be as well trained as guards farther back.
- Some of the first guards may be walking wounded who are distracted by their own condition.
- You know something about the area where you are captured and may know the location of nearby friendly units.

The way you escape depends on what you can think of to fit the situation. The only general rules are to escape early and escape when the enemy is distracted.

Once you escape, it may not be easy to contact friendly troops, even when you know where they are. You should contact a friendly unit as you would if you were a member of a lost patrol. Time your movement so that you pass through enemy units at night and arrive at a friendly unit at dawn. A good way to make contact is to find a ditch or shallow hole to hide in where you have cover from both friendly and enemy fire. At dawn, attract the attention of the friendly unit by an action such as waving a white cloth, shouting, or showing a panel. When the friendly unit has been alerted, shout who you are and what your situation is, and ask for permission to move toward the unit.

NIGHT-VISION EQUIPMENT

Poor visibility adds to command and control problems. Modern technology has produced devices that soldiers can use to reduce the effects of limited visibility. Reconnaissance, surveillance, and target acquisition (RSTA) devices available in a Bradley-equipped platoon include the following:

- *AN/PVS-4 Individual Weapon Night-Vision Device.* A small, lightweight, image-intensification device used on the M16A1 rifle. It can also be hand-held. It is a 3.8X telescopic device and has a range of 400 meters in starlight and 600 meters in moonlight.

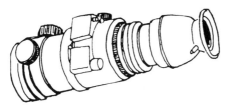

AN/PVS-4.

- *AN/PVS-5 Night-Vision Goggles.* This is both an active and a passive night-vision device worn on the head. It has a built-in infrared light source for close-up viewing within 2 meters. This mode can be used to read maps, orders, and overlays, or for vehicle maintenance. The goggles have a range of 150 meters in the passive mode.

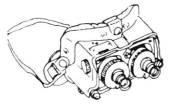

AN/PVS-5.

- *AN/TAS-5 Dragon Thermal Night-Vision Sight.* This is a passive thermal-imagery system with a range of 1,200 meters.

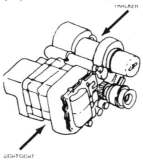

AN/TAS-5.

- *AN/VVS-2 Night-Vision Driver's Viewer.* This image-intensification device is mounted in the Bradley driver's station and has a range in excess of 150 meters. It can observe rounds fired from the 25-millimeter gun and the 7.62-millimeter coaxial machine gun out to greater ranges.

AN/VVS-2.

- *Integrated Sight Unit (ISU).* The ISU is a thermal-imagery sight on the Bradley with 4X and 12X magnification.

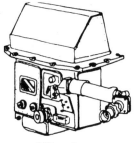

ISU periscope.

CODE OF CONDUCT
FOR MEMBERS OF THE
ARMED FORCES OF THE UNITED STATES

1. I am an American, fighting in the forces which guard my country and our way of life. I am prepared to give my life in their defense.
2. I will never surrender of my own free will. If in command, I will never surrender the members of my command while they still have means to resist.
3. If I am captured I will continue to resist by all means available. I will make every effort to escape and aid others to escape. I will accept neither parole nor special favors from the enemy.
4. If I become a prisoner of war, I will keep faith with my fellow prisoners. I will give no information or take part in any action which might be harmful to my comrades. If I am senior, I will take command. If not, I will obey the lawful order of those appointed over me and will back them up in every way.
5. When questioned, should I become a prisoner of war, I am required to give name, rank, service number, and date of birth. I will evade answering further questions to the utmost of my ability. I will make no oral or written statements disloyal to my country and its allies or harmful to their cause.
6. I will never forget that I am an American, fighting for freedom, responsible for my actions, and dedicated to the principles which made my country free. I will trust in my God and in the United States of America.

18

NBC (Nuclear, Biological, Chemical Warfare)

Avoidance is the most important fundamental of NBC defense. Passive avoidance measures include operations and communication security, dispersion, and hardening units by proper training, equipment, and position improvement.

MARKING CONTAMINATION

When contamination is found, it must be marked to prevent other soldiers from being exposed, and then reported. The only exception to marking an area is if the marking would help the enemy avoid contamination. If this exception is approved by the commander, the contaminated area must still be reported. When marking an area, place the markers facing away from the contamination. Markers are placed at roads, trails, and other likely points of entry.

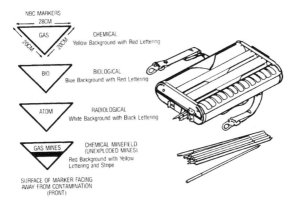

NBC MARKERS

GAS — CHEMICAL
Yellow Background with Red Lettering

BIO — BIOLOGICAL
Blue Background with Red Lettering

ATOM — RADIOLOGICAL
White Background with Black Lettering

GAS MINES — CHEMICAL MINEFIELD
(UNEXPLODED MINES)
Red Background with Yellow Lettering and Stripe

SURFACE OF MARKER FACING
AWAY FROM CONTAMINATION
(FRONT)

NBC contamination marking set.

PASSING ALARMS AND SIGNALS

The vocal alarm for any chemical or biological hazard or attack is the word "gas." The person giving the alarm stops breathing, masks, and shouts "Gas" as loudly as possible. Everyone hearing this immediately masks and passes the alarm.

The first person to hear or see the M8 automatic chemical alarm sound or flash also stops breathing, masks, and yells "Gas."

The all-clear signal is given by word of mouth through the chain of command. The signal is given by leaders after testing for contamination proves negative.

PROTECTING AGAINST NBC ATTACKS

Hardening includes all the things you can do to make yourself more resistant to enemy strikes. Foxholes and bunkers, tanks, and other armored vehicles provide protection. Existing natural and man-made terrain features, such as caves, ditches, ravines, culverts, overpasses, and tunnels, can be used as expedient shelters.

MISSION-ORIENTED PROTECTIVE POSTURE (MOPP)

MOPP is the use of protective clothing and equipment. Wearing MOPP gear can cause heat and mental stress and reduce your efficiency. The leader weighs the needs of individual protection against unit efficiency. Leaders use standard MOPP levels to increase or decrease protection.

MOPP Zero

The protective mask, skin decon kit, and detector papers are carried. The overgarment, overboots, chemical protective helmet cover, and gloves are stowed nearby.

MOPP 1

The overgarment is worn. M9 paper is affixed to the overgarment, and the chemical protective helmet cover is worn.

MOPP 2

Add the overboots to MOPP 1.

MOPP 3

The protective mask and hood are added.

MOPP 4

A pair of rubber gloves and cotton liners are put on. The overgarment is closed, and the hood is pulled down and adjusted.

Mask Only

This is not a MOPP level. Only the mask with hood is worn. All exposed skin must be covered with ordinary clothing.

NUCLEAR ATTACK

An enemy nuclear attack rarely is preceded by a warning. The first indication will be a flash of intense light and heat. Initial radiation comes with the light. Blast and hurricanelike winds follow within seconds. There will be a short time to take action, as follows:

- Drop down immediately in a prone, head-on position.
- Protect your exposed skin areas, especially your eyes, face, neck, and hands, which are vulnerable to injury from the dust, sand, and debris blown by the blast wave. Stay down until the blast wave passes in both directions.
- If you are in a tank or other armored vehicle, brace yourself. Stay buttoned up.
- If you are in a building or other shelter, drop to the floor. Get under a desk or table, and keep out of the way of doors and windows. Broken glass fragments flying through the air are dangerous.

- Get out of a wheeled vehicle. You will be safer lying prone than inside a wheeled vehicle.
- If flying in an aircraft, land. If a suitable landing area is not available or dazzle effects prevent landing, turn the aircraft away from the blast and initiate a full-power climb.

Characteristics of Nuclear Explosions

The following are characteristics of nuclear explosions:

Blast

Blast produces an intense shock wave and high winds that create flying debris. It may collapse shelters and some fighting positions.

Thermal Radiation

Thermal radiation (heat and light) causes burns and starts fires. The bright flash at the time of the explosion can cause a temporary loss of vision or permanent eye damage if you look at the explosion, especially at night.

Nuclear Radiation

Nuclear radiation can cause casualties and delay movements. It may last for days and cover large areas of terrain. It occurs in two stages, initial and residual:

- *Initial radiation* is emitted directly from the fireball in the first minute after the explosion. It travels at the speed of light along straight lines and has high penetrating power.
- *Residual radiation* lingers after the first minute. It comes from the radioactive material originally in a nuclear weapon or from material, such as soil and equipment, made radioactive by the explosion.

EMP

EMP is a massive surge of electrical power. It is created the instant a nuclear detonation occurs and is transmitted at the speed of light in all directions. It can damage solid-state components of electrical equipment (radios, radars, etc.). Equipment can be protected by disconnecting it from its power source and placing it in or behind some type of shielding material (armored vehicle or dirt wall) out of the line of sight to the explosion. If no warning is received prior to a burst, there is no effective means of protecting operating equipment.

Effects on Soldiers

Exposure of the human body to nuclear radiation causes damage to the cells in all parts of the body. The damage is the cause of "radiation sickness." The early symptoms of radiation sickness will usually appear one to six hours after exposure. These symptoms may include headache, nausea, vomiting, and diarrhea. There is no first aid for you once you have been exposed to nuclear radiation. The only help is to get as comfortable as possible while undergoing the early symptoms. If the radiation dose was small, the symptoms will probably go away and not recur. If the symptoms recur, go to an aid station.

Effects on Equipment and Supplies

Blast can crush sealed or partly sealed objects such as food cans, barrels, fuel tanks, and helicopters. Rubble from crumbling buildings can bury supplies and equipment. Heat can ignite dry wood, fuel, tarps, and other flammable material. Nuclear radiation can contaminate food and water.

Post-strike Actions

Take the following actions after a nuclear explosion:
- Assess the situation—how to repair and reinforce your position, assist casualties, improve protection against fallout.
- Put out fires before they can spread.
- Check weapons systems—they may be unserviceable because of sand or dirt blown into them. Field stripping and cleaning may be required before firing.
- Cover foxholes and shelter openings against fallout (shelter half will do).
- MOPP gear will keep fallout off your skin and out of your body.

CHEMICAL AND BIOLOGICAL WEAPONS

Enemy forces have both chemical and biological weapons. These weapons may be used separately or together, with or without nuclear weapons. Regardless of how they are used, you must be able to survive an attack.

Characteristics

Chemical agents are like poisonous pesticides but are far more powerful. They are meant to kill or injure you and are released to cover large areas. They may be released as gases, liquids, or sprays. The enemy may use a mixture of agents to cause confusion and casualties. Artillery, rockets, mortars, aircraft bombs, and land mines can deliver the agents.

Biological agents are disease-producing germs. They create a disease hazard where none exists naturally. They may be dispersed as sprays by generators or delivered by explosives, bomblets, missiles, or aircraft. They may also be spread by the release of germ-carrying flies, mosquitoes, fleas, and ticks. The U.S. Army does not employ these agents, but other armies may.

Toxins are poisonous substances produced by living things (such as snake venom). Toxins are not living things, and in this sense they are chemicals. They would be used in combat in the same way as chemical-warfare agents, and they may disable or kill without warning.

Effects on Equipment

Chemical and biological agents have little direct effect on equipment. Liquid chemical agents can restrict the use of equipment until it is decontaminated.

Effects on Terrain

Liquid agents may restrict the use of buildings. Because it is difficult to decontaminate terrain, it is best to wait for the weather to decontaminate terrain naturally. Bypass contaminated areas if not wearing protective clothing.

Effects on Soldiers

Chemical and biological agents may enter your body through your eyes, nose, mouth, or skin. They can disable or kill.

Liquid agents may be dispersed on you, your equipment, the terrain, and foliage. The agents may linger for days and endanger you when you are unprotected.

Biological agents are hard to detect in the early stages of use. If you find out or suspect that the enemy is using biological agents, report it to your leader.

Decontamination

Chemical-agent decontamination of soldiers and individual equipment is accomplished using the M258A1 decontaminating kit. Instructions for its use are printed on the container. This kit is especially made for skin decontamination, but you may use it to decontaminate some personal equipment.

Unit equipment is decontaminated with DS2 decontaminating solution, soapy water, solvents, or slurry. Decontaminate optical instruments by blotting them with rags, wiping with lens-cleaning solvent, and then letting dry.

Biological-agent decontamination of your body is done by showering with soap and hot water. Use germicidal soap if available. Wash contaminated clothing in hot, soapy water if you cannot send it to a field laundry.

19

Radio Sets, Procedures, and Field Antennas

Radios, a common means of communications, are particularly suited for use when you are on the move. Small handheld or backpack radios that communicate for only short distances are found at squad and platoon level. As the need grows to talk over greater distances and to more units, the size and complexity of radios increase.

ENVIRONMENT

Factors that affect the range of radios are weather, terrain, power, antenna, and the location of the radio. Man-made objects such as bridges and buildings may affect radio transmission. Interference may also come from power lines, electrical generators, bad weather, other radio stations, and enemy jamming. You can correct many of the causes of poor radio communications by using common sense. For example, make sure you are not trying to communicate from under a steel bridge.

RULES FOR RADIO USE

Observe the following rules for radio use:
- Listen before transmitting.
- Avoid excessive radio checks.
- Make messages clear and concise. If possible, write them out before transmitting.
- Speak clearly, slowly, and in natural phrases, and enunciate each word. If receiving operator must write, allow time for writing.
- Always assume the enemy is listening.
- If jammed, notify higher headquarters by established procedures.
- Maintain whip antennas in a vertical position.
- Make sure radio is turned off before starting vehicle.

PROWORDS

The following are frequently used prowords:

ALL AFTER—Part of the message to which I refer is all of that which follows.

ALL BEFORE—Part of the message to which I refer is all of that which precedes.

AUTHENTICATE—Station called is to reply to the challenge that follows.

AUTHENTICATION IS—Transmission authentication of this message is.

BREAK—Indicates the separation of text from other parts of the message.

CORRECT—What you have transmitted is correct.

CORRECTION—Error has been made in this transmission. Transmission will continue with the last word correctly transmitted.

I READ BACK—The following is my response to your instructions to read back.

I SAY AGAIN—I am repeating transmission or part indicated.

I SPELL—I shall spell the next word phonetically.

OUT—This is the end of my transmission to you and no answer is required.

OVER—This is the end of my transmission to you and a response is necessary. Go ahead: transmit.

READ BACK—Repeat this entire transmission back to me exactly as received.

ROGER—Have received your last message satisfactorily.

SAY AGAIN—Say again all of your last transmission.

SILENCE—Cease transmission on this net immediately. (If repeated three or more times, silence will be maintained until lifted.)

SILENCE LIFTED—Silence is lifted (when an authentication system is in force, the transmission imposing and lifting silence is to be authenticated).

SPEAK SLOWER—You are transmitting too fast—slow down.

WAIT—I must pause for a few seconds.

WAIT, OUT—I must pause longer than a few seconds.

WILCO—Have received your last message, understand it, and will comply.

SECURITY

Radio is one of the least secure means of communicating. Each time you talk, your voice travels in all directions. The enemy can listen to your transmissions to get information about you and your unit, or to locate your position to destroy you with artillery fire. Communications security keeps unauthorized persons from gaining information of value from radio and telephone transmissions. It includes the following:

- Using authentication to make sure that the other communicating station is a friendly one.
- Using only approved codes.
- Designating periods when all radios are turned off.
- Restricting the use of radio transmitters and monitoring radio receivers.
- Operating radios on low power.
- Enforcing net discipline and radiotelephone procedure (all stations must use authorized prosigns and prowords, and must transmit official traffic only).
- Using radio sites with hills or other shields between them and the enemy.
- Using directional antennas when feasible.

RADIO SETS AND RECEIVER-TRANSMITTERS
Radio Sets AN/VRC-12, -46, -47, and -49

These radio sets provide short range, two-way, frequency-modulated (FM), radiotelephone communication between vehicles or crew-served weapons. They provide the fast and flexible means of communication necessary in combat operations. Installation kits, provided for specific vehicles, include control boxes, cables, and audio accessories necessary for extending the use of the particular set to various crew members and for furnishing intercommunication facilities.

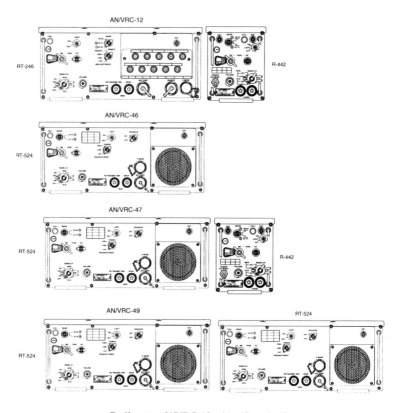

Radio sets AN/VRC-12, -46, -47, and -49.

Receiver-Transmitter, Radio RT-246/VRC, and Receiver-Transmitter, Radio RT-524/VRC

General

These receiver-transmitters are frequency-modulated. They are identical, except that the RT-246 has ten preset channels while the RT-524 has none, and the RT-524 has a built-in speaker.

Characteristics and Capabilities

- Frequency range: 30.00–75.95 MHz.
- Type of signals: voice.
- Preset frequencies: ten (RT-246 only).
- Transmission planning range: moving, 15 miles (24 kilometers); stationary, 20 miles (32 kilometers).
- Type of operation: push-to-talk.

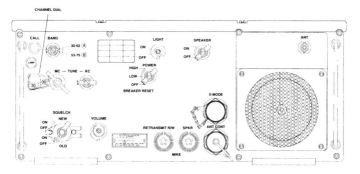

Receiver-transmitter RT-524/VRC control panel.

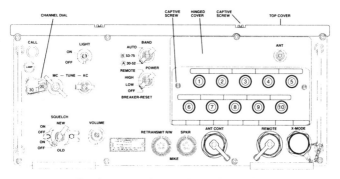

Receiver-transmitter, radio RT-246/VRC.

- Type of control: local or remote.
- Antenna: center-fed whip.
- Number of channels: 920.
- Types of squelch: noise and tone operated.
- Pertinent publication: TM 11-5820-401-10, as changed.

Receiver, Radio R-442/VRC
General

The frequency-modulated receiver, radio R-442/VRC, is used in conjunction with the receiver-transmitter RT-246 or RT-524. This receiver gives the operator a facility for monitoring a frequency in addition to a frequency tuned on the receiver-transmitter. It is common practice for a commander to tune the RT-246 to his own command net and to monitor the next higher headquarters command net on the R-442.

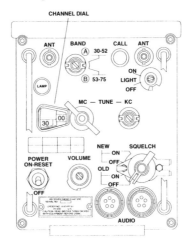

Receiver R-442/VRC control panel.

Characteristics and Capabilities

- Frequency range: 30.00–75.95 MHz.
- Type of signals: voice.
- Preset frequencies: none.
- Antenna: multisection whip.
- Types of squelch: noise and tone operated.
- Pertinent publication: TM 11-5820-401-10, as changed.

Radio Set AN/VRC-12
General

A receiver-transmitter RT-246, a receiver R-442, and an antenna AS-1729 or AT-912 are components of radio set AN/VRC-12. Listed below are the steps necessary to place this set in operation.

Operating Instructions

- Connect audio accessories to control, intercommunication set C-2298/VRC.
- Place the monitor switch in the ALL position.
- Adjust the VOLUME on the control, intercommunication set C-2298/VRC (final adjustment is made at the discretion of the operator).
- Turn the MAIN PWR switch on the amplifier AM-1780/VRC to the NORM position.
- Set the POWER CKT BKR switch to ON.
- If all crew members are to operate the receiver-transmitter, turn the RADIO TRANS switch to CDR & CREW.
- Turn the POWER switch on the receiver-transmitter RT-246 to the LOW position.
- Adjust the VOLUME control on the RT-246 to MAXIMUM.
- If manual tuning is to be used: Turn the BAND switch to A or B, depending on the frequency desired; turn the MC-TUNE and KC-TUNE knobs until the desired frequency appears on the channel dial.
- If pushbutton tuning is to be used: Turn the BAND switch to AUTO; push in the pushbutton for the desired frequency. *Note:* Presetting frequencies is a maintenance function.
- Squelch. The accompanying chart describes the function of the SQUELCH switch and the type of communication provided in each of the four positions. *Note:* Do not move the locking bar that separates the two sectors of the switch. This is a maintenance function.

Position	Transmit To	Receive From
	Tone Activated (New Series)	Tone Activated (New Series)
ON		
	Noise Activated (Old Series)	
NEW		
	Tone Activated (New Series)	Tone Activated (New Series)
OFF		
	Noise Activated (Old Series)	Noise Activated (Old Series)
	Noise Activated (Old Series)	Noise Activated (Old Series)
ON		
	(*)	Tone Activated (New Series)
OLD		
	Noise Activated (Old Series)	Noise Activated (Old Series)
OFF		
	Tone Activated (New Series)	Tone Activated (New Series)

* Transmission to other New Series Radios is only possible if the New Series Radios receiving the transmission are not in the New ON position. Primary consideration when using Old Series Radios in the same net with New Series Radios is that the New Series Radios must be in the Old OFF or ON position.

- Set the POWER switch to REMOTE if you desire to control power and frequency selection from control, frequency selector C-2742/VRC.
- Turn the POWER switch on the receiver R-442/VRC to ON-RESET.
- Adjust the VOLUME control on the R-442/VRC to MAXI-MUM.
- Turn the BAND switch to A or B, depending on the frequency desired.
- Turn the MC-TUNE and KC-TUNE knobs until the desired frequency appears on the channel dial.
- Turn the SQUELCH switch to ON (see above).

NEW RADIOS

- *AN/PRC-119 SINCGARS.* Fielding of SINCGARS equipment began in 1988 and is ongoing. It replaces the PRC 77, AN/VRC-12, -46, -47, and -49 radio sets. It operates in the frequency range of 30.00 to 87.975 MHz with 2320 channels and weighs 18.3 pounds with battery.

- *AN/PRC-126 VHF FM Radio Set.* This equipment was fielded in 1989–90 as the squad radio (small-unit radio), replacing the PRT-4/PRR-9 and the PRC 68. It operates in the same range as the PRC-119, with a short-range transmission of 500 meters (short antenna) and 3 kilometers (long antenna). The PRC 126 weighs 2.8 pounds with battery.

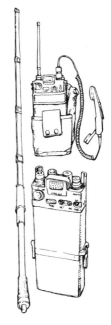

AN/PRC-126 VHF FM radio.

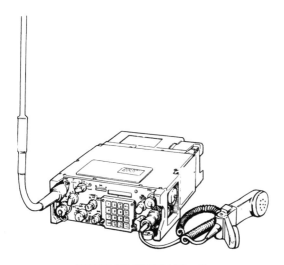

AN/PRC-119 SINCGARS radio.

FIELD EXPEDIENT ANTENNAS

Expedient antennas are temporary antennas designed and constructed by the user to increase the range of tactical radio sets. Antennas that are components of tactical radio sets are, for the most part, vertical antennas, resulting in the signal being radiated equally in all directions. Expedient antennas increase the operating range of a given radio set, providing increased efficiency through the use of an antenna specifically designed for the operating frequency in use, elevation of the antenna above the ground, or concentrating the radiated signal along a given direction. Field expedient antennas are easily constructed from field wire using poles on trees for support. Whatever antenna is used, remember that the most important considerations are site location and location of the radio set. Before deciding to construct a field expedient, other considerations or operating hints that may improve communications are as follows:

- Use a headset to receive weak signals.
- Speak slowly and distinctly directly into the microphone or handset.
- Use an RC-292 antenna, if available.
- Use CW in place of voice for increased range on AM radios.

General

Steel wires should be clipped off, leaving only the copper wires. The copper wires are twisted together and placed into the center hole of the aux antenna connector, or the antenna connector, making sure the wires do not touch any other part of the radio set.

If the whip antenna of your radio becomes damaged, try a piece of communication wire tied to a broomstick or a tree limb. Insert the end of the wire in the antenna connector. If you then hold the stick or limb in a vertical position, you should be able to communicate. It will not be as effective as it would have been with the whip antenna, but this antenna is definitely better than no antenna at all.

Vertical Antennas

Vertical field expedient antennas improve radio set performance by virtue of height above the ground. The most effective height above the ground is equal to one-half wavelength of the operating frequency in meters. Elevation above this height requires ground plane elements.

Improvised Whip Antenna

Whip antennas may become broken during use, with no replacement antenna readily available. If this should happen, it is possible to improvise a satisfactory replacement by using telephone cable WD-1/TT or by lashing the broken antenna pieces together.

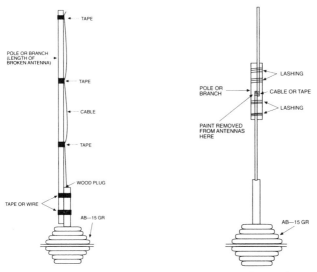

Emergency repair of whip antenna using field wire WD-1/TT.

Emergency repair of whip antenna using broken antenna sections.

Patrol Antenna

The patrol antenna is used primarily with FM radios. It is used extensively in heavily wooded areas with the portable radio set AN/PRC-77 to increase line-of-sight communications. Antenna performance increases with height above the ground up to 13 meters.

Length in meters . . . . ½ wavelength of operating frequency
Height . . . . Variable (lead-in not over 13 meters)
Radiation . . . . 360 degrees

Bent Bamboo Antenna

The bent bamboo antenna is a variation of the patrol antenna using different construction materials.

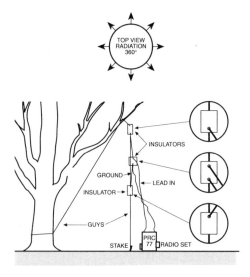

Patrol antenna. To determine length of antenna in meters, divide 142.5 by your operating frequency. Example: Constant = 142.5 divided by op. freq. 45.0 = 3.17 meters. OR, constant = 468 divided by op. freq. 45.0 = 10.4 feet.

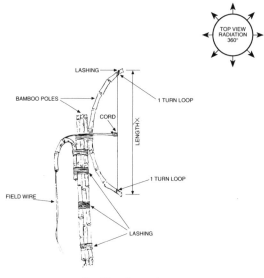

Bent bamboo antenna.

Ground Plane Antenna

The ground plane antenna is used with FM radios. It is used in place of the Antenna Equipment RC-292 when such an antenna is not available. The length of the antenna elements listed below may be used for all frequencies of the VRC-12 family radios.

Length . . . . Antenna Element—2 meters
Ground Plane Elements—2½ meters
Range . . . . Under most conditions will increase the range of the set
Radiation . . . . 360 degrees

Note: Portions of the RC-292 may be used to construct a modified version of this field expedient antenna. Only the vertical element, antenna base, ground plane elements, and lead-in cord are needed. The antenna may be erected by fastening insulator material to the top of the vertical elements, attaching a guy rope, and pulling the assembled elements up in a tree.

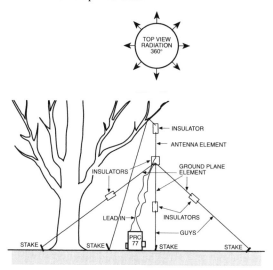

Ground plane antenna.

Horizontal Antennas

When the situation does not require mobility and the antenna group RC-292 is not available, you can get greater distance by using the long-wire horizontal antenna. The physical length in meters of one wavelength for a given operating frequency can be computed as follows:

$$\text{length (meters)} = \frac{285}{\text{operating freq (MHz)}}$$

All horizontal antennas described here are fed by connecting the receiver-transmitter to one end of the antenna. Antenna efficiency can be estimated by use of the following table.

Antenna Efficiency. Using WD-1 Field Wire and the VRC-12 family radios:

Antenna Length (wavelengths)	Power Gain Factor
1	1.2
2	1.4
4	2.1
6	3.1
8	4.3

Note: Due to technical characteristics, antenna efficiency begins to decrease when antenna length exceeds eight wavelengths.

Radiation Patterns

In a half-wavelength antenna, maximum radiation occurs in the two directions that are at right angles to the antenna itself with no radiation off the ends. The direction of maximum radiation moves closer to the direction of the antenna itself as the length of the antenna increases.

The radiation patterns can be modified to make them more directional through the use of a resistor connected to one end of the antenna. The antenna may be made of WD-1/TT wire and the resistor fashioned from the carbon pole in a flashlight battery. The radio should be connected to one end of the antenna with the resistor connected between the opposite end and the ground. The antenna must be a minimum of two wavelengths of the transmitting frequency. Maximum signal is radiated off the end of the antenna toward the resistor, and it tends to reject or reduce signals from other directions. The directivity is of value for anti-jamming and other communications security considerations.

A suspended antenna causes considerable pull on the radio set at the connection. Difficulty may be experienced in keeping the antenna

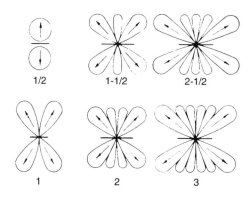

Radiation patterns for H- to 3-wavelength antennas.

connected to the binding post. One method of overcoming the difficulty is as follows: Remove the regular whip antenna from the mounting base. Place in the mounting base a broken stub, which most surely will be available. Drill a hole through the broken stub, push the end of the antenna through the hole, and tie the antenna to the stub. The connection to the radio set is already on the stub. This expedient will keep the weight of the wire from pulling the wire away from the binding post. Be sure to remove the paint from the area on the stub where the antenna is connected.

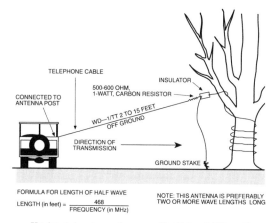

Horizontal antenna for use with AM and FM radios.

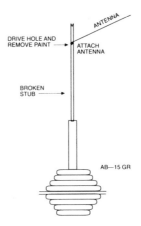

Expedient method of connecting a horizontal antenna.

Long-Wire Antenna

The long-wire antenna is used with both AM and FM radios to increase the range. It is normally used in open terrain where installation can be accomplished with ease.

Length . . . .   5 or 7 wavelengths of operating frequency
Height . . . .   3 meters
Range . . . .   Up to 2 to 3 times the operating range of set
Resistor . . . .   400–700 ohms
Radiation . . . .   Without resistor—From both ends
                                 With resistor—Off resistor end only

Long-wire antenna.

Vertical Half-Rhombic Antenna

The vertical half-rhombic antenna has the advantage of being smaller in physical size than the horizontal antenna and requires only one pole for construction. It can be made directional with the use of a resistor. The principal disadvantage is that if the angle between the antenna wire and surface of the earth is too small, the signal will be radiated at an upward angle that may be above the intended receiver. A typical vertical half-rhombic antenna consists of 100 feet of field wire WD-1/TT, erected over a single 30-foot support base. One leg of the antenna terminates at the resistor; the other end is connected from the insulator to the radio by a 5-foot lead-in wire.

Length. . . . .   2 wavelengths of operating frequency, with a 5-foot lead-in

Height . . . .   20 meters

Range . . . .   Up to 2 to 3 times operating range of set

Resistor . . . .   400–700 ohms

Radiation. . . . .   Without resistor—Equally off both ends

With resistor—Off resistor end only

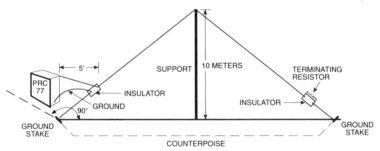

Vertical half-rhombic antenna.

Note: A counterpoise is used as an additional ground in everyday climate. When the counterpoise is used, it is placed on top of the ground and is installed from one ground stake to the other, and then to the battery case clip. If the counterpoise is not used, the ground lead-in is connected from the ground stake to the battery case clip. The insulators and the resistor are installed approximately knee high.

Doublet Antenna

The doublet antenna is primarily used with low-powered high-frequency AM or SSB radios. It is used in place of the radio's organic antennas to increase the range.

Length. . . . .   ½ wavelength of operating frequency
Height . . . .   Variable
Range . . . .   Up to 2 to 3 times operating range of set
Radiation. . . . .   Off broad side of antenna

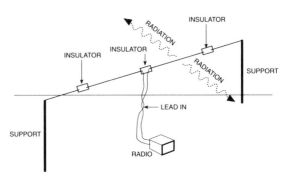

Doublet antenna.

20

Field Expedient Antiarmor Devices

There are many weapons you can use to destroy a tank or an armored personnel carrier. The weapons most frequently used are the LAW, Dragon, TOW, mines, and high-explosive, dual-purpose rounds of the M203 grenade launcher. There may be times, however, when you will not have these weapons available. In such cases, you may have to use field expedient devices. In order to construct some of these devices, you must know how to prime charges, electrically and nonelectrically.

FLAME DEVICES
Flame devices are used to obscure the vision of a vehicle's crew and to set the vehicle afire.

Molotov Cocktail
A Molotov cocktail is made with a breakable container (usually a bottle), a gas and oil mixture, and a cloth wick. To construct it, fill the container with the mixture, and then insert the cloth wick into the container. The wick must extend both into the mixture and out of the bottle. Light the

wick before throwing the container. When the container hits the vehicle and breaks, the mixture will ignite, burning both the vehicle and the personnel around it.

Eagle Fireball

An eagle fireball is made with an ammunition can, a gas and oil mixture, a white phosphorus grenade wrapped with detonating cord, tape, a nonelectric blasting cap, a fuse igniter, and a grapnel (or rope with bent nails).

To construct an eagle fireball, fill the ammunition can with the mixture. Wrap the grenade with detonating cord, and attach a nonelectric firing system to the end of the detonating cord. Place the grenade inside the can with the time fuse extending out. Make a slot in the can's lid for the fuse to pass through when the lid is closed. If available, attach a rope with bent nails or a grapnel to the can. When you throw the can onto a vehicle, the bent nails or the grapnel will help hold the can there. Before throwing the can, fire the fuse igniter.

Molotov cocktail.

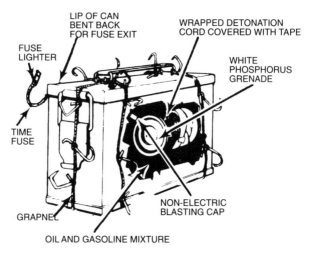

Eagle fireball.

Eagle Cocktail

An eagle cocktail is made of a plastic or rubberized bag (a waterproof bag or a sandbag lined with a poncho), a gas and oil mixture, a smoke grenade, a thermite grenade, tape, string, and communications wire or cord.

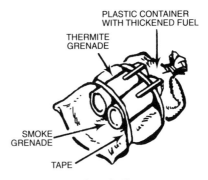

Eagle cocktail.

To construct an eagle cocktail, fill the bag with the mixture. Seal the bag by twisting its end and then taping or tying it. Attach the thermite and the smoke grenades to the bag using tape, string, or communications wire. When attaching the grenades, do not bind the safety levers on the grenades. Tie a piece of string or cord to the safety pins of the grenades. Before throwing the eagle cocktail, pull the safety pins in both grenades.

EXPLOSIVE DEVICES

Towed Charge

A towed charge is made of rope or communications wire, mines or blocks of explosives, electrical blasting caps, tape, and electrical firing wire.

To construct a towed charge, link a series of armed antitank mines together with a rope or communications wire. If mines are not available, use about 25 to 50 pounds of explosives attached on a board (sled charge). Anchor one end of the rope on one side of the road, and run its other end to a safe position from which the charge may be pulled onto the road. Attach an electric firing system to each mine (or to the explosive), and connect those systems to the firing wire. Tape the firing wire to the rope running to the position from which the charge is pulled onto the road. At that position, conduct a circuit check, and then connect the firing wire to a blasting machine.

Just before a vehicle reaches the site of the towed charge, pull the charge onto the road so that it will be run over by the vehicle. When the vehicle is over it, fire the charge.

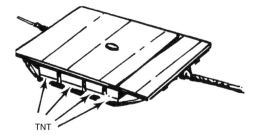

Towed charge.

Pole Charge

A pole charge is made of explosives (TNT or C4), nonelectric blasting caps, time fuse, detonating cord, tape, string or wire, fuse igniters, and a pole long enough for the mission. Prime the desired amount of explosives with two nonelectric firing systems, and attach the explosives to a board or some other flat material. The amount of explosives you use depends on the target to be destroyed. Tie or tape the board with the explosives to the pole. The time fuse should be only about 6 inches long. Before putting a pole charge on a target, fire the fuse igniters.

Some good places to put a pole charge on a vehicle are under the turret, over the engine compartment, in the suspension system, and in the main gun tube (if the charge is made small enough to fit in the tube).

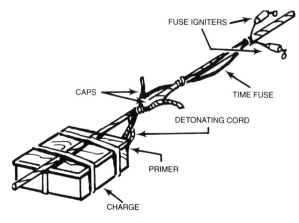

Pole charge.

Satchel Charge

A satchel charge is made of explosives (TNT or C4), nonelectric blasting caps, time fuse, detonating cord, tape, fuse igniters, and some type of satchel. The satchel can be an empty sandbag, a demolitions bag, or other material. To construct the device, fill the satchel with the amount of explosives needed for the mission. Prime the explosives with two nonelectric firing systems. Use only about 6 inches of time fuse. Seal the satchel with string, rope, or tape, and leave the time fuse and igniters hanging out of the satchel. Before throwing a satchel charge onto a target, fire the fuse igniters.

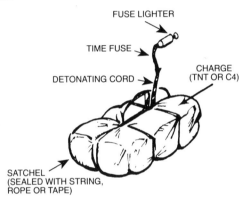

FUSE LIGHTER

TIME FUSE

DETONATING CORD

CHARGE (TNT OR C4)

SATCHEL (SEALED WITH STRING, ROPE OR TAPE)

Satchel charge.

WEAK POINTS OF ARMORED VEHICLES

To use expedient devices, you must know the weak points of armored vehicles. The following are some of the common weak points:

- The suspension system.
- The fuel tanks.
- The ammunition storage compartments.
- The engine compartment.
- The turret ring.
- The armor on the sides, top, and rear (normally not as thick as that on the front).

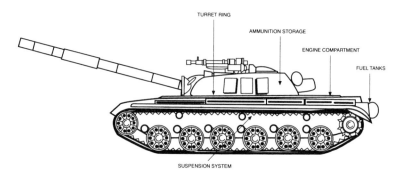

Weak points of armored vehicles.

BUTTONED-UP ARMORED VEHICLES

If an armored vehicle is "buttoned-up" and you have no antiarmor weapons, fire your rifle at the vision blocks, at any optical equipment mounted outside the vehicle, into the engine compartment, at any external fuel tanks, or at the hatches. That will not destroy the vehicle but may hinder its ability to fight.

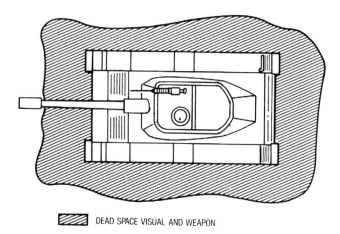

DEAD SPACE VISUAL AND WEAPON

Dead space.

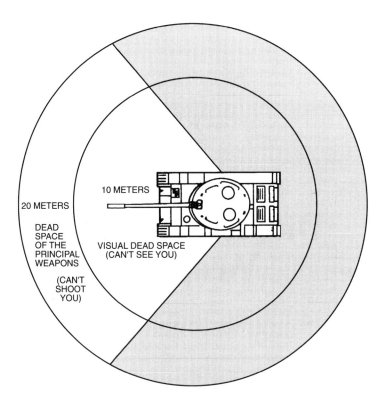

PRINCIPAL DIRECTION OF FIRE AND OBSERVATION
(When turret is to the front and the hatches closed)

MOST FAVORABLE DIRECTION OF ATTACK
(When turret is to the front)

Dead space, 10 meters and 20 meters.

21

Directed-Energy Weapons

This chapter introduces directed-energy weapons (DEW) and gives an overview of how to defend against them. These new weapons are radically different in operation and effect from any other weapon in use. They include lasers, microwave radiation emitters, and particle beam generators. Weapon prototypes have been developed using laser and microwave radiation emitter technology.

CHARACTERISTICS

The following are characteristics of DEW:
- DE (directed energy) is another line-of-sight, direct-fire device. Directed-energy weapons rely upon subatomic particles or electromagnetic waves that impact at or near the speed of light. The time of flight to the target, then, is essentially zero.
- Laser weapons produce intense heat and light on a target; these can burn out optics and blind their operators.
- High-power microwave weapons can burn out electrical systems and components or create an electrical upset.

- A DEW gunner is not required to lead a target, and traditional resupply problems are nonexistent.
- DE weapons attack armored vehicles at their most vulnerable points: their "eyes" (optics) and soft electronics.

LASER WEAPONS

The most vulnerable targets of laser weapons are optics, specifically vehicle sights and sighting systems. The two general categories of optical devices on the battlefield today are the *direct-view devices* and the *electro-optical devices.*

In addition to eyeglasses, contact lenses, and sun-wind-dust goggles, direct-view devices include the following magnifying devices: binoculars; Dragon daysight (X6); daysight (ISU, X4, and X12); backup sight (X4); M60 series tank sights; and M1 series tank sights (105 series telescopes and .50-caliber sights).

Electro-optical devices include image intensifiers—AN/PVS 4, AN/PVS 5, and AN/VVS 2 (driver's night viewer); thermal devices— thermal night sight (ISU), Dragon night sight, and tank thermal sight (TTS); and infrared devices—infrared TOW tracker and infrared Dragon tracker.

Direct-View Optics

A laser weapon targeted on see-through optics will cause damage to the eyes of the operator. The beam passes through the optical device to the eye and burns it, causing either temporary loss of vision (dazzle) or permanent blindness. When the optical device has a magnifying capability, the beam strength is magnified and causes even greater injury to the eye.

Electro-Optics

A laser weapon attacks optics that are not see-through by burning the sensor or reticle inside the device. Some of the electrical circuits inside the device may also be damaged by the heat surge, which does not, however, have any effect on the operator.

Personal Injury

Even when not using optical devices, soldiers are susceptible to laser weapons. Laser energy from friendly or enemy systems can cause temporary or permanent damage to the naked, unprotected eye. Laser weapons have a greater effect in darkness than in daylight because the eye is more sensitive to light at night.

Protective Equipment
Protective spectacles, filters, and lenses are being fielded to protect soldiers and optics against lasers.

MICROWAVE WEAPONS
High-powered microwave weapons cause electronic "kills" or electrical upset in electronic equipment. These weapons are effective against command posts, sensors, radar, computers, optical devices, fusing, engines, and a whole variety of electronic communications that use transistors or integrated circuits.

TACTICAL CONSIDERATIONS
With directed energy weapons, an additional direct-fire system now exists that can injure soldiers or damage equipment, but this fact does not change the nature of tactics. Standard defensive techniques employed against any direct-fire weapon will provide equal or better protection against personal injury from directed energy weapons because such weapons have no bursting radius. You should observe the following defensive techniques:
- Use terrain for cover and concealment.
- Use weather (fog and rain).
- Use smoke to conceal movement.
- Use artillery, mortars, and direct-fire weapons to suppress known or suspected locations of DE weapons.
- Use shoot-and-move tactics to prevent friendly positions from being pinpointed.

Equipment Preparation
Observe the following tactics for preparing equipment:
- Position vehicles and weapons in covered and concealed locations to minimize exposure of glass surfaces to the enemy.
- Cover or shield external glass surfaces until needed. Tape, canvas, empty sandbags, or other materials can be used as covers.

- Open optical protective doors only during required observation or when engaging targets.
- Use a minimum number of optical or electro-optical devices to search for the enemy; protect the rest until they are required for firing weapons.
- Tubular extensions may be fabricated for objective lenses. These decrease detection except from almost head-on.

Soldier Preparation

Prepare soldiers by doing the following:

- Train soldiers to know when they have been engaged by DE weapons and what action they can take, e.g., switching from damaged electro-optical devices to direct-view devices while using laser-protective spectacles.
- Conduct first-aid classes to prepare soldiers to aid injured buddies.
- Teach soldiers that wounds caused by a laser or other direct-fire weapon system occur in the absence of noise and that the device will probably leave no detectable signature. Although laser burns on the retina do not produce pain, they do cause dark spots in the soldier's vision.
- Train soldiers to wear their protective spectacles whenever they are outside their vehicles, outside their foxholes, or looking out from their foxholes.

APPENDIX A
NATO Armored Vehicles

Chieftain—British
Large shallow turret with long, sloping front.
Long gun tube with bore evacuator in center.
High, flat engine decks.
6 road wheels with skirting plates covering support rollers.

Centurion—British
Large square turret.
Bore evacuator ⅔ down from muzzle.
6 road wheels with skirting plates covering support rollers.

AMX30—French
Large squat turret.
Long gun tube, no bore evacuator.
Flat engine decks.
5 road wheels with support rollers.

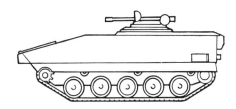

AMX10—French
Large cupola set to the left.
Long thin gun (20mm).
Flat hull with long, sloping front plate.
5 road wheels with support rollers.

Leopard—German
Large rounded flat turret.
Bore evacuator ⅔ from muzzle.
Long sloping-sided hull with horizontal exhaust louvres at rear.
7 road wheels with support rollers.

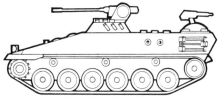

Marder—German
Small turret placed centrally on hull.
Gun mounted on turret.
Long hull with inward-sloping sides, domed cupola at rear.
6 road wheels with support rollers.

M551—United States
Turtle-shaped turret.
Long front slope, square-sided hull.
Short, stubby gun tube.
5 large road wheels, no support rollers.

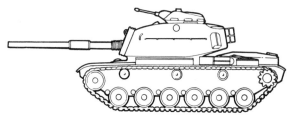

M60—United States
High rear deck.
Tortoise-shell-shaped turret.
6 road wheels with 3 support rollers.
Prominent cupola.

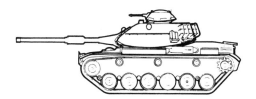

M60A1—United States
Wedge-shaped turret.
Bore evacuator ⅓ down from muzzle, no blast deflector.
6 road wheels with support rollers.

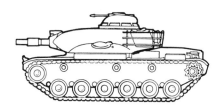

M60A2—United States
Long, narrow, and square-sided turret.
Short, stubby gun tube.
6 road wheels with support rollers.

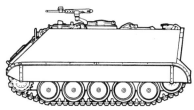

M113—United States
.50 cal mg, pintle mounted.
Rectangular, box-shaped hull.
Track—5 road wheels, no support rollers.

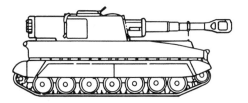

M109A1SP—United States
Long gun tube.
7 evenly spaced road wheels.
Large, boxy turret mounted rear of center.

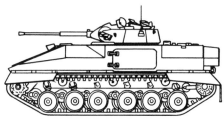

MCV 80—British
High rear deck.
Small, shallow turret.
Flat engine decks.
6 road wheels.

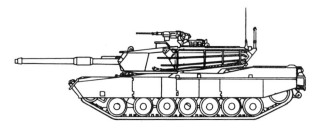

M1 Abrams—United States
Low, boxy.
Low turret—no cupola.
7 road wheels covered with skirt.

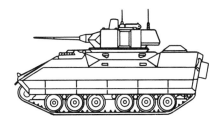

M2 Bradley—United States
High profile.
Distinctive turret in center with tow launcher on left side.
6 road wheels, space between 3rd and 4th road wheel.
Skirt over road wheels.

APPENDIX B
Former Soviet Union Vehicles

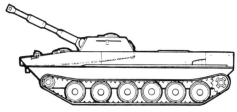

PT 76
Cone-shaped turret set well forward.
Short gun with evacuator at center, muzzle brake at end.
Wide, long, and square hull.
Narrow back, 6 road wheels, no support rollers.

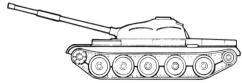

T62
Smooth, round (pear-shaped) turret.
Long gun with evacuator ⅓ down from muzzle.
Flat engine deck.
5 road wheels, with large gaps between #3, #4, #5, no support rollers.

T72
Turret centrally mounted on chassis.
Support rollers and 6 road wheels.
V-shaped mud deflector on front slope.
IR searchlight mounted to left of gun tube.

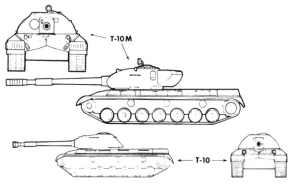

T-10
Turret round well forward, well sloped.
Long gun tube, bore evacuator near end of muzzle break.
Hull, narrow; splash guard, wide.
7 road wheels, 3 support rollers.

ZSU 23-4
Shallow and square-sided turret.
4 antiaircraft guns.
Square-sided hull.
6 road wheels, no support rollers.

ZSU 57-2
Large, square, and open-topped turret.
Twin tapering barrels with slotted muzzle brake.
4 road wheels, no support rollers.

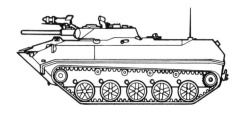

BMD
Same turret and armament as BMP.
Driver's hatch centered below main gun.
5 road wheels, 4 support rollers.
Found with airborne units.

BMP
Circular and cone-shaped turret.
Short gun with missile mounted above.
Low, wide hull.
6 road wheels with support rollers.

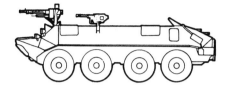

BTR 60P
May have small turret.
MG toward front.
Large, boatlike hull with sharp square nose.
Wheeled—4 large wheels each side.

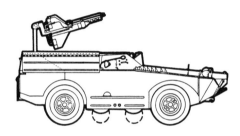

BRDM
No turret.
Armament may vary from pintle-mounted machine gun to anti-tank missiles.
Long, sloping hood and raised troop compartment.
4 wheels.

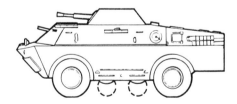

BRDM-2
Small, cone-shaped turret, centered on hull.
MG mounted in turret.
Square-shaped hull with distinct undercut at nose.
Wheeled—2 each side.

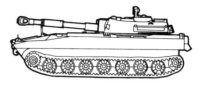

SAU 122
PT-76–type chassis with 7 road wheels.
Turret location is rear of center.
IR searchlight top left of turret.
Double-baffle muzzle brake and bore evacuator.

APPENDIX C
Map Symbols

UNIT SIZE

Squad/crew	Smallest unit/UK section	• (single dot in box)
Section or unit larger than a squad but smaller than a platoon	Unit larger than a US squad/ UK section but smaller than a platoon equivalent	• • (two dots in box)
Platoon or detachment	Platoon/troop equivalent	• • • (three dots in box)
Company, battery, or troop	Company/battery/squadron equivalent	│ (one vertical line in box)
Battalion or squadron	Battalion equivalent	│ │ (two vertical lines in box)
Group or regiment	Regiment/group equivalent	│ │ │ (three vertical lines in box)
Brigade	Brigade equivalent	X (in box)
Division	Division	XX (in box)
Corps	Corps	XXX (in box)
Army	Army	XXXX (in box)

(Continued)

UNIT SIZE *(Continued)*

Army group or front	Army group/front	<u>XXXXX</u>
Special size indicator for a nonorganic or temporary grouping	Battalion task force	
	Company team	

BRANCH OR FUNCTION

Adjutant General (personnel services and administration)	**AG**
Aerial observation	Air Force (surveillance) Army
Airborne (normally associated with another branch symbol)	
Air cavalry	
Air defense	

(Continued)

BRANCH OR FUNCTION *(Continued)*

Amphibious	
Amphibious engineer	
Antiarmor	
Armor	
Armored cavalry	
Army aviation **Rotary wing**	
Fixed wing	
Attack helicopter	
Bridging	
Cavalry or reconnaissance	

(Continued)

BRANCH OR FUNCTION *(Continued)*

Chemical (NBC)	
Chemical (NBC decontamination)	DECON
Chemical (reconnaissance)	
Chemical (smoke generator)	SMOKE
Civil Affairs (US only)	CA
Data processing unit	DPU
Dental	D
Engineer	
Electronic warfare	EW
Field artillery	●

(Continued)

BRANCH OR FUNCTION *(Continued)*

Finance/Pay		
Infantry		
	Light	
	Mechanized **APC**	
	BIFV (mounted)	
	BIFV (dismounted)	
	Motorized	
Maintenance		
Medical		
Military Intelligence **(at corps and below insert is CEWI)**		MI

(Continued)

BRANCH OR FUNCTION *(Continued)*

Military Police	MP
Motorized	
Mountain	
Ordnance	
Petroleum supply	
Psychological operations	
Quartermaster	
Ranger	RGR
Rocket artillery	
Service	SVC

(Continued)

BRANCH OR FUNCTION *(Continued)*

Signal/communications	
Sound ranging	
Special forces	**SF**
Supply	
Supply and maintenance	
Supply and transportation	
Support	**SPT**
Surface-to-air missile	
Surface-to-surface missile	
Transportation	

(Continued)

BRANCH OR FUNCTION *(Continued)*

Unmanned air reconnaissance (RPV, etc)	

WEAPONS AND EQUIPMENT

Select the appropriate weapon symbol.

(light automatic weapon)	(gun)

Add horizontal bars (one for medium or two for heavy) to denote the size.

(medium machine gun)	(heavy gun)

If a weapon has a high trajectory, a O is placed at the base of the shaft. If the weapon has a flat trajectory, a ⌒ is placed at the base of the shaft.

(medium morter)	(light antitank gun)

If the weapon is primarily for air defense, a ⌒ is placed at the base of the shaft.

(air defense missle)	(air defense gun)

If the weapon is rocket launched, a ⌃ is placed at the head of the shaft. If a weapon is also a tracked, self-propelled vehicle, a ⌒ is placed below the weapon symbol.

(rocket launcher)	(a tracked, self-propelled medium howitzer)

(Continued)

WEAPONS AND EQUIPMENT *(Continued)*

Examples of weapons symbols are shown below.

Description	Symbol		
	LIGHT	**MEDIUM**	**HEAVY**
Air defense gun			
Antitank gun			
Antitank missile, self-propelled			
Antitank rocket launcher			
Flamethrower	 portable	 vehicular	
Gun in air defense role, self-propelled			
Gun in antitank role			
Howitzer			

(Continued)

WEAPONS AND EQUIPMENT *(Continued)*

	LIGHT	MEDIUM	HEAVY
Machine gun/automatic weapon			
Mortar			
Multibarrel rocket launcher			
Surface-to-air missile			
Surface-to-surface missile			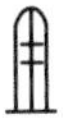

VEHICLES

Armored personnel carrier (APC)	
Armored engineer vehicle	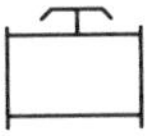
Armored vehicle launch bridge (AVLB)	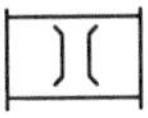

(Continued)

VEHICLES *(Continued)*

Bradley infantry fighting vehicle (BIFV)	
Cavalry fighting vehicle (CFV)	
Tank	Light　　Medium　　Heavy

LOCATIONS

A solid line symbol represents a present or actual location.	
A broken line symbol indicates a future or projected location.	
Basic symbols other than the headquarters symbol may be placed on a staff that is extended or bent as required. The end of the staff indicates the precise location.	

POINTS

	OWN	ENEMY
General or unspecified point (Exact location is the tip at the bottom of the symbol)		
Coordinating point (Exact location is the center of the symbol)	⊗	⊗
Contact point		
Start point	SP	SP
Release point	RP	RP

	Own	**Enemy**
Strongpoint (May be combined with unit size symbol)	SP 6 SP 5	SP 2

Checkpoint	8
Linkup point	● 8

(Continued)

POINTS *(Continued)*

Passage point	PP 8
Point of departure	PD
Pop-up point	PUP
Rally point	RALLY
Rendezvous point (Letter in circle appears in alphabetical sequence for number of points required)	A RDVU

LINES

Front lines	Own present	
	Own planned	
	Enemy present	

(Continued)

LINES *(Continued)*

Front lines (cont.)	Enemy anticipated or suspect	
General tactical boundary	Own present	**X X**
	Own planned	**X X**
	Enemy present	**E N — III — E N**
	Enemy anticipated or suspect	**E N --- III --- E N**
Obstacle line (Tips point toward the enemy)		
Fortified line		

ROUTES

Attack General symbol for main attack—double arrowhead	
General symbol for other than main attack—single arrowhead	

(Continued)

ROUTES *(Continued)*

Attack (cont.)

Double arrowhead for direction of main attack and axis of advance for the main attack

Single arrowhead for supporting direction of attack and supporting axis of advance

Axis of advance

Actual

ALPHA

Proposed with date and time effective

RED EFF 040500Z NOV

Axis of advance for unit designated to conduct main attack

TF 2-7

Bypass

Bypass easy

Bypass difficult

Bypass impossible

(Continued)

ROUTES *(Continued)*

Direction of attack.

Direction of attack is shown graphically as an arrow extending from the line of departure. The arrow is not normally labeled.

Follow and support mission

OBSTACLES

Abatis	
Booby trap	
Nonexplosive antitank	
Trip wire	
Wire	

(Continued)

OBSTACLES *(Continued)*

Point	
Planned abatis reinforced with antipersonnel mines	
Executed or fired demolition reinforced with antitank mines	
Booby-trapped nonexplosive antitank obstacle with target serial number	

Linear

Antitank ditch
(A rectangle need not be used when the obstacle is drawn to scale on the overlay. Teeth point toward the enemy.)

Under preparation   Completed

Unspecified

Wire
(enemy under preparation)

Minefields
  Indicators
  Antipersonnel mine

  Antitank mine

(Continued)

OBSTACLES *(Continued)*

Antitank mine with antihandling device	
Mine cluster	
Mine, type unspecified	
Conventional A planned minefield consisting of unspecified mines	
A completed minefield consisting of **unspecified mines**	
Scatterable minefield (DTGs used for self-destruct mines)	
Conventional row mining (outline drawn to scale)	
Nuisance **Nuisance minefield**	

(Continued)

OBSTACLES *(Continued)*

Phony Phony minefield	
Protective Protective minefield	
Antitank ditch reinforced with antitank mines	
Tactical Tactical minefield of scatterable antitank mines, effective till 101200Z	
Completed antitank minefield (drawn away from the location and connected by a vector)	

FIRE PLANNING

Basic Concentration/point	
Linear concentration/line	

(Continued)

FIRE PLANNING *(Continued)*

Rectangular target	
Target reference point (TRP)	X1300Z
Concentrations and barrages Linear concentration	AG 1201
Targets and final protective fires Friendly targets (not enemy) are represented by one of the following symbols, as appropriate. Targets for friendly fires are normally designated using two letters followed by four numbers. A linear concentration, target number 1201, on a friendly target effected at 100700Z	1201 AT100700Z
Final protective fire (identified by unit designation)	A/1-3

NBC

(Height of burst in meters)

(Target number)

(Delivery unit and time on target)

(Weapon type and yield)
(For chemical weapons type of agent is written here)

APPENDIX D
Hasty Protective Minefield Record

INSTRUCTIONS

1. Designate an easily identifiable reference point on the ground (a tree, a stump, a stake, or the like). Orient the form (the blank form on the next page) by tying in the center point of circles to the designated reference point on the ground.

2. Tie in reference point to a landmark, such as a road junction, house corner, etc., that can be found on a standard military map.

3. Complete the azimuth block.

4. Complete the following information in the identification block: unit, ref. pt., remarks, map and sheet no., OIC, name, SSAN.

5. Starting from the reference point, record the magnetic azimuth in degrees (°) and distance in paces (P) of each leg from the friendly position toward the enemy position and from right to left or left to right across each row of mines.

However, all rows must be recorded in the same direction. Whichever direction is used, the starting points of the rows must be marked A1, B1, etc., and the ending points marked A2, B2, etc. as shown in the example. Each mine in each row will be numbered sequentially from the starting point to the last mine in the row.

6. Fill in the tabular block (see example).

7. Fill in the scale being used where space is provided "scale 2CM= " and fill in the pace (P) readings in the right margin.

8. Make all minefield reports (intention, initiation, completion, transfer, and change) by some secure means.

9. Note what has been used to identify A1 and B1, e.g., 2x4 driven flush with ground, steel picket or fence post wrapped with engineer tape, etc.

Row	Type	Actuation	Mine number
A	M16A1	TRIPWIRE	1, 2, 6
	M21	CONTROLLED	3, 4, 5
B	M16A1	TRIPWIRE	1, 3
	M1BA1	PRESSURE	2
Remarks:			

DA FORM 1355-1-R.

SCALE: 2cm = 25 paces

IDENTIFICATION BLOCK

Unit	2ND PLT, A Co 1-4TH 2BDE, 1CANDIV
Ref Pt	TREE STUMP SIDE of ROAD
Remarks:	POINTS A1, A2, B1, B2 ARE MARKED WITH 2" x 2" STAKES
Map & Sheet No	TALBOT 5568
Name of OIC	Lt ALLAN
Signature	E. Allan
Time & Date	1700 6 JAN 75
Mines removed	
Mines transferred	

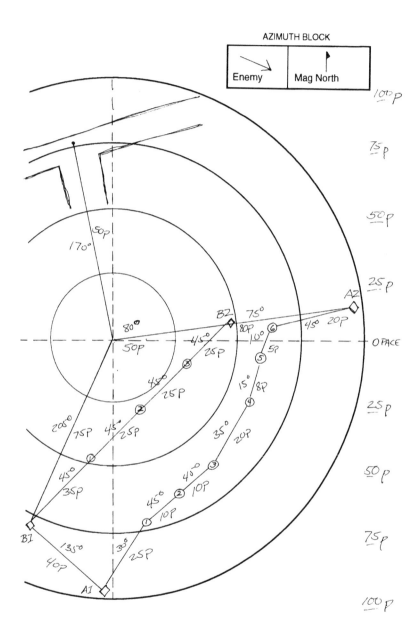

AZIMUTH BLOCK

Enemy | Mag North

APPENDIX E
Platoon and Squad Organization

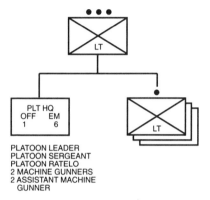

PLATOON LEADER
PLATOON SERGEANT
PLATOON RATELO
2 MACHINE GUNNERS
2 ASSISTANT MACHINE
  GUNNER

Light infantry platoon organization.

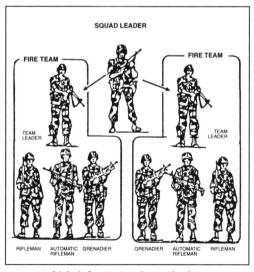

Light infantry squad organization.

APPENDIX F
Organic and Supporting Weapons

	M9 Pistol	M1 6A2	M249 MG	M203	M60
WEIGHT (lbs)	2.6	8.7	15.5	11	23
LENGTH (in)	8.5	39	41.1	39	43
MAX RANGE (m)	1,800	3,600	3,600	400	3,750
ARMING RANGE (m)	N/A	N/A	N/A	14	N/A
MIN SAFE RANGE (m)	N/A	N/A	N/A	31	N/A
RATE OF FIRE					
CYCLIC (rpm)	N/A	700-800	800	N/A	550
RAPID (m)	N/A	N/A	200*	35	200
SUSTAINED	60	16	85	35	100
EFFECTIVE RANGE					
AREA (m)	N/A	800	800	350	1,100
POINT	50	580	600	160	600
MOVING (m)	N/A	200	N/A	N/A	N/A
AMMUMITION					
TYPE	BALL	BALL, TRACER, DUMMY, PRACTICE, and BLANK	BALL, TRACER, DUMMY, PRACTICE, and BLANK	HE,WP, CS, ILLUM, TP, and BUCK-SHOT	BALL, TRACER, and BLANK
EXAMPLE LOAD (rds)	30	210	600		

* With barrel change.

Organic weapons.

	M72 LAW	M136 AT4	M47 DRAGON
WEIGHT (lbs)	4.7	14.8	68.5
LENGTH (in)	22/35	40	44
MAX RANGE(m)	1,000	2,100	1,000
ARMING RANGE (m)	10	30	65
MIN SAFE RANGE (m)	30	30	65
EFFECTIVE RANGE			
STATIONARY (m)	200	300	1,000
MOVING (m)	125	300	100
BACKBLAST (m)	50	60	50

Antitank weapons.

	FRAG	WP	THERMITE	CONCUSS
WEIGHT (lbs)	1	2	2	1
RANGE (m)	40	30	25	40
		(Thrown by average soldier)		
PACKING (box)	30	N/A	16	20
BURST RADIUS (m)	15	17		2
		60-sec burn	40-sec burn	

	M21 ANTITANK MINE	M14 APERS MINE (Toe Popper)	M16A1 APERS MINE (Bouncing Betty)	M18A1 APERS MINE (Claymore)
WEIGHT (lbs)	18	3.6	8.3	3.5
PACKING (box)	4 mines 4 fuzes	90 ea mines and deton	4 fuzes tripwire	6 mines w/accy
BURST RADIUS	1 tank	1 indiv	30 meters	50 meters (eff) 250 meters(max)

Grenades and mines.

	M2 (.50 CAL)	MK 19	M202 FLASH	M3 RAAWS
WEIGHT (lbs)	84	76	26.7	22
LENGTH (in)	66	43	34.7	42.6
MAX RANGE (m)	6,765	2,212	N/A	
ARMING RANGE (m)	N/A	18	N/A	
MIN SAFE RANGE (m)	N/A	28	20	50 (HEAT)
				500 (illum)
				250 (HE)
				50 (SMOKE)
				50 (TNG)
RATE OF FIRE				
CYCLIC (rpm)	500	375	N/A	
RAPID (rpm)	40*	60	N/A	
SUSTAINED (rpm)	40*	40	N/A	6
EFFECTIVE RANGE				
AREA (m)	1,830	2,212	750	
POINT (m)	1,200	1,500	200	
STATIONARY (m)	N/A	N/A	N/A	700 (HEAT)
MOVING (m)	N/A	N/A	N/A	250
BACKBAST (m)			50	60
BURST RADIUS (m)			20	
AMMUNITION				
TYPE	BALL, AP, TRACER, API, API-T, INCEN, and BLANK	HEDP, HE, TP, and BUCKSHOT		HEAT, ILLUM, HE, SMOKE, TP, and TNG

*With barrel change

Supporting weapons.

WEAPON	AMMUNITION MODEL	TYPE	METERS MIN RANGE	MAX RANGE***	RATE OF FIRE
M224 60-mm	M720/M888	HE	70	3,500*	30 rounds per minute for 4 minutes**, then 20 rounds per minute, sustained
	M722	WP	70	3,500	
	M72	ILLUM	200	3,200	
	M302A1	WP	33	1,625	
	M83A3	ILLUM	725	950	
	M49A4	HE	45	1,925	
M29AI 81-mm	M374A2	HE	70	4,600	12 rounds per minute for 2 minutes, then 5 rounds per minute, sustained
	M374A3	HE	73	4,725	
	M375A2	WP	73	4,775	
	M301A3	ILLUM	100	2,950	
M252 81-mm	M821/M889	HE	83	5,600	30 rounds per minute for 2 minutes, then 15 rounds per minute, sustained
	M374A3	HE	73	4,775	
	M819	RED P	300	4,875	
	M375A3	WP	73	4,775	
	M853A1	ILLUM	300	5,050	
	M301A1	ILLUM	100	2,950	
M30 107-mm	M329A2	HE	770	6,850	18 rounds per minute for 1 minute, then 9 rounds per minute for 5 minutes, then 3 rounds per minute, sustained
	M328A1	WP	720	5,650	
	M335A2	ILLUM	400	5,500	
M120 120-mm	M57	HE	200	7,200	15 rounds per minute for 1 minute, then 4 rounds per minute, sustained
	M68	SMOKE	200	7,200	
	M91	ILLUM	200	7,100	

*Bipod mounted, charge 4 maximum range handheld is 1,300 meters.

**Charge 2 and above, 30 rounds per minute can be sustained with charge 0 or 1.

***Rounded to nearest 25 meters.

Mortars.

	M102	M119	M198
CALIBER	105-mm	105-mm	155-mm
MAX RANGE (For HE) (m)	11,500	14,000	18,100
PLANNING RANGE (m)	11,500	11,500	14,600
MIN RANGE (m)	DIRECT FIRE	DIRECT FIRE	DIRECT FIRE
DANGER CLOSE RANGE	600	600	600
RATE OF FIRE			
MAXIMUM (rpm)	10	10	4
SUSTAINED (rpm)	3	3	2
PROJECTILE			
TYPE	HE, WP, ILLUM, HEP-T, APICM, CHEM, APERS, RAP	HE, M760, ILLUM, HEP-T, APICM, CHEM, RAP	HE, WP, ILLUM, SMOKE, CHEM, NUC, RAP, FASCAM, CPHD, AP/DPICM
FUZES			
TYPE	PD, VT, MT, MTSQ, CP, DELAY	PD, VT, MT, MTSQ, CP, DELAY	PD, VT, CP MT, MTSQ, DELAY

LEGEND:

AP—Armor-piercing
APERS—Antipersonnel
APICM—Antipersonnel Improved
    Conventional Munitions
CHEM—Chemical
    CP—Concrete Piercing
CPHD—Copperhead
DPICM—Dual-Purpose Improved
    Conventional Munitions
FASCAM—Family of Scatterable Mines

HEP-T—High-Explosive Plastic Tracer
ILLUM—Illumination
MT—Mechanical Time
MTSQ—Mechanical Time Super Quick
NUC—Nuclear
PD—Point Detonating
RAP—Rocket Assisted Projectile
VT—Variable Time
WP—White Phosphorus

Artillery.

Chain of Command

(Fill in the names)

Commander in Chief _____
Secretary of Defense _____
Secretary of the Army _____
Chief of Staff, U.S. Army _____
CG, TRADOC or FORSCOM _____
Theater Commander _____
Army Group Commander _____
Army Commander _____
Corps Commander _____
Division Commander _____
Brigade Commander _____
Bn/Sqdn Commander _____
Co/Btry/Trp Commander _____
Platoon Leader _____
Section Leader _____
Squad Leader _____
Fire Team Leader _____

Selected Acronyms and Abbreviations

ADA	Air defense artillery
AG	Adjutant General
APC	Armored personnel carrier
AR	Automatic rifle
ASL	Assistant squad leader
AT	Antitank
ATGM	Antitank guided missile
AVLB	Armored vehicle launch bridge
BFV	Bradley fighting vehicle
BIFV	Bradley infantry fighting vehicle
BMP	A Soviet infantry fighting vehicle
BP	Battle position
BRDM	A Russian vehicle used by reconnaissance units
BTR	A Soviet wheel vehicle
CEWI	Combat electronics warfare and intelligence
CFV	Cavalry fighting vehicle
CP	Command post
CSS	Combat service support
CW	Continuous wave
DEW	Directed energy weapons
DLIC	Detachment left in contact
DTG	Date time group
EA	Engagement area
EMP	A massive surge of electrical power

EPW	Enemy prisoners of war
FDC	Fire direction center
FEBA	Forward edge of battle area
FIST	Fire support team
FLOT	Forward line of own troops
FO	Forward observer
FPF	Final protective fires
FPL	Final protective line
FRAGO	Fragmentary order
FSO	Fire support officer
GL	Grenade launcher
HE	High explosives
HHC	Headquarters and headquarters company
ISU	Periscope
ITV	Improved TOW vehicle
KIA	Killed in action
LAW	Light antitank weapon
LD	Line of departure
LMG/COAX	Light machine gun/coaxial
LOGPAC	Logistical package
LZ	Landing zone
METT-T	Mission, enemy, terrain and weather, troops and equipment, time available
MOPP	Mission-oriented protective posture
NBC	Nuclear, biological, and chemical warfare
OCOKA	Observation, cover and concealment, obstacles, key terrain, avenues of approach
OP	Observation post
OPCON	Operational control
OPORD	Operation order
OPSEC	Operations security
OT	Observer-target
PAC	Personnel and administration center
PL	Phase line
PSG	Platoon sergeant
PUP	Pop-up point
PW	Prisoner of war
PZ	Pickup zone

RATELO	Radiotelephone operator
RDVU	Rendezvous point
RP	Release point
RPV	Remotely piloted vehicle
RS	Road space
SAW	Squad automatic weapon
SF	Special forces
SL	Squad leader
SOP	Standing operating procedure
TF	Task force
TL	Team leader
TOW	Tube-launched, optically tracked, wire-guided
TRP	Target reference point
VT	Variable time (a type of fuse)
WIA	Wounded in action
WP	White phosphorus
XO	Executive officer

References

For further information about the subjects discussed in this guide, you should refer to the following publications:

FM 3-100   *NBC Operations,* September 1985
FM 6-30   *Observed Fire Procedures,* June 1985
FM 7-8   *The Infantry Rifle Platoon and Squad,* April 1992
FM 7-10   *The Infantry Rifle Company,* December 1990
FM 20-32   *Mine/Countermine Operations,* December 1985
FM 21-11   *First Aid for Soldiers,* October 1985
FC 21-26   *Map Reading and Land Navigation,* June 1986
FM 21-75   *Combat Skills of the Soldier,* August 1984
FM 22-100   *Military Leadership,* October 1983
FM 90-4   *Air Assault Operations,* March 1987
FM 90-8   *Counterguerrilla Operations,* August 1986
FM 90-10-1   *Infantryman's Guide to Combat in Built-up Areas,* July 1992 (draft)
FM 90-26   *Airborne Operations,* December 1990
FM 100-5   *Operations,* 1993 (draft)
FM 101-5-1   *Operational Terms and Symbols,* October 1985

Index